# THE CONSTITUTION:
# OUR WRITTEN LEGACY

# THE CONSTITUTION:
# OUR WRITTEN LEGACY

Joseph A. Melusky
Department of History and Political Science
Saint Francis College
Loretto, Pennsylvania

KRIEGER PUBLISHING COMPANY
MALABAR, FLORIDA

Original Edition 1991
Reprint 1992, 1994, 2002

Printed and Published by
KRIEGER PUBLISHING COMPANY
KRIEGER DRIVE
MALABAR, FLORIDA 32950

Library of Congress Cataloging-in-Publication Data

Melusky, Joseph Anthony.
        The Constitution : our legacy / Joseph A. Melusky.
            p.    cm.
        Includes Bibliographical references.
        ISBN 0-89464-334-7 (Cloth) (alk. paper)
        ISBN 0-89464-550-1 (Paper)
        1. United States--Constitutional history.   I. Title.
KF4541.M43    1990
342.73`029--dc20
[347.30229]                                                        89-19963
                                                                        CIP

10   9   8   7   6   5

For my son, Mike

May you be as durable and resilient as the Constitution has been.

# CHRONOLOGICAL CONTENTS

# TOPICAL CONTENTS

# PREFACE

Not long ago, Walter Berns remarked that no law school or political science department in the country offers a course on the Constitution. Courses on constitutional law are common, but courses on the Constitution itself are not. Ralph Lerner, a political scientist, and Philip B. Kurland, a constitutional law scholar, proposed to prepare a small volume of primary source materials on issues that confronted the Framers. The planned volume was intended to serve as a textbook for a course like the one that Berns described. Instead, Kurland and Lerner's project expanded and they produced a five-volume anthology entitled, *The Founders' Constitution.*[1] As such, the need for a smaller volume of primary materials for use as a textbook in the undergraduate classroom remains. This book is designed to meet this need.

The United States Constitution belongs not only to judges, lawyers, and other legal experts; it belongs to the American people and should be understood by them. It is difficult to enjoy the benefits—and fulfill the responsibilities—of citizenship unless one knows what they are. As Thomas Jefferson said, "[i]f a nation expects to be ignorant and free ... it expects what never was and never will be." In a related vein, James Madison observed, "[k]nowledge will forever govern ignorance and a people that mean to be their own governors must arm themselves with the power that knowledge brings." Awareness of constitutional principles is a prerequisite of informed and responsible citizenship. The purpose of this book is to help the reader develop a better understanding and appreciation of such principles.

The Constitution's bicentennial stimulated various programs aimed at public education. This book grew out of one such program sponsored by the Pennsylvania Humanities Council. The PHC recruited political scientists and historians to moderate discussion groups for the general public and in-service courses for elementary and secondary teachers in communities throughout Pennsylvania starting in 1985. Participants were supplied with a collection of primary materials on the Constitution. I used these materials as I taught several of these in-service courses for the PHC. Recalling Berns's comments and Kurland

---

[1]  As cited by Ralph Lerner in Jennifer Newton's, "The Founders' Constitution," 7 *Humanities* 1 (February 1986): 7-9, at p. 7. The book was published by the University of Chicago Press in 1987.

and Lerner's efforts, I anticipated that one of the most pressing problems that would face instructors trying to develop undergraduate courses on the Constitution would be to find a single suitable collection of original materials. With the PHC's backing, I set out to adapt the original reader to this purpose. Although I retained the original title for the sake of continuity, this is an expanded and substantially-revised version of the earlier work.

This book's premise is that the Constitution remains viable today because it contains vague, open-ended, and flexible language. The meaning of ambiguous provisions can be adapted to meet changing circumstances without the need for frequent amendments to the written text. But this adaptability means that the Constitution's "meaning" is not always self-evident and precise. To determine what the Constitution meant when it was written, what it has meant at different points in history, and what it means today, it is necessary to look beyond the four corners of the document itself to writings of early and later statesmen, justices, and others who have interpreted and applied it.

This book has several distinctive features. First, it relies exclusively on primary source materials. Many historical treatments of the Framers and the constitutional convention are already available. Books about the Constitution, laws, judges, and courts are also available. But anthologies presenting the original thoughts and words of the Framers themselves, earlier works that influenced them, key documents of their times, and more recent interpretations are not so common. This book relies solely on primary materials to enable readers to draw their own conclusions without being overly dependent upon and influenced by the opinions of secondary commentators. Instead of relying on some contemporary author to tell readers "what the Framers really meant," for example, readers can make that determination for themselves after reading what the Framers themselves said.

Second, the coverage of this reader is broad. Selections run from the Magna Carta (1215) through the Supreme Court's opinion in *Bowers v. Hardwick* (1986)—a span of 771 years. Important documents, letters, statutes, judicial opinions, and other writings that shed light on the evolving meaning of constitutional principles are included. In this way, readers can study not only the Constitution itself, but previous works that influenced the Framers and Court decisions that applied the Constitution to later controversies as well.

Third, this book is relatively brief. While there is an undeniable element of subjectivity involved in selecting readings, I tried to include only fundamentally important sources. For instance, if a case established a landmark principle or if a case applied such a principle in an unusual context, it was a strong candidate for inclusion. If, on the other hand, a case was a link in a chain of legal decisions that produced a gradual shift in the application of the original landmark principle, it was excluded. Readings were also edited in the interest of brevity. Only material that is essential to understanding the main point of a selection was included; potentially interesting but non-essential information was omitted.

Fourth, this book is designed to be accessible for diverse audiences. This is not another casebook for an upper-level course on constitutional law or civil liberties. Its intended audience includes students with no prior experience in the subject. Selections are heavily edited to make them understandable to a general readership. Case selections are frequently short. Introductory essays provide necessary background information and context. In short, this is a "user friendly" collection of materials intended to introduce readers to the Constitution. It should be equally appropriate for undergraduate survey courses and general public discussion groups.

Fifth, this book is designed to be flexible. Readings are organized in chronological fashion to help the reader gain a sense of the historical development of constitutional values and ideals. In the event that some instructors would prefer a thematic approach, a topical guide to the readings is also provided. As noted, introductory passages establish historical, political, and conceptual background for the readings. I tried to supply enough information so that relatively inexperienced readers can understand the selections, but not so much detail and commentary that my own words intrude upon the primary materials themselves. "Discussion Points" follow each reading. Instructors might use these ideas as the basis of assignments or for in-class discussions. Finally, a bibliography developed by the Commission on the Bicentennial of the United States Constitution is included for those interested in additional sources. Depending on instructor objectives, student level, time constraints, and the like, it would be fairly easy to adapt this anthology by using only certain sections or, conversely, by supplementing it with outside readings. I hope that my organization of the materials does not restrict choice and that instructors will use the book in ways that suit their own needs.

The original version of this work was funded by an Exemplary Project Award from the National Endowment for the Humanities. The text of the reader was first conceived by Dr. Craig Eisendrath, Executive Director of the PHC. It was shaped by the advice of scholars serving as discussion leaders. It was originally compiled and introduced by Dr. Joseph P. O'Grady and Dr. George Stow, Professors of History at

LaSalle University, with editorial assistance by Dr. Joseph J. Kelly, Associate Director of the PHC. Assistance was also provided by Dr. Richard Beeman, Director of the Philadelphia Center for Early American Studies at the University of Pennsylvania; Judge Louis H. Pollack, Judge of the U.S. District Court for Eastern Pennsylvania; Harris Wofford, Philadelphia attorney and PHC member; Minna Novick, educational consultant; and Dana Lobell, PHC staff member.

I want to thank the Pennsylvania Humanities Council for cooperating in this venture and I especially want to thank Dr. Kelly for his advice and encouragement. Additionally, I solicited recommendations for revisions from all instructors who moderated PHC discussion groups using the original collection of readings. In particular, I want to acknowledge the helpful suggestions I received from Dr. Thomas Baldino of Juniata College, Dr. Kent F. Moors of Duquesne University, and Dr. Frank Dawson of the Pennsylvania State University, Fayette Campus. I also want to thank Dr. Duncan MacDonald of the Council of Chief State School Officers for his perceptive comments. Needless to say, the responsibility for any errors of fact or judgment is mine.

# INTRODUCTION

A constitution serves as the supreme law of the land. Statutes inconsistent with its provisions are invalid. Most constitutions provide general frameworks for governments. They establish structures and specify how public officials will be selected. They delegate powers to governmental institutions and actors. And some constitutions place limits on such powers while recognizing certain rights that are retained by individuals.

The United States Constitution was written in 1787. At the time, a written constitution was highly unusual. Today, only a few nations lack written constitutions. In such countries, the "constitution" consists of legislative acts, judicial decisions, and customs that have not been collected in a single document. Israel and Great Britain are contemporary examples of nations with such unwritten constitutions.

No other constitution in the world has lasted as long as that of the United States. Nearly two-thirds of the world's 160 national constitutions have been written or revised since 1970. Only 14 predate World War II. Approximately 53.5 percent of the independent nations of the world have been under more than one constitution since the Second World War. The average nation has had two constitutions since 1945. Syria and Thailand have each had nine constitutions over the past 40 years.[2] By contrast, the American Constitution has been remarkably durable.

The original American Constitution contained just 4,223 words—the equivalent of about 17 typewritten and double-spaced pages. A number of state constitutions are considerably longer. The first ten amendments (termed "articles"), the Bill of Rights, were added almost immediately. Only 16 amendments have been added subsequently, however. And two of these amendments—the eighteenth establishing and the twenty-first repealing prohibition respectively—cancel each other. How has this short, written Constitution been able to serve for so long?

The Constitution's durability can be traced in large part to the way it was written. Some provisions describe governmental powers; others

---

[2] These figures and related information can be found in Mark W. Cannon's, "Why Celebrate the Constitution?" *National Forum: Toward the Bicentennial of the Constitution* 64 (Fall 1984): 3.

describe individual rights. But many of these provisions were written in highly general, open-ended language. For example, Article One, Section Eight lists congressional powers. Clause 18 concludes this Section with the statement that Congress will have the power to make "all laws necessary and proper for carrying into execution the foregoing powers . . ." How does one distinguish a "necessary and proper" law from an unnecessary and improper one? The Framers didn't say. Similarly, the Sixth Amendment guarantees the accused the "right to a speedy trial . . . by an impartial jury." What is a "speedy" trial? An "impartial" jury? The Framers didn't specify.

The use of such open-ended language can be traced both to the authors' inability to resolve their disputes more concretely and to their recognition that they were writing something more important than a traffic code. The flexibility of the Constitution's language permits it to evolve as times change. The Framers laid down a series of fundamental concepts and principles, but they left the precise meaning of their words to future generations. Constitutional ambiguities enable us to regard it as a "living" document.

Courts are often asked to interpret and reinterpret the Constitution in an ongoing effort to apply it to contemporary matters. In the process, judges rely on precedent, the text of the Constitution itself, and the intent of the Framers. Judges are not free to substitute their own views of wise public policy for the law. Their discretion is limited. However, judging is not purely mechanical.

It can be difficult to determine, with certainty, what the Framers really intended. Further, even if their intentions can be ascertained, judges should not disregard two-hundred-plus years of legal developments since the Framers' time. For example, the Fourth Amendment prohibits "unreasonable searches and seizures." What is the literal definition of an "unreasonable search"? Furthermore, did the Framers intend to address wiretaps, spike mikes, airplane overflights, infrared telescopes, and other forms of modern surveillance? Of course not. Yet their choice of open-ended language permits courts to apply the Fourth Amendment to such activities today. To this end, one can argue that the Framers "intended" to protect a general sphere of personal privacy against unreasonable governmental intrusions and that technology-enhanced eavesdropping can, under some conditions, constitute such unreasonable intrusion.

If the Constitution were more explicit, fewer disputes would arise about its meaning and it wouldn't make much difference who the judges were. On the other hand, the document would require revision to meet every technological advance. As it is, textual ambiguities sometimes allow different judges to interpret the same provision differently. While some might object to such uncertainty, it is this ambiguity that lets the Constitution evolve with the times.

The Framers of the Constitution tried to create a stronger central government than they had under the much-criticized Articles of Confederation. But with the memory of British rule still fresh, they sought ways to limit governmental power and avoid tyranny.

The first three Articles established the three departments of the national government. Article I established a bicameral national legislature—the United States Congress. Article II outlined the powers of the Nation's chief executive officer—the President of the United States. Article III provided for a national court system, including the United States Supreme Court. Article I, Section 9 identified some limits on congressional power. Both the President and federal judges could be impeached. Separate departments were assigned separate powers and responsibilities. Additionally, these separate departments were designed so that no single one would be self sufficient. Branches were to be functionally interdependent as power checked and balanced power. Further, a federal system was devised so that certain powers would be retained at the state and local levels. In these ways, the Framers were trying to establish a strong but limited central government.

Article IV dealt with intergovernmental relations and federalism. Article V provided an amendment mechanism so the Constitution could be changed to meet future developments without the need for armed rebellion or other extreme upheaval. Article VI announced the supremacy of the Constitution to contrary enactments and Article VII stated that ratification would require the approval of nine States.

Some argued for the inclusion of a written Bill of Rights—as the powers of the central government were spelled out in writing, limits on that government and the rights of individuals against the state should be spelled out as well. A written statement makes fundamental principles seem more permanent. Subsequently, all governmental actions would be judged against these written standards. In this way, parties who offended the prevailing conventional opinion of the moment would be treated fairly. Further, the actions of future politicians could be judged against more enduring standards than popular opinion of their day. The fact that something may be popular would not necessarily mean that it was constitutionally permissible. In light of the persuasiveness of such arguments, a written Bill of Rights was added.

Over the years, additional amendments have been adopted. Some have modified the power of the national government. Some have limited the powers of state governments. Some have expanded voting rights. Some have changed governmental structures and processes. And some have limited the behavior of private individuals.

Before proceeding any further, the reader should carefully examine the text of the Constitution and its amendments. The document appears in its present entirety in the Appendix.

\* \* \* \* \* \* \* \* \* \* \* \* \* \* \* \* \* \* \* \* \* \* \* \* \* \* \* \* \* \* \*

*Discussion Points:*

1. Construct an index to the Constitution that identifies in summary fashion what sections of the document do. Use this index as you continue your readings.
2. Make a list of constitutional provisions that seem ambiguous to you.
3. List constitutional principles that illustrate the principle of "checks and balances." Cite examples of how the "separate" departments interact.
4. In *Myers v. United States* (1926), Justice Brandeis observed that the point of the American political system was not to promote efficiency but to "preclude the exercise of arbitrary power." What did he mean? List specific constitutional provisions that illustrate his point.
5. Constitutional amendments serve a number of purposes:
   a. List amendments that increase or decrease the power of the national government;
   b. List amendments that decrease the power of state governments;
   c. List amendments that expand voting rights;
   d. List amendments that change governmental structures and processes;
   e. List amendments that limit the behavior of individuals.

---

Item five is based on exercises found in John J. Patrick and Richard C. Remy's, *Lessons on the Constitution* (Washington, D.C.: Social Science Education Consortium, Inc. and Project '87, a joint effort of the American Historical Association and the American Political Science Association, 1986): 185–91.

# PART I:
# PHILOSOPHICAL ROOTS
# OF THE AMERICAN
# CONSTITUTION

# CHAPTER 1

# THE MAGNA CARTA (1215)

The "Great Charter" is considered the forerunner of constitutional government. Wrung by the English barons from King John, it was a promise by John that he would provide more reasonable governance in the future. For years, governmental authority was based on the "divine right" of kings which assumed that the king ruled on earth on God's behalf. It was accepted that God created the state, chose the king, and endowed him with the right to rule. The Magna Carta marked the first time that men successfully limited this absolute authority of the king.

The King heavily taxed the barons' estates. Many were also angry that King John lost Normandy—where some of the barons had extensive holdings—to France. In 1213, a group of barons and church leaders drew up a list of rights they wanted the King to promise them. King John twice refused. The barons raised an army to force him to acquiesce. Seeing no chance of victory, he met the barons at Runnymede and placed his seal on the document on June 15, 1215 (he signed a revised draft four days later).

John's predecessor had unified the country. The barons did not attempt to break England into autonomous feudal states. Instead, they tried to restrain the abuses of the central government by stipulating that the King, like everyone else, was bound by the law. If the King failed to comply with law, the document said that he could be compelled to do so.

Specifically, Chapter 39 stated that the government could not take actions against an individual without giving him the benefit of "the lawful judgment of his peers"—what we have come to call "due process" of law. Chapters 55 and 61 notified the King that, in the event of future misgovernance, the barons would exercise their right to revolt. The Magna Carta symbolized the supremacy of law, the conviction that even the King was bound by the law.

\* \* \* \* \* \* \* \* \* \* \* \* \* \* \* \* \* \* \* \* \* \* \* \* \* \* \*

1. In the first place we have granted to God, and by this our present

charter confirmed for us and our heirs for ever that the English church shall be free, and shall have her rights entire, and her liberties inviolate and we will that it be thus observed. We have also granted to all freemen of our kingdom, for us and our heirs forever, all the underwritten liberties to be had and held by them and their heirs, of us and our heirs for ever. . . .

16. No one shall be distrained for performance of greater service for a knight's fee, or for any other free tenement, than is due therefrom.

17. Common pleas shall not follow our court, but shall be held in some fixed place.

18. Inquests shall not be held elsewhere than in their own county-courts, and that in manner following,—We, or, if we should be out of the realm, our chief justiciar, will send two justiciars through every county four times a year, who shall, along with four knights of the county chosen by the county, hold the said assizes in the county court, on the day and in the place of meeting of that court.

19. And if any of the said assizes cannot be taken on the day of the county court, let there remain of the knights and freeholders, who were present at the county court on that day, as many as may be required for the efficient making of judgments, according as the business be more or less. . . .

38. No bailiff for the future shall, upon his own unsupported complaint, put anyone to his "law," without credible witnesses brought for this purpose.

39. No freeman shall be taken or [and] imprisoned or disseised or exiled or in any way destroyed, nor will we go upon him nor send upon him, except by the lawful judgment of his peers or [and] by the law of the land. . . .

55. All fines made with us unjustly and against the law of the land, and all amercements imposed unjustly and against the law of the land, shall be entirely remitted, or else it shall be done concerning them according to the decision of the five-and-twenty barons or according to the judgment of the majority of the same, along with the aforesaid Stephen, archbishop of Canterbury, if he can be present, and such others as he may wish to bring with him for this purpose. . . .

61. Since, moreover, for God and the amendment of our kingdom and for the better allaying of the quarrel that has arisen between us and our barons, we have granted all these concessions, desirous that they should enjoy them in complete and firm endurance for ever, we give and grant to them the under-written security, namely, that the barons choose five-and-twenty barons of the kingdom, whomsoever they will, who shall be bound with all their might, to observe and hold, and cause

to be observed, the peace and liberties we have granted and confirmed to them by this our present Charter, so that if we, or our justiciar, or our bailiffs or any one of our officers, shall in anything be at fault toward anyone, or shall have broken any one of the articles of the peace or of this security, and the offense be notified to four barons of the foresaid five-and-twenty, the said four barons shall repair to us and, laying the transgression before us, petition to have that transgression redressed without delay. And if we shall not have corrected the transgression within forty days, reckoning from the time it has been intimated to us, the four barons aforesaid shall refer that matter to the rest of the five-and-twenty barons, and those five-and-twenty barons shall, together with the community of the whole land, distrain and distress us in all possible ways, namely, by seizing our castles, lands, possessions, and in any other way they can, until redress has been obtained as they deem fit, saving harmless our own person, and the persons of our queen and children; and when redress has been obtained, they shall resume their old relations towards us. . . .

And we shall procure nothing from anyone, directly or indirectly, whereby any part of these concessions and liberties might be revoked or diminished; and if any such thing has been procured, let it be void and null, and we shall never use it personally or by another.

\* \* \* \* \* \* \* \* \* \* \* \* \* \* \* \* \* \* \* \* \* \* \* \* \* \* \* \* \*

*Discussion Points:*

1. Look for parallels between the Magna Carta and the United States Constitution. Pay particular attention to the following ideas:
   a. freedom of religion
   b. the right to be confronted with witnesses against the accused and the right of the accused to have compulsory processes for obtaining witnesses in his or her favor
   c. due process of law
   d. protection against excessive fines
   e. holding leaders accountable for their transgressions
   f. supremacy of the Charter to contrary actions
   g. intention that the Charter remain in effect for posterity.

# CHAPTER 2

# THE MAYFLOWER COMPACT (1620)

The passengers on the Mayflower recognized that they were outside the jurisdiction of the London Company and they had to decide which laws would govern them while they were at sea. They also had to decide under what jurisdiction they would establish their colony. To resolve these matters, 41 of the Pilgrims drew up an agreement and signed it at sea on November 21 (then November 11), 1620. The document was the basis of the government formed for the Plymouth Colony.

The Compact combined the settlers into a "civil body Politick" that would frame "just and equal laws" and provide for the "general good" of the Colony. The signers agreed to form a government and obey its laws. The authority of this government, then, was derived from the consent of those who were to be governed.

The Mayflower Compact was a social contract reflecting political thought of the seventeenth century. It served as a model for many similar compacts in New England. When a group sought to launch a new settlement or plantation, one of its first steps was to adopt a "plantation covenant." The Mayflower Compact is important because it serves as an early example of self-government and influenced the development of American republicanism and democracy.

\* \* \* \* \* \* \* \* \* \* \* \* \* \* \* \* \* \* \* \* \* \* \* \* \* \* \*

In the name of God, Amen. We, whose names are underwritten, the loyal subjects of our dread sovereign Lord King James, by the grace of God, of Great Britain, France, and Ireland, king, defender of the faith, &c. Having undertaken for the glory of God, and advancement of the Christian faith and honor of our king and country, a voyage to plant the first colony in the northern parts of Virginia, do by these presents solemnly and mutually in the presence of God, and one of another, covenant and combine ourselves together into a civil body Politick, for our better ordering and preservation and furtherance of the ends aforesaid; and by virtue hereof do enact, constitute, and frame such just and equal laws, ordinances, Acts, constitutions, and offices, from time to time, as shall be thought to be most meet and convenient for the general good of the Colony; unto which we promise all due submission and obedience. In witness whereof we have hereunto subscribed our names at Cape Cod the eleventh of November . . . 1620.

\* \* \* \* \* \* \* \* \* \* \* \* \* \* \* \* \* \* \* \* \* \* \* \* \* \* \* \* \* \*

*Discussion Points:*

1. It was noted above that the Mayflower Compact was a social contract reflecting seventeenth century political thought. Consider this claim while reading excerpts from the works of Thomas Hobbes and John Locke. In what ways were the signers of the Mayflower Compact adopting a social contract?

# CHAPTER 3

# THOMAS HOBBES, *LEVIATHAN* (1651)

The Framers of the United States Constitution were influenced by the writings of the "social contract" theorists. In general terms, these theorists posited that once men lived in a state of nature where they were selfish, competitive, and insecure. Conflicts were common. These natural men were, however, capable of reason. To live more secure lives, they drafted a social contract in which they agreed to enter into civil society. They agreed to establish a government and to give it the power to make and enforce laws that limited individual liberty. This government was designed to promote security and its authority came from the consent of the governed. Civil men would retain certain of their "natural" rights against the government. If the government violated these rights, the contract would be abridged and consent could be withdrawn. In this way, the social contract theorists explained the origins of governmental authority and challenged the doctrine of the divine right of kings.

Thomas Hobbes (1588–1679) was one of the most prominent of these theorists. He argued that there was no sense of community in the state of nature; men were unconnected and alone. Natural man was exclusively self-interested, concerned only with satisfying his own desires. The Hobbesian natural state was a place of absolute liberty. Man had an absolute right to everything, including the right to kill others. As such, the Hobbesian natural man was in constant fear for his very life. No man could feel safe and secure. In Hobbes's own words, the life of the natural man was "solitary, poor, nasty, brutish, and short."

Hobbes, however, believed that natural men were capable of using reason to alleviate their perpetual fear and anxiety. All men share the basic right of self-preservation. On this basis, Hobbes maintained that men agreed to create an artificial entity to advance at least this minimal objective. They agreed to create a tremendously powerful state—a "Leviathan"—to protect them from one another. In the process, they exchanged the extreme liberty of the state of nature for the security of civil society. Civil man retained one right: the right to life. Since the

9

state was created to protect the lives of the contractors, the contract would be violated if the state failed to do so and consent could be withdrawn.

Hobbes's advocacy of a powerful state stemmed from his perception of the degree of conflict present in the state of nature. He saw the natural state as a place of intolerable insecurity. As such, he thought that the contractors would be so desperate that they would be willing to sacrifice almost all of their natural rights to the Leviathan they created.

* * * * * * * * * * * * * * * * * * * * * * * * * * * *

Nature has made men so equal in the facilities of body and mind, as that though there be found one man sometimes manifestly stronger in body, or of quicker mind than another, yet when all is reckoned together, the difference between man and man is not so considerable, as that one man can thereupon claim to himself any benefit to which another man may not pretend as well as he. For as to the strength of the body, the weakest has strength enough to kill the strongest, either by secret machinations, or by confederacy with others that are in the same danger with himself.

And as to the faculties of the mind . . . I find yet a greater equality among men than that of strength. For prudence is but experience, which equal time equally bestows on all men in those things they equally apply themselves unto. . . .

From this equality or ability arises equality of hope in the attaining of our ends. And therefore if any two men desire the same thing, which nevertheless they cannot both enjoy, they become enemies . . . and . . . endeavor to destroy or subdue one another. . . .

. . . [M]en have no pleasure, but on the contrary a great deal of grief, in keeping company where there is no power able to over-awe them all. . . .

So that in the nature of man we find three principal causes of quarrel: First, competition; secondly, diffidence; thirdly, glory.

The first makes men invade for gain; the second, for safety; and the third, for reputation. . . .

Hereby it is manifest that, during the time men live without a common power to keep them all in awe, they are in that condition which is called war; and such a war as is of every man against every man. . . .

. . . . In such condition, there is no place for industry, because the fruit thereof is uncertain; and consequently no culture of the earth; no navigation nor use of the commodities that may be imported by sea; no commodious building; no instruments of moving, and removing, such things as require much force; no knowledge of the face of the earth; no account of time; no arts; no letters; no society and, which is the worst of all, continual fear, and danger of violent death; and the life of man, solitary, poor, nasty, brutish, and short. . . .

To this war of every man against every man this also is consequent; that nothing can be unjust. The notions of right and wrong, justice and injustice, have there no place. Where there is no common power, there is no law; where no law, no injustice. Force and fraud are in war the two cardinal virtues. . . .

The passions that incline men to peace are fear of death, desire of such things as are necessary to commodious living, and a hope by their industry to obtain them. And reason suggests convenient articles of peace, upon which men may be drawn to agreement. . . .

The *right of nature*, which writers commonly call *jus naturale*, is the liberty each man has to use his own power as he will himself for the preservation of . . . his own life, and consequently of doing anything which in his own judgment and reason he shall conceive to be the aptest means thereunto.

By *liberty* is understood . . . the absence of external impediments, which impediments may often take away part of a man's power to do what he would, but cannot hinder him from using the power left him, according as his judgment and reason shall dictate to him.

A law of nature, *lex naturalis*, is a precept or general rule, found out by reason, by which a man is forbidden to do that which is destructive of his life, or takes away the means of preserving the same, and to omit that by which he thinks it may be best preserved. . . .

And because the condition of man, as has been declared in the precedent chapter, is a condition of war of everyone against everyone, in which case everyone is governed by his own reason, and there is nothing he can make use of that may not be a help unto him in preserving his life against his enemies; it follows that in such a condition every man has a right to everything, even to one another's body. And therefore, as long as this natural right of every man to everything endures, there can be no security to any man, how strong or wise soever he be, of living out the time which nature ordinarily allows men to live. And consequently it is a precept or general rule of reason that every man ought to endeavor peace, as far as he has hope of obtaining it, and, when he cannot obtain it, that he may seek, and use, all helps and advantages of war. The first branch of which rule contains the first, and fundamental law of nature, which is to seek peace and follow it. The second, the sum of the right of nature, which is, by all means we can, to defend ourselves.

From this fundamental law of nature by which men are commanded to endeavor peace is derived this second law; that a man be willing, when others are so too, as far-forth, as for peace and defence of himself, he shall think it necessary to lay down this right to all things and be contented with so much liberty against other men as he would allow other men against himself. For as long as every man holds this right of doing anything he likes, so long are all men in the condition of war. But if other men will not lay down their right, as well as he, then there is no reason for anyone to divest himself of his, for that were to expose himself to prey, which no man is bound to, rather than to dispose himself to peace. This is that law of the Gospel: whatsoever you require that others should do to you, that do ye to them. . . .

Whensoever a man transfers his right or renounces it, it is either in consideration of some right reciprocally transferred to himself, or for some other good he hopes for thereby. For it is a voluntary act; and of the voluntary acts of every man the object is some *good to himself.* And therefore there be some rights which no man can be understood . . . to have abandoned or transferred. As first a man cannot lay down the right of resisting them that assault him by force to take away his life, because he cannot be understood to aim thereby at any good to himself. . . . And lastly, the motive and end for which this renouncing and transferring of right is introduced, is nothing else but the security of a man's person in his life and in the means of so preserving life as not to be weary of it. . . . The mutual transferring of right is that which men call *contract.* . . .

The only way to erect such a common power, as may be able to defend them from the invasion of foreigners and the injuries of one another . . . is to confer all their power and strength upon one man, or upon one assembly of men, that may reduce all their wills, by plurality of voices, unto one will. . . . This is more than consent or concord; it is a real unity of them all, in one and the same person, made by covenant of every man with every man, in such manner as if every man should say to every man, I authorize and give up my right of governing myself, to this man, or to this assembly of men, on this condition, that thou give up thy right to him, and authorize all his actions in like manner. This done, the multitude so united in one person is called a Commonwealth, in Latin, *civitas.* This is the generation of that great *Leviathan,* or rather, to speak more reverently, of that *mortal* god to which we owe, under the *immortal* God, our peace and defense. For by this authority, given him by every particular man in the commonwealth, he has the use of so much power and strength conferred on him that by terror thereof he is enabled to form the wills of them all, to peace at home, and mutual aid against their enemies abroad. And in him consists the essence of the commonwealth; which, to define it, is one person of whose acts a great multitude, by mutual covenants one with another, have made themselves every one the author, to the end he may use the strength and means of them all, as he shall think expedient, for their peace and common defense.

And he that carries this person is called Sovereign, and said to have *sovereign power*; and every one besides, his subject. . . .

The difference of commonwealths consists in the difference of the sovereign. . . . When the representative is one man, then is the commonwealth a monarchy; when an assembly of all that will come together, then it is a democracy, or popular commonwealth; when an assembly of a part only, then it is called an aristocracy. . . .

\* \* \* \* \* \* \* \* \* \* \* \* \* \* \* \* \* \* \* \* \* \* \* \* \* \* \* \* \* \* \*

*Discussion Points:*

1. Review the Mayflower Compact in light of Hobbes's views on the social contract.
2. Review the Preamble to the United States Constitution in light of Hobbes's views on the social contract.
3. There is one ground for revolution in the Hobbesian civil society. What is it? List examples of developments that could justify a decision by citizens to withdraw their consent from the state.
4. Reflect upon Hobbes's idea that unlimited liberty—as men enjoyed in the state of nature—produces anxiety and insecurity. Do you agree that there is such a thing as too much freedom? Explain.

# CHAPTER 4

# JOHN LOCKE, *SECOND TREATISE,*
# *OF CIVIL GOVERNMENT* (1690)

John Locke (1632–1704), another social contract theorist, had a profound influence on the American Revolution. Like Hobbes, he used the state of nature as a starting point in his analysis of the origins and limits of governmental power. Unlike Hobbes, whose state of nature was little more than a perilous jungle, Locke presented a relatively more optimistic view of the natural state.

Locke saw natural men as largely free and equal, but all possessed God-given natural rights. All were subject to the laws of God and all were required to respect His natural laws. Such early shared agreement about fundamental values was absent from the Hobbesian natural state. Locke thought natural men were somewhat interconnected. They lived as members of a primitive community in which they were capable of treating one another with some degree of empathy and respect. The universal, natural laws of God bound natural men to respect the lives of their fellows. They lived in a community of mankind with God as their sovereign.

But Lockean natural men were still primarily interested in satisfying their selfish interests. When several desired the same thing, conflict inevitably followed. Man's passionately-selfish side made him unable to live in complete accordance with natural laws. Further, it was not always clear to conflicting parties how natural law applied to their immediate dispute; they were blinded by self-interest. They needed an impartial third party to adjudicate these disputes and to resolve conflicts peaceably. At this point, they employed reason.

Locke's natural men formed a social contract in which they exchanged some of their natural freedom for increased security and convenience. They established a state and empowered it to draft liberty-limiting laws that could be used to resolve disputes. But they insisted on retaining certain natural rights even after entering into civil society. They retained the rights to life, liberty, and property. A broad area of individual conduct would be beyond the control of the state. If the state violated the contract by abridging such rights, consent could be withdrawn.

As noted, Hobbes saw the state of nature as a place of extreme peril and intolerable insecurity. As such, his contractors were so desperate to live more secure lives that they relinquished almost all of their natural rights when entering into civil society. They retained only the right to life as they abided by the laws of their Leviathan. The Lockean state of nature, by contrast, was relatively less perilous; it was a place of inconvenient insecurity. For this reason, Locke's contractors retained more rights against their more limited state. In short, grounds for revolution are more varied in a Lockean civil society than in a Hobbesian one.

\* \* \* \* \* \* \* \* \* \* \* \* \* \* \* \* \* \* \* \* \* \* \* \* \* \*

[The state of nature is] a state of perfect freedom . . . [and] . . . also of equality, wherein all the power and jurisdiction is reciprocal, no one having more than another. . . .

But though this be a state of liberty, yet it is not a state of license. . . . The state of nature has a law of nature to govern it, which obliges every one, and reason, which is that law, teaches all mankind, who will but consult it, that being all equal and independent, no one ought to harm another in his life, health, liberty, or possessions: for men being all the workmanship of one omnipotent, and infinitely wise maker . . . sharing all in one community of nature, there cannot be supposed any such subordination among us, that may authorize us to destroy one another, as if we were made for one another's uses. . . .

. . . [T]he execution of the law of nature is, in that state, put into every man's hands, whereby every one has a right to punish the transgressors of that law to such a degree, as may hinder its violation. . . . [E]ach transgression may be punished to that degree, and with so much severity, as will suffice to make it an ill bargain for the offender, give him cause to repent, and terrify others from doing the like. . . .

. . . [In] political society . . . the community comes to be umpire, by settled standing rules; indifferent, and the same to all parties. And by men having authority from the community for the execution of those rules, decides all the differences that may happen between any members of that society concerning any matter of right, and punishes those offenses which any member hath committed against the society with such penalties as the law has established. . . .

Wherever, therefore, any number of men are so united into one society as to quit every one his executive power of the law of nature, and to resign it to the public, there and there only is a political or civil society. . . . For hereby he authorizes the society . . . to make laws for him as the public good of the society shall require. . . . And this puts men out of a state of nature into that of a commonwealth, by setting up a judge on earth with authority to determine all the controversies and redress the injuries that may happen to any member of the commonwealth. . . .

If man in the state of nature be so free . . . [to] be absolute lord of his own person and possessions; equal to the greatest and subject to no body, why will he part with his freedom . . . and subject himself to the dominion and control of any other power? To which 'tis obvious to answer, that though in the state of nature he hath such a right, yet the enjoyment of it is very uncertain and constantly exposed to the invasion of others . . . the enjoyment of the property he has in this state is very unsafe, very unsecure. This makes him willing to quit this condition which, however free, is full of fears and continual dangers; and 'tis not without reason that he seeks out and is willing to join in society with others who are already united, or have a mind to unite for the mutual preservation of their lives, liberties, and estates, which I call by the general name property.

The great and chief end, therefore, of men's uniting into commonwealths, and putting themselves under government, is the preservation of their property, to which in the state of nature there are many things wanting.

First, There wants an established, settled, known law, received and allowed by common consent to be the standard of right and wrong, and the common measure to decide all controversies between them. . . .

Secondly, In the state of nature there wants a known and indifferent judge, with authority to determine all differences according to the established law. . . .

Thirdly, In the state of nature there often wants power to back and support the sentence when right, and to give it due execution. . . .

Thus mankind, notwithstanding all the privileges of the state of nature, being but in an ill condition while they remain it, are quickly driven into society. Hence it comes to pass, that we seldom find any number of men live any time together in this state. The inconveniences that they are therein exposed to by the irregular and uncertain exercise of the power every man has of punishing the transgressions of others, make them take sanctuary under the established laws of government, and therein seek the preservation of their property. . . . And in this we have the original right and rise of both the legislative and executive power as well as of the governments and societies themselves.

The reason why men enter into society is the preservation of their property; and the end why they choose and authorize a legislative is that there may be laws made, and rules set, as guards and fences to the properties of all the members of the society to limit the powers and moderate the dominion of every part and member of the society. For since it can never be supposed to be the will of the society that the legislative should have a power to destroy that which everyone designs secure by entering into society, and for which the people submitted themselves to legislators of their own making; whenever the legislators endeavor to take away and destroy the property of the people, or to reduce them to slavery under arbitrary power, they put themselves into a state of war with the people, who are thereupon absolved from any further obedience, and are left to the common refuge which God hath provided for all men against force and violence. Whensoever, therefore, the legislative shall transgress this fundamental rule of society, and . . . endeavor to grasp themselves or put into the hands of any other an absolute power over the lives, liberties, and estates of the people, by this breach of trust they forfeit the power the people had put into their hands for quite contrary ends, and it devolves to the people; who have a right to resume their original liberty, and by the establishment of a new legislative (such as they shall think fit), provide for their own safety and security. . . .

But 'twill be said, this hypothesis lays a ferment for frequent rebellion. To which I answer:

First, No more than any other hypothesis. For when the people are . . . generally ill treated . . . [they] will be ready upon any occasion to ease themselves of a burden that sits heavy upon them.

Secondly, I answer such revolutions happen not upon every little mismanagement in public affairs . . . [but in response to] a long train of abuses, prevarications, and artifices. . . .

The end of government is the good of mankind; and which is best for mankind, that the people should be always exposed to the boundless will of tyranny, or that the rulers should be sometimes liable to be opposed when they grow exorbitant in the use of their power? . . .

\* \* \* \* \* \* \* \* \* \* \* \* \* \* \* \* \* \* \* \* \* \* \* \* \* \* \* \* \* \* \* \*

*Discussion Points:*

1. Review the Mayflower Compact in light of Locke's views on the social contract.

2. Review the Preamble to the Constitution in light of Locke's views on the social contract.
3. A social contract is a device through which people consent to establish and empower a government. At the same time, the contract may limit governmental power by describing the rights of citizens. Review the United States Constitution. Is it sensible to call it an American social contract? Why or why not? List examples of constitutional provisions that empower governmental institutions. List examples of provisions that limit governmental power or guarantee individual rights.
4. Locke envisioned multiple grounds for revolution. What are they? List examples of developments that could justify a decision by citizens to withdraw their consent from the state.
5. Compare and contrast Hobbes and Locke regarding the state of nature and the powers of the state.

# PART II:
# HISTORICAL ROOTS OF THE AMERICAN CONSTITUTION

# CHAPTER 5

# THE DECLARATION OF INDEPENDENCE (1776)

The Continental Congress approved a Resolution of Independence on July 2, 1776. Thomas Jefferson was charged with drafting a formal Declaration of Independence that would justify the American Revolution to the world. A final draft was approved on July 4, 1776. The document combined general concepts and an abstract theory of governmental authority with a list of specific grievances against King George III.

Jefferson's writing had a distinctively Lockean flavor. In the opening paragraphs, Jefferson invoked natural law in support of the claim that the King had violated the colonists' rights. Like Locke, Jefferson argued that all men are created equal, they enjoy certain natural rights, they create governments to defend these rights, governmental authority rests on the consent of the governed, and that consent can be withdrawn if the government becomes destructive of those rights. Jefferson followed these general principles with a 27-paragraph bill of particulars in which he chronicled ways in which the Crown had become destructive of the colonists' rights.

\* \* \* \* \* \* \* \* \* \* \* \* \* \* \* \* \* \* \* \* \* \* \* \* \* \*

The unanimous Declaration of the thirteen United States of America,

When in the course of human events, it becomes necessary for one people to dissolve the political bands which have connected them with another, and to assume among the Powers of the earth, the separate and equal station to which the Laws of Nature and of Nature's God entitle them, a decent respect to the opinions of mankind requires that they should declare the causes which impel them to the separation.

We hold these truths to be self-evident, that all men are created equal, that they are endowed by their Creator with certain unalienable Rights, that among these are Life, Liberty and the Pursuit of Happiness. That to secure these rights, Governments are instituted among

Men, deriving their just powers from the consent of the governed, That whenever any Form of Government becomes destructive of these ends, it is the right of the people to alter or to abolish it, and to institute new Government, laying its foundation on such principles and organizing its powers in such form, as to them shall seem most likely to effect their Safety and Happiness. Prudence, indeed, will dictate that Governments long established should not be changed for light and transient causes; and accordingly all experience hath shown, that mankind are more disposed to suffer, while evils are sufferable, than to right themselves by abolishing the forms to which they are accustomed. But when a long train of abuses and usurpations, pursuing invariably the same Object evinces a design to reduce them under absolute Despotism, it is their right, it is their duty, to throw off such Government, and to provide new Guards for their future security.—Such has been the patient sufferance of these Colonies; and such is now the necessity which constrains them to alter their former Systems of Government. The history of the present King of Great Britain is a history of repeated injuries and usurpations, all having in direct object the establishment of an absolute Tyranny over these States. To prove this, let Facts be submitted to a candid world.

He has refused his Assent to Laws, the most wholesome and necessary for the public good.

He has forbidden his Governors to pass Laws of immediate and pressing importance, unless suspended in their operation till his Assent should be obtained; and when so suspended, he has utterly neglected to attend to them.

He has refused to pass other Laws for the accommodation of large districts of people, unless those people would relinquish the right of Representation in the Legislature, a right inestimable to them and formidable to tyrants only.

He has called together legislative bodies at places unusual, uncomfortable, and distant from the depository of their Public Records, for the sole purpose of fatiguing them into compliance with his measures.

He has dissolved Representative Houses repeatedly, for opposing with manly firmness his invasions on the rights of the people.

He has refused for a long time, after such dissolutions, to cause others to be elected; whereby the Legislative Powers, incapable of Annihilation, have returned to the People at large for their exercise; the State remaining in the mean time exposed to all the dangers of invasion from without, and convulsions within.

He has endeavoured to prevent the population of these States; for that purpose obstructing the Laws for Naturalization of Foreigners; refusing to pass others to encourage their migration hither, and raising the conditions of new Appropriations of Lands.

He has obstructed the Administration of Justice, by refusing his Assent of Laws for establishing Judiciary Powers.

He has made Judges dependent on his Will alone, for the tenure of their offices, and the amount and payment of their salaries.

He has erected a multitude of New Offices, and sent hither swarms of Officers to harass our People, and eat out their substance.

He has kept among us, in times of peace, Standing Armies without the Consent of our legislature.

He has affected to render the Military independent of and superior to the Civil Power.

He has combined with others to subject us to a jurisdiction foreign to our constitution, and unacknowledged by our laws; giving his Assent to their acts of pretended Legislation:

For quartering large bodies of armed troops among us:

For protecting them, by a mock Trial, from Punishment for any Murders which they should commit on the Inhabitants of these States:

For cutting off our Trade with all parts of the world:

For imposing taxes on us without our Consent:

For depriving us in many cases, of the benefits of Trial by Jury:

For transporting us beyond Seas to be tried for pretended offences:

For abolishing the free System of English Laws in a neighbouring Province, establishing therein an Arbitrary government, and enlarging its Boundaries so as to render it at once an example and fit instrument for introducing the same absolute rule into these Colonies:

For taking away our Charters, abolishing our most valuable Laws, and altering fundamentally the Forms of our Government:

For suspending our own Legislature, and declaring themselves invested with Power to legislate for us in all cases whatsoever.

He has abdicated Government here, by declaring us out of his Protection and waging War against us.

He has plundered our seas, ravaged our Coasts, burnt our towns, and destroyed the lives of our people.

He is at the time transporting large armies of foreign mercenaries to compleat the works of death, desolation and tyranny, already begun with circumstances of Cruelty & perfidy scarcely paralleled in the most barbarous ages, and totally unworthy the Head of a civilized nation.

He has constrained our fellow Citizens taken Captive on the high Seas to bear Arms against their Country, to become the executioners of their friends and Brethren, or to fall themselves by their Hands.

He has excited domestic insurrections amongst us, and has endeavoured to bring on the inhabitants of our frontiers, the merciless Indian Savages, whose known rule of warfare, is an undistinguished destruction of all ages, sexes and conditions.

In every stage of these Oppressions We have Petitioned for Redress in the most humble terms: Our repeated Petitions have been answered only by repeated injury. A Prince, whose character is thus marked by every act which may define a Tyrant, is unfit to be the ruler of a free People.

Nor have We been wanting in attention to our British brethren. We have warned them from time to time of attempts by their legislature to extend an unwarrantable jurisdiction over us. We have reminded them of the circumstances of our emigration and settlement here. We have appealed to their native justice and magnanimity, and we have conjured them by the ties of our common kindred to disavow these usurpations, which, would inevitably interrupt our connections and correspondence. They too have been deaf to the voice of justice and of consanguinity. We must, therefore, acquiesce in the necessity, which denounces our Separation, and hold them, as we hold the rest of mankind, Enemies in War, in Peace Friends.

We, therefore, the Representatives of the united States of America, in General Congress, Assembled, appealing to the Supreme Judge of the world for the rectitude of our intentions, do, in the Name, and by Authority of the good People of these Colonies, solemnly publish and declare, That these United Colonies are, and of Right ought to be Free and Independent States; that they are absolved from all Allegiance to the British Crown, and that all political connection between them and the State of Great Britain, is and ought to be totally dissolved; and that as Free and Independent States, they have full Power to levy War, conclude Peace, contract Alliances, establish Commerce, and to do all other Acts and Things which Independent States may of right do. And for the support of this Declaration, with a firm reliance on the Protection of Divine Providence, we mutually pledge to each other our Lives, our Fortunes and our sacred Honor.

\* \* \* \* \* \* \* \* \* \* \* \* \* \* \* \* \* \* \* \* \* \* \* \* \* \* \* \* \* \*

*Discussion Points:*

1. List points on which Jefferson appears to have been influenced by Locke. Be specific.
2. Compare and contrast Hobbes, Locke, and Jefferson regarding the rights of men in civil society.
3. Study the charges leveled against the King by the colonists. Do

you detect any recurrent themes in the offenses attributed to the King?

4. Why do you think the signers of the Declaration of Independence tried to justify the American Revolution in the eyes of the world?

# CHAPTER 6

# THE ARTICLES OF CONFEDERATION
# (1777)

The Second Continental Congress assembled in 1775 as a provisional government to direct action against the British. In order to establish an authorized central government, delegates to that Congress formed a committee, chaired by Pennsylvania's John Dickinson, to draft articles of confederation and submit them to the states in 1777. In March, 1781, after all thirteen states had ratified the articles, a formal and authorized government assumed powers. This government lasted until 1789.

The Articles of Confederation created a central government with very limited powers, an understandable development in light of colonial experiences with the King. With memory of British rule so fresh, there was considerable reluctance to establish another powerful centralized government. Additionally, familiarity had developed with the governmental machinery that already operated at the state level. Such considerations influenced the shape of the Articles of Confederation.

The Articles did not provide for an independent chief executive officer for the nation. To do so, some argued, would be to create an American King. Neither did the Articles provide for a national court system. A Congress was established, in which each state would have a single vote. But this Congress was given limited powers. Congress had the power to declare war, to enter into treaties, and to establish and control the armed forces. But Congress could not compel states to respect treaties. Nor could Congress draft soldiers. Consequently, congressional power to conduct foreign relations effectively was questionable. Further, Congress could not regulate interstate and foreign commerce. It could neither collect taxes directly from the people nor compel states to pay a share of governmental costs. Instead, it relied on states to collect monies and to forward funds to defray expenses. Soon complaints were heard that the Articles of Confederation were too weak and were in need of revision.

Some were dissatisfied because Congress was unable to construct stable trade agreements with foreign nations. Some were dissatisfied because states sometimes used their taxing powers to the advantage of in-state businesses and to the disadvantage of out-of-state businesses trying to conduct commercial transactions across state lines. Some were dissatisfied because Congress could not draft troops to provide adequate protection against Indian raids, piracy, and so on. Some were dissatisfied because Congress was unable to enact retaliatory tariffs which might have induced Britain to relax trade and shipping restrictions imposed against the United States. Such dissatisfactions fueled mounting sentiment that the Articles of Confederation should be revised to establish a stronger national government.

\* \* \* \* \* \* \* \* \* \* \* \* \* \* \* \* \* \* \* \* \* \* \* \* \* \* \*

Whereas the Delegates of the United States of America in Congress assembled did on the fifteenth day of November in the Year of our Lord One Thousand Seven Hundred and Seventyseven, and in the Second Year of the Independence of America agree to certain articles of Confederation and perpetual Union between the States of Newhampshire, Massachusetts-bay, Rhodeisland, and Providence Plantations, Connecticut, New York, New Jersey, Pennsylvania, Delaware, Maryland, Virginia, North-Carolina, South-Carolina and Georgia in the Words following. . . .

ARTICLE I. The stile of this confederacy shall be "The United States of America."

ARTICLE II. Each State retains its sovereignty, freedom and independence, and every power, jurisdiction and right, which is not by this confederation expressly delegated to the United States, in Congress assembled.

ARTICLE III. The said States hereby severally enter into a firm league of friendship with each other, against all force offered to, of attacks made upon them, or any of them, on account of religion, sovereignty, trade, or any other pretence whatever.

ARTICLE IV. The better to secure and perpetuate mutual friendship and intercourse among people of the different States in this Union, the free inhabitants of each of these States, paupers, vagabonds and fugitives from justice excepted, shall be entitled to all privileges and immunities of free citizens in the several States; and the people of each State shall have free ingress and regress to and from any other State, and shall enjoy therein all the privileges of trade and commerce, subject to the same duties, impositions and restrictions as the inhabitants thereof respectively, provided that such restrictions shall not extend so far as to prevent the removal of property imported into any State, to any other State of which the owner is an inhabitant; provided also that no imposition, duties or restriction shall be laid by any State, on the property of the United States, or either of them.

If any person guilty of, or charged with treason, felony, or other high misdemeanor in any State, shall flee from justice, and be found in any of the United States, he shall upon demand of the Governor or Executive power, of the State from which he fled, be delivered up and removed to the State having jurisdiction of his offence.

Full faith and credit shall be given in each of these States to the records, acts and judicial proceedings of the courts and magistrates of every other State.

ARTICLE V. For the more convenient management of the general interests of the United States, delegates shall be annually appointed in such manner as the legislature of each State shall direct, to meet in Congress on the first Monday in November, in every year, with a power reserved to each State, to recall its delegates, or any of them, at any time within the year, and to send others in their stead, for the remainder of the year.

No State shall be represented in Congress by less than two, not by more than seven members; and no person shall be capable of being a delegate for more than three years in any term of six years; nor shall any person, being a delegate, be capable of holding any office under the United States, for which he, or another for his benefit receives any salary, fees or emolument of any kind.

Each State shall maintain its own delegates in a meeting of the States, and while they act as members of the committee of the States.

In determining questions in the United States, in Congress assembled, each State shall have one vote.

Freedom of speech and debate in Congress shall not be impeached or questioned in any court, or place out of Congress, and the members of Congress shall be protected in their persons from arrests and imprisonments, during the time of their going to and from, any attendance on Congress, except for treason, felony, or breach of the peace.

ARTICLE VI. No State without the consent of the United States in Congress assembled, shall send any embassy to, or receive any embassy from, or enter into any conference, agreement, alliance or treaty with any king prince or state; nor shall any person holding any office of profit or trust under the United States, or any of them, accept of any present, emolument, office or title of any kind whatever from any king, prince or foreign state; nor shall the United States in Congress assembled, or any of them, grant any title of nobility.

No two or more States shall enter into any treaty, confederation or alliance whatever between them, without the consent of the United States in Congress assembled, specifying accurately the purposes for which the same is to be entered into, and how long it shall continue.

No State shall lay any imposts or duties, which may interfere with any stipulations in treaties, entered into by the United States in Congress assembled, with any king, prince or state, in pursuance of any treaties already proposed by Congress, to the courts of France and Spain.

No vessels of war shall be kept up in time of peace by any State, except such number only, as shall be deemed necessary by the United States in Congress assembled, for the defence of such State, or its trade: nor shall any body of forces be kept up by any State, in time of peace, except such number only, as in the judgment of the United States, in Congress assembled, shall be deemed requisite to garrison the forts necessary for the defence of such State; but every State shall always keep up a well regulated and disciplined militia, sufficiently armed and accoutered, and shall provide and constantly have ready for use, in public stores, a due number of field pieces and tents, and a proper quantity of arms, ammunition and camp equipage.

No State shall engage in any war without the consent of the United States in Congress assembled, unless such State be actually invaded by enemies, or shall have received certain advice of a resolution being formed by some nation of Indians to invade such State, and the danger is so imminent as not to admit of a delay, till the United States in Congress assembled can be consulted: nor shall any State grant commissions to any ships or vessels of war, nor letters of marque or reprisal, except it be after a declaration of war by the United States in Congress assembled, and then only against the kingdom or state and the subjects thereof, against which war has been so declared, and under such regulations as shall be established by the United States in Congress assembled, unless such State is infested by pirates, in which case vessels of war may be fitted out for that occasion, and kept as long as the danger shall continue, or until the United States in Congress assembled shall determine otherwise.

ARTICLE VII. When land-forces are raised by any State for the common defence, all officers of or under the rank of colonel, shall be appointed by the Legislature of each State respectively by whom such forces shall be raised, or in such manner as such State shall direct, and all vacancies shall be filled up by the State which first made the appointment.

ARTICLE VIII. All charges of war, and all other expenses that shall be incurred for the common defence or general welfare, and allowed by the United States in Congress assembled, shall be defrayed out of a common treasury, which shall be supplied by the several States, in proportion to the value of all land within each State, granted to or surveyed for any person, as such land and the buildings and improvements thereon shall be estimated according to such mode as the United States in Congress assembled, shall from time to time direct and appoint.

The taxes for paying that proportion shall be laid and levied by the authority and direction of the Legislature of the several States within the time agreed upon by the United States in Congress assembled.

ARTICLE IX. The United States in Congress assembled, shall have the sole and exclusive right and power of determining on peace and war, except in the cases mentioned in the sixth article—of sending and receiving ambassadors—entering into treaties and alliances, provided that no treaty of commerce shall be made whereby the legislative power of the respective States shall be restrained from imposing such imposts and duties on foreigners, as their own people are subjected to, or from prohibiting the exportation or importation of any species of goods or commodities whatsoever—of establishing rules for deciding in all cases, what captures on land or water shall be legal, and in what manner prizes taken by land or naval forces in the service of the United States shall be divided or appropriated—of granting letters of marque and reprisal in times of peace—appointing courts for the trial of piracies and felonies committed on the high seas and establishing courts for receiving and determining finally appeals in all cases of captures, provided that no member of Congress shall be appointed a judge of any of the said courts.

The United States in Congress assembled shall also be the last resort on appeal in all disputes and differences now subsisting or that hereafter may arise between two or more States concerning boundary, jurisdiction or any other cause whatever: which authority shall always be exercised in the manner following. Whenever the legislative or executive authority or lawful agent of any State in controversy with another shall present a petition to Congress, stating the matter in question and praying for a hearing, notice thereof shall be given by order of Congress to the legislative or executive authority of the other State in controversy, and a day assigned for the appearance of the parties by their lawful agents, who shall then be directed to appoint by joint consent, commissioners or judges to constitute a court for hearing and determining the matter in question: but if they cannot agree, Congress shall name three persons out of each of the United States, and from the list of such persons each party shall alternately strike out one, the petitioners beginning, until the number shall be reduced to thirteen; and from the number not less than seven, nor more than nine names as Congress shall direct, shall in the presence of Congress be drawn out by lot, and the persons whose names shall be so drawn or any five of them, shall be commissioners or judges, to hear and finally determine the controversy, so always as a major part of the judges who shall hear the cause shall agree in the determination: and if either party shall neglect to attend at the day appointed, without showing reasons, which Congress shall judge sufficient, or being present shall refuse to strike, the Congress shall proceed to nominate three persons out of each State, and the Secretary of Congress shall strike in behalf of such party absent or refusing: and the judgment and sentence of the court to be appointed, in the manner before prescribed, shall be final and conclusive; and if any of the parties shall refuse to submit to the authority of such court, or to appear or defend their claim or cause, the court shall nevertheless proceed to pronounce sentence, or judgment, which shall in like manner be final and decisive, the judgment or sentence and other proceedings being in either case transmitted to Congress, and lodged among the acts of Congress for the security of the parties concerned: provided that every commissioner, before he sits in judgment, shall take an oath to be administered by one of the judges of the supreme or superior court of the State where the cause shall be tried, "well and truly to hear and determine the matter in question, according to the best of his judgment, without favour, affection or hope of reward:" provided also that no State shall be deprived of territory for the benefit of the United States.

All controversies concerning the private right of soil claimed under different grants of two or more States, whose jurisdiction as they may respect such lands, and the States which passed such grants are adjusted, the said grants or either of them being at the same time claimed to have originated antecedent to such settlement of jurisdiction, shall on the petition of either party to the Congress of the United States, be finally determined as near as may be in the same manner as is before prescribed for deciding disputes respecting territorial jurisdiction between different States.

The United States in Congress assembled shall also have the sole and exclusive right and power of regulating the alloy and value of coin struck by their own authority, or by that of the respective States—fixing the standard of weights and measure throughout the United

States—regulating the trade and managing all affairs with the Indians, not members of any of the States, provided that the legislative right of any State within its own limits be not infringed or violated—establishing and regulating post-offices from one State to another, throughout all the United States, and exacting such postage on the papers passing thro' the same as may be requisite to defray the expenses of the said office—appointing all officers of the land forces, in the service of the United States, excepting regimental officers—appointing all the officers of the naval forces, and commissioning all officers whatever in the service of the United States—making rules for the government and regulation of the said land and naval forces, and directing their operations.

The United States in Congress assembled shall have authority to appoint a committee, to sit in the recess of Congress, to be denominated "a Committee of the States," and to consist of one delegate from each State; and to appoint such other committees and civil officers as may be necessary for managing the general affairs of the United States under their direction—to appoint one of their number to preside, provided that no person be allowed to serve in the office of president more than one year in any term of three years; to ascertain the necessary sums of money to be raised for the service of the United States, and to appropriate and apply the same for defraying the public expenses—to borrow money, or emit bills on the credit of the United States, transmitting every half year to the respective States an account of the sums of money so borrowed or emitted,—to build and equip a navy—to agree upon the number of land forces, and to make requisitions from each State for its quota, in proportion to the number of white inhabitants in such State; which requisition shall be binding, and thereupon the Legislature of each State shall appoint the regimental officers, raise the men and cloath, arm and equip them in a soldier like manner, at the expense of the United States; and the officers and men so cloathed, armed and equipped shall march to the place appointed, and within the time agreed on by the United States in Congress assembled: but if the United States in Congress assembled shall, on consideration of circumstances judge proper that any State should not raise men, or should raise a smaller number than its quota, and that any other State should raise a greater number of men than the quota thereof, such extra number shall be raised, officered, cloathed, armed and equipped in the same manner as the quota of such State, unless the legislature of such State shall judge that such extra number cannot be safely spared out of the same, in which case they shall raise officer, cloath, arm and equip as many of such extra number as they judge can be safely spared. And the officers and men so cloathed, armed and equipped, shall march to the place appointed, and within the time agreed on by the United States in Congress assembled.

The United States in Congress assembled shall never engage in a war, nor grant letters of marque and reprisal in time of peace, nor enter into any treaties or alliances, nor coin money, nor regulate the value thereof, nor ascertain the sums and expenses necessary for the defence and welfare of the United States, or any of them, nor emit bills, nor borrow money on the credit of the United States, nor appropriate money, nor agree upon the number of vessels of war, to be built or purchased, or the number of land or sea forces to be raised, nor appoint a commander in chief of the army or navy, unless nine States assent to the same: nor shall a question on any other point, except for adjourning from day to day be determined, unless by the votes of a majority of the United States in Congress assembled.

The Congress of the United States shall have power to adjourn to any time within the year, and to any place within the United States, so that no period of adjournment be for a longer duration than the space of six months, and shall publish the journal of the proceedings monthly, except such parts thereof relating to treaties, alliances or military operations, as in their judgment require secrecy; and the yeas and nays of the delegates of each State on any question shall be entered on the journal, when it is desired by any delegate; and the delegates of a State, or any of them, at his or their request shall be furnished with a transcript of the said journal, except such parts as are above excepted, to lay before the Legislatures of the several States.

ARTICLE X. The committee of the States, or any nine of them, shall be authorized to execute, in the recess of Congress, such of the powers of Congress as the United States in Congress assembled, by the consent of nine States, shall from time to time think expedient to vest them with; provided that no power be delegated to the said committee, for the exercise of which, by the articles of confederation, the voice of nine States in the Congress of the United States assembled is requisite.

ARTICLE XI. Canada acceding to this confederation, and joining in the measures of the United States, shall be admitted into, and entitled to all the advantages of this Union: but no other colony shall be admitted into the same, unless such admission be agreed to by nine States.

ARTICLE XII. All bills of credit emitted, monies borrowed and debts contracted by, or under the authority of Congress, before the assembling of the United States, in pursuance of the present confederation, shall be deemed and considered as a charge against the United

States, for payment and satisfaction whereof the said United States, and the public faith are hereby solemnly pledged.

ARTICLE XIII. Every State shall abide by the determinations of the United States in Congress assembled, on all questions which by this confederation are submitted to them. And the articles of this confederation shall be inviolably observed by every State, and the Union shall be perpetual; nor shall any alteration at any time hereafter be made in any of them; unless such alteration be agreed to in a Congress of the United States, and be afterwards confirmed by the Legislatures of every State.

And whereas it has pleased the Great Governor of the world to incline the hearts of the Legislatures we respectively represent in Congress, to approve of, and to authorize us to ratify the said articles of confederation and perpetual union. Know ye that we the undersigned delegates, by virtue of the power and authority to us given for the purpose, do by these presents, in the name and in behalf of our respective constituents, fully and entirely ratify and confirm each and every of the said articles of confederation and perpetual union, and all and singular the matters and things therein contained: and we do further solemnly plight and engage the faith of our respective constituents, that they shall abide by the determinations of the United States in Congress assembled, on all questions, which by the said confederation are submitted to them. And that the articles thereof shall be inviolably observed by the States we re[s]pectively represent, and that the Union shall be perpetual.

In witness whereof we have hereunto set our hands in Congress. Done at Philadelphia in the State of Pennsylvania the ninth day of July in the year of our Lord one thousand seven hundred and seventy-eight, and in the third year of the Independence of America.

\* \* \* \* \* \* \* \* \* \* \* \* \* \* \* \* \* \* \* \* \* \* \* \* \* \* \* \* \* \* \* \* \* \*

*Discussion Points:*

1. Review some of the criticisms voiced against the Articles of Confederation. Do you detect any recurrent theme(s)?
2. Some of the weaknesses of the Articles of Confederation were listed earlier. Do you detect any additional weaknesses?

# CHAPTER 7

# THE NORTHWEST ORDINANCE (1787)

Land ordinances passed in 1784 and 1785 provided for the Northwest Territory to be surveyed, parceled into segments, and sold at auction. The impoverished Congress was eager to sell these holdings in that they represented a source of income that did not depend on the unreliable contributions of the states. Immediate public response failed to meet congressional expectations.

One of the last acts of the Articles of Confederation Congress was the Northwest Ordinance of 1787. The Act provided for the political organization of the region. It described the basic rights and liberties of settlers. It specified that states carved out of this territory would be admitted to the Union on an equal footing with the original states. As such, Congress avoided future conflicts regarding the relationship of colonies and territories to the central government—a problem that England had not been able to resolve.

* * * * * * * * * * * * * * * * * * * * * * * * * * * * *

*Be it ordained by the United States in Congress assembled,* That the said territory, for the purposes of temporary government, be one district, subject, however, to be divided into two districts, as future circumstances may, in the opinion of Congress, make it expedient. . . .

*Be it ordained by the authority aforesaid,* That there shall be appointed from time to time by Congress, a governor, whose commission shall continue in force for the term of three years, unless sooner revoked by Congress; he shall reside in the district. . . .

There shall be appointed from time to time by Congress, a secretary, whose commission shall continue in force for four years unless sooner revoked; he shall reside in the district and have a freehold estate therein in 500 acres of land, while in the exercise of his office. . . .

There shall also be appointed a court to consist of three judges, any two of whom to form a court, who shall have a common law jurisdiction, and reside in the district, and have each therein a freehold estate in 500 acres of land while in the exercise of their offices; and their commissions shall continue in force during good behavior.

The governor and judges, or a majority of them, shall adopt and publish in the district such laws of the original States, criminal and civil, as may be necessary and best suited to the circumstances of the district, and report them to Congress from time to time: which laws shall be in force in the district until the organization of the General Assembly therein, unless disapproved of by Congress; but afterwards the Legislature shall have authority to alter them as they shall think fit. . . .

Previous to the organization of the general assembly, the governor shall appoint such magistrates and other civil officers in each county or township, as he shall find necessary for the preservation of the peace and good order in the same: After the general assembly shall be organized, the powers and duties of the magistrates and other civil officers shall be regulated and defined by the said assembly; but all magistrates and other civil officers not herein otherwise directed, shall, during the continuance of this temporary government, be appointed by the governor. . . .

So soon as there shall be five thousand free male inhabitants of full age in the district, upon giving proof thereof to the governor, they shall receive authority, with time and place, to elect representatives from their counties or townships to represent them in the general assembly: *Provided*, That, for every five hundred free male inhabitants, there shall be one representative, and so on progressively with the number of free male inhabitants shall the right of representation increase, until the number of representatives shall amount to twenty-five; after which, the number and proportion of representatives shall be regulated by the legislature: *Provided*, That no person be eligible or qualified to act as a representative unless he shall have been a citizen of one of the United States three years, and be a resident in the district, or unless he shall have resided in the district three years, and, in either case, shall likewise hold in his own right, in fee simple, two hundred acres of land within the same: *Provided, also,* That a freehold in fifty acres of land in the district, having been a citizen of one of the states, and being resident in the district, or the like freehold and two years residence in the district, shall be necessary to qualify a man as an elector of a representative.

The representatives thus elected, shall serve for the term of two years. . . .

The general assembly or legislature shall consist of the governor, legislative council, and a house of representatives. . . .

And the governor, legislative council, and house of representatives, shall have authority to make laws in all cases, for the good government of the district, not repugnant to the principles and articles in this ordinance established and declared. And all bills, having passed by a majority in the house, and by a majority in the council, shall be referred to the governor for his assent; but no bill, or legislative act whatever, shall be of any force without his assent. The governor shall have power to convene, prorogue, and dissolve the general assembly, when, in his opinion, it shall be expedient. . . .

And, for extending the fundamental principles of civil and religious liberty, which form the basis whereon these republics, their laws and constitutions are erected; to fix and establish those principles as the basis of all laws, constitutions, and governments, which forever hereafter shall be formed in the said territory: to provide also for the establishment of States, and permanent government therein, and for their admission to a share in the federal councils on an equal footing with the original States, at as early periods as may be consistent with the general interest:

It is hereby ordained and declared by the authority aforesaid, That the following articles shall be considered as articles of compact between the original States and the people and States in the said territory and forever remain unalterable, unless by common consent, to wit:

ART. 1. No person, demeaning himself in a peaceable and orderly manner, shall ever be molested on account of his mode of worship or religious sentiments, in the said territory.

ART. 2. The inhabitants of the said territory shall always be entitled to the benefits of the writ of *habeas corpus*, and of the trial by jury; of a proportionate representation of the people in the legislature; and of judicial proceedings according to the course of the common law. All persons shall be bailable, unless for capital offences, where the proof shall be evident or the presumption great. All fines shall be moderate; and no cruel or unusual punishments shall be inflicted. No man shall be deprived of his liberty or property, but by the judgment of his peers or the law of the land; and, should the public exigencies make it necessary, for the common preservation, to take any person's property, or to demand his particular services, full compensation shall be made for the same. And, in the just preservation of rights and property, it is understood and declared, that no law ought ever to be made, or have force in the said territory, that shall, in any manner whatever, interfere with or affect private contracts or engagements, *bona fide*, and without fraud, previously formed.

ART. 3. Religion, morality, and knowledge, being necessary to good government and the happiness of mankind, schools and the means of education shall forever be encouraged. The utmost good faith shall always be observed towards the Indians; their lands and property shall never be taken from them without their consent; and, in their property, rights, and liberty, they shall never be invaded or disturbed, unless in just and lawful wars authorized by Congress; but laws founded in justice and humanity, shall from time to time be made for preventing wrongs being done to them and for preserving peace and friendship with them.

ART. 4. The said territory, and the States which may be formed therein, shall forever remain a part of this Confederacy of the United States of America, subject to the Articles of Confederation, and to such alterations therein as shall be constitutionally made; and to all the acts and ordinances of the United States in Congress assembled, comformable thereto. The inhabitants and settlers in the said territory shall be subject to pay a part of the federal debts contracted or to be contracted, and a proportional part of the expenses of government, to be apportioned on them by Congress according to the same common rule and measure by which apportionments thereof shall be made on the other States; and the taxes for paying their proportion shall be laid and levied by the authority and direction of the legislatures of the district or districts, or new States, as in the original States, within the time agreed upon by the United States in Congress assembled. The legislatures of those districts or new States, shall never interfere with the primary disposal of the soil by the United States in Congress assembled, nor with any regulations Congress may find necessary for securing the title in such soil to the *bona fide* purchasers. No tax shall be imposed on lands the property of the United States; and, in no case, shall non-resident proprietors be taxed higher than residents. The navigable waters leading into the Mississippi and St. Lawrence, and the carrying places between the same, shall be common highways and forever free, as well to the inhabitants of the said territory as to the citizens of the United States, and those of any other States that may be admitted into the confederacy, without any tax, impost, or duty therefor.

ART. 5. There shall be formed in the said territory, not less than three nor more than five States. . . .

And, whenever any of the said States shall have sixty thousand free inhabitants therein, such State shall be admitted, by its delegates, into the Congress of the United States, on an equal footing with the original States in all respects whatever, and shall be at liberty to form a permanent constitution and State government: *Provided*, the constitution and government so to be formed, shall be republican, and in conformity to the principles contained in these articles; and, so far as it can be consistent with the general interest of the confederacy, such admission shall be allowed at an earlier period, and when there may be a less number of free inhabitants in the State than sixty thousand.

ART. 6. There shall be neither slavery nor involuntary servitude in the said territory, otherwise than in the punishment of crimes whereof the party shall have been duly convicted; *Provided, always,* That any person escaping into the same, from whom labor or service is lawfully claimed in any one of the original States, such fugitive may be lawfully reclaimed and conveyed to the person claiming his or her labor or service as aforesaid. . . .

\* \* \* \* \* \* \* \* \* \* \* \* \* \* \* \* \* \* \* \* \* \* \* \* \* \* \* \* \* \* \*

*Discussion Points:*

1. Recall Hobbes and Locke regarding social contracts. The Northwest Ordinance established a governmental system, defined the rights of citizens, and detailed the status of new states. As such, one might argue that it was a "social contract." On the other hand, Congress wrote the Ordinance *for* the settlers; they did not write it themselves. Discuss fully. In doing so, comment on the fact that when new States qualified for admittance into the union, citizens could draft their own republican state constitutions.

2. Compare and contrast provisions of the Ordinance with related provisions in the Constitution. Comment specifically on the following:
   a. supremacy of the Ordinance or the Constitution to other laws
   b. religious liberty
   c. right to trial by jury
   d. protection against excessive bails and fines
   e. prohibition of cruel and unusual punishments
   f. protection against deprivation of liberty or property without the judgment of one's peers (due process?)
   g. guarantee of just compensation in the event that private property is taken for public use
   h. taxation
   i. protection of navigation, shipping, and commerce
   j. guarantee of a "republican" form of government
   k. slavery.

# CHAPTER 8

# JAMES MADISON, THE LAST DAY OF THE CONSTITUTIONAL CONVENTION (SEPTEMBER 17, 1787)

Criticisms of the Articles of Confederation mounted in the mid-1780s. In September of 1786, delegates from five states met in Annapolis to discuss such matters. The small turnout disappointed the nationalists in attendance, but they persuaded Congress to support a second meeting in Philadelphia "to render the constitution of the Federal Government adequate to the exigencies of the Union." Congress announced the convention would be held in May 1787 for "the sole and express purpose of revising the Articles of Confederation."

In the meantime, a group of impoverished farmers led by Daniel Shays rebelled against high taxes, high interest rates, and mortgage foreclosures in Massachusetts. State militiamen put down the rebellion before United States troops were able to arrive on the scene. These developments motivated some delegates to take part in the Philadelphia convention so the national government could be strengthened. All in all, fifty-five delegates from twelve states attended. They exceeded their charge and drafted a new Constitution.

Despite similarities in their backgrounds, the delegates represented diverse areas and interests. Their disagreements were many and, frequently, severe. Large-state delegates clashed with those from small states. Nationalists clashed with advocates of states' rights. Numerous compromises were necessary to draft the new document. One produced a bicameral legislature. Each state would receive two seats in the Senate, but seats in the House of Representatives would be apportioned on the basis of population. Further, Representatives would be elected through a direct popular vote but, in light of some doubts about the capabilities of the general electorate, Senators would be selected by state legislators. Also, the delegates decided to let states set their own suffrage requirements and subsequently, the vote was widely denied to women, blacks, and others. Another compromise involved population counts. It was decided for purposes both of apportioning House seats and taxation that slaves would be counted as three-fifths of all other persons. Additionally, the delegates decided that Congress could not halt the importation of new slaves before 1808. Thus, it is readily apparent that the delegates sometimes compromised ideals and principles in their attempts to resolve their disputes and draft the new Constitution.

When the delegates ended their deliberations and heard the new Constitution read in finished form, some expressed fear that they had created an imperfect document. These reservations are evident in James Madison's notes on the last day of the Convention.

* * * * * * * * * * * * * * * * * * * * * * * * * * * * *

Monday, September 17

In Convention, the 109th day, the engrossed Constitution being read, Dr. Franklin rose with a speech in his hand, which he had reduced to writing for his own conveniency, and which Mr. Wilson read in the words following:

Mr. President:

I confess that there are several parts of this constitution which I do not at present approve, but I am not sure I shall never approve them, for having lived long, I have experienced many instances of being obliged by better information or fuller consideration, to change opinions even on important subjects, which I once thought right, but found to be otherwise. It is therefore that the older I grow, the more apt I am to doubt my own judgment, and to pay more respect to the judgment of others. Most men indeed as well as most sects in Religion, think themselves in possession of all truth, and that wherever others differ from them it is so far error. Steele, a Protestant in a Dedication tells the Pope, that the only difference between our Churches in their opinions of the certainty of their doctrine is, the Church of Rome is infallible and the Church of England is never in the wrong. But though many private persons think almost as highly of their own infallibility as that of their sect, few express it so naturally as a certain French lady, who in a dispute with her sister, said, "I don't know how it happens, Sister but I meet with no body by myself, that's always in the right,"—*Il n'y a que moi qui a tojours raison.*

In these sentiments, Sir, I agree to this Constitution with all its faults, If they are such; because I think a general Government necessary for us, and there is no form of Government but what may be a blessing to the people if well administered, and believe farther that this is likely to be well administered for a course of years, and can only end in Despotism, as other forms have done before it, when the people shall become so corrupted as to need despotic Government, being incapable of any other. I doubt too whether any other Convention we can obtain may be able to make a better Constitution. For when you assemble a number of men to have the advantage of their joint wisdom, you inevitably assemble with those men, all their prejudices, their passions, their errors of opinion, their local interests, and their selfish views. From such an Assembly can a perfect production be expected? It therefore astonishes me, Sir, to find this system approaching so near to perfection as it does; and I think it will astonish our enemies, who are waiting with confidence to hear that our councils are confounded like those of the Builders of Babel; and that our States are on the point of separation, only to meet hereafter for the purpose of cutting one another's throats. Thus I consent, Sir, to this Constitution because I expect no better, and because I am not sure, that it is not the best. The opinions I have had of its errors, I sacrifice to the public good—I have never whispered a syllable of them abroad—Within these walls they are born, and here they shall die—if every one of us in returning to our Constituents were to report the objections he has had to it, and endeavor to gain partizans in support of them, we might prevent its being generally received, and thereby lose all the salutary effects and great advantages resulting naturally in our favor among foreign Nations as well as among ourselves, from our real or apparent unanimity. Much of the strength and efficiency of any Government in procuring and securing happiness to the people, depends on opinion, on the general opinion of the goodness of the Government, as well as of the wisdom and integrity of its Governors. I hope therefore that for the sake of posterity, we shall act heartily and unanimously in recommending this Constitution (if approved by Congress and confirmed by the Conventions) wherever our influence may extend, and turn our future thoughts and endeavors to the means of having it well administered.

On the whole, Sir, I cannot help expressing a wish that every member of the Convention who may still have objections to it, would with me, on this occasion doubt a little of his own infallibility—and to make manifest our unanimity, put his name to this instrument.—He then moved that the Constitution be signed by members and offered the following as a convenient form viz. 'Done in Convention, by the unanimous consent of the States present the 17th of September—In Witness whereof we have hereunto subscribed our names'. . .

Mr. Randolph then rose and with an allusion to the observations of Dr. Franklin, apologized for his refusing to sign the Constitution, notwithstanding the vast majority and venerable names that would give sanction to its wisdom and its worth. He said however that he did not mean by this refusal to decide that he should oppose the Constitution without doors. He meant only to keep himself free to be governed by his duty as it should be prescribed by his future judgment—He refused to sign, because he thought the object of the convention would be frustrated by the alternative which it presented to the people. Nine States will fail to ratify the plan and confusion must ensue. With such a view of the subject he ought not, he could not, by pledging himself to support the plan, restrain himself from taking such steps as might appear to him most consistent with the public good.

Mr. Governeur Morris said that he too had objections, but considering the present plan as the best that was to be attained, he should take it with all its faults. The majority had determined in its favor and by that determination he should abide. The moment this plan goes forth all other considerations will be laid aside—and the great question will be, shall there be a national Government or not? and this must take place or a general anarchy will be the alternative. . .

Mr. Hamilton expressed his anxiety that every member should sign . . . No man's ideas were more remote from the plan than his own were known to be; but it is impossible to deliberate between anarchy and Convulsion on one side, and the chance of good to be expected from the plan on the other. . .

Mr. Gerry described the painful feelings of his situation, and the embarrassment under which he rose to offer any further observations of the subject which had been finally decided. Whilst the plan was depending, he had treated it with all the freedom he thought it deserved. He now felt himself bound as he was to treat it with the respect due to the Act of the Convention—He hoped he should not violate that respect in declaring on this occasion his fears that a Civil war may result from the present crisis of the United States—In Massachusetts, particularly he saw the danger of this calamitous event—In that State there are two parties, one devoted to Democracy, the worst he thought of all political evils, the other as violent in the opposite extreme. From the collision of these in opposing and resisting the Constitution, confusion was greatly to be feared. He had thought it necessary for this and other reasons that the plan should have been proposed in a more mediating shape, in order to abate the heat and opposition of parties—As it had been passed by the Convention, he was persuaded it would have a contrary effect—He could not therefore by signing the Constitution pledge himself to abide by it at all events... Alluding to the remarks of Dr. Franklin, he could not he said but view them as levelled at himself and the other gentlemen who meant not to sign; ...

On motion of Dr. Franklin.

New Hampshire: ay. Massachusetts: ay. Connecticut: ay. New Jersey: ay. Pennsylvania: ay. Delaware: ay. Maryland: ay. Virginia: ay. North Carolina: ay. South Carolina: divided. Georgia: ay. (Ayes-10; noes-0; divided-1.) ...

The members then proceeded to sign the instrument.

Whilst the last members were signing it Dr. Franklin looking towards the President's Chair, at the back of which a rising sun happened to be painted, observed to a few members near him, that Painters had found it difficult to distinguish in their art a rising from a setting sun. I have, said he, often and often in the course of the Session, and the vicissitudes of my hopes and fears as to its issue, looked at that behind the President without being able to tell whether it was rising or setting; But now at length I have the happiness to know that it is a rising and not a setting sun.

The Constitution being signed by all the Members except Mr. Randolph, Mr. Mason, and Mr. Gerry who declined giving it the sanction of their names, the Convention dissolved itself by the Adjournment sine die—

\* \* \* \* \* \* \* \* \* \* \* \* \* \* \* \* \* \* \* \* \* \* \* \* \* \* \* \*

*Discussion Points:*

1. Why did Franklin sign the Constitution? Why did he advocate that the delegates unanimously endorse it?
2. Why did Randolph refuse to sign the Constitution? Did he oppose it or did he, in effect, abstain? Explain.
3. Why did Gouverneur Morris sign the Constitution? Do you see any similarity between his position and Franklin's?
4. Why did Hamilton sign the Constitution? Do you see any similarity between his position and Franklin's?
5. Why did Gerry refuse to sign the Constitution?

# PART III:
# THE RATIFICATION DEBATES

# CHAPTER 9

# *THE FEDERALIST* PAPERS (1787–1788)

After the Constitution was written, ratification remained. It was decided that special state ratification meetings would be held and that the Constitution would stand approved when it received the support of nine states. New York was a strong state. If New York failed to ratify, the nation would lack geographical unity. Commercial and economic implications of such a refusal were also important. Further, other states might follow New York's example. For such reasons, the State's ratification was considered crucial.

James Madison, Alexander Hamilton, and John Jay wrote a series of 85 letters to newspapers in New York. The letters appeared from October 27, 1787 through May 28, 1788 and were published in book form in June of 1788. In these letters, the authors offered a philosophical defense of the proposed Constitution in an effort to persuade New Yorkers to ratify it. These *Federalist* papers have long been recognized as an outstanding contribution to the literature on constitutional democracy and federalism, and even as a classic of Western political thought. George Washington predicted that the work "will merit the notice of posterity because in it are candidly discussed the principle of freedom and the topics of government which will always be interesting to mankind. . . ." These letters stand as the best place to look to learn what the writers of the Constitution had in mind.

The letters were published under the pseudonym *Publius* because the authors were unwilling, for political reasons, to be identified with particular selections. As a result, some controversy surrounds the authorship of some of the pieces. Nevertheless, most agree that Hamilton wrote 51 letters, Jay 5, and Madison 29. It seems safe to attribute numbers 1, 69, 70, and 78 to Hamilton and numbers 10, 51, 57, and 62 to Madison.

\* \* \* \* \* \* \* \* \* \* \* \* \* \* \* \* \* \* \* \* \* \* \* \* \* \* \* \*

## ALEXANDER HAMILTON, *THE FEDERALIST*, NO. 1

In this selection, Hamilton explained the reasons for writing *The Federalist* papers. He noted that the letters would discuss the insufficiency of the Articles of Confederation, the need for a stronger central government, similarities between the proposed Constitution and existing state constitutions, and the additional security that the Constitution would provide.

\* \* \* \* \* \* \* \* \* \* \* \* \* \* \* \* \* \* \* \* \* \* \* \* \* \* \* \*

After an unequivocal experience of the inefficiency of the subsisting federal government, you are called upon to deliberate on a new Constitution for the United States of America. The subject speaks its own importance; comprehending in its consequences nothing less than the existence of the UNION, the safety and welfare of the parts of which it is composed, the fate of an empire in many respects the most interesting in the world. It has been frequently remarked that it seems to have been reserved to the people of this country, by their conduct and example, to decide the important question, whether societies of men are really capable or not of establishing good government from reflection and choice, or whether they are forever destined to depend for their political constitutions on accident and force. If there be any truth in the remark, the crisis at which we are arrived may with propriety be regarded as the era in which that decision is to be made; and a wrong election of the part we shall act may, in this view, deserve to be considered as the general misfortune of mankind.

This idea will add the inducements of philanthropy to those of patriotism, to heighten the solicitude which all considerate and good men must feel for the event. Happy will it be if our choice should be directed by a judicious estimate of our true interests, unperplexed and unbiased by considerations not connected with the public good. But this is a thing more ardently to be wished than seriously to be expected. The plan offered to our deliberations affects too many particular interests, innovates upon too many local institutions, not to involve in its discussion a variety of objects foreign to its merits, and of views, passions and prejudices little favorable to the discovery of truth.

Among the most formidable of the obstacles which the new Constitution will have to encounter may readily be distinguished the obvious interest of a certain class of men in every State to resist all changes which may hazard a diminution of the power emolument, and consequence of the offices they hold under the State establishments; and the perverted ambition of another class of men, who will either hope to aggrandize themselves by the confusions of their country, or will flatter themselves with fairer prospects of elevation from the subdivision of the empire into several partial confederacies than from its union under one government. . . .

And yet, however just these sentiments will be allowed to be, we have already sufficient indications that it will happen in this as in all former cases of great national discussion. A torrent of angry and malignant passions will be let loose. To judge from the conduct of the opposite parties, we shall be led to conclude that they will mutually hope to evince the justness of their opinions, and to increase the number of their converts by the loudness of their declamations and the bitterness of their invectives. An enlightened zeal for the energy and efficiency of government will be stigmatized as the offspring of a temper fond of despotic power and hostile to the principles of liberty. An over-scrupulous jealousy of danger to the rights of the people, which is more commonly the fault of the head than of the heart, will be represented as mere pretense and artifice, the stale bait for popularity at the expense of the public good. It will be forgotten, on the one hand, that jealousy is the usual concomitant of love, and that the noble enthusiasm of liberty is apt to be infected with a spirit of narrow and illiberal distrust. On the other hand, it will be equally forgotten that the vigor of government is essential to the security of liberty; that, in the contemplation of a sound and well-informed judgment, their interest can never be separated; and that a dangerous ambition more often lurks behind the specious mask of zeal for the rights of the people than under the forbidden appearance of zeal for the firmness and efficiency of government. . . .

I propose, in a series of papers, to discuss the following interesting particulars:—THE UTILITY OF THE UNION TO YOUR POLITI-CAL PROSPERITY—THE INSUFFICIENCY OF THE PRESENT CONFEDERATION TO PRESERVE THAT UNION—THE NE-CESSITY OF A GOVERNMENT AT LEAST EQUALLY ENER-GETIC WITH THE ONE PROPOSED, TO THE ATTAINMENT OF THIS OBJECT—THE CONFORMITY OF THE PROPOSED CON-STITUTION TO THE TRUE PRINCIPLES OF REPUBLICAN GOVERNMENT—ITS ANALOGY TO YOUR OWN STATE CON-STITUTION—and lastly, THE ADDITIONAL SECURITY WHICH ITS ADOPTION WILL AFFORD TO THE PRESERVATION OF THAT SPECIES OF GOVERNMENT, TO LIBERTY, AND TO PROPERTY.

\* \* \* \* \* \* \* \* \* \* \* \* \* \* \* \* \* \* \* \* \* \* \* \* \* \* \* \*

*Discussion Points:*

1. Recall the social contract theorists' emphasis on reason and the consent of the governed. In this light, discuss Hamilton's observation that the country was attempting to determine whether "good government" could be established "from reflection and choice."
2. Hamilton suggested that some would oppose ratification out of self-interest. Give examples of the kinds of parties and institutions he had in mind.
3. Hamilton warned that some of the proposed Constitution's opponents would be motivated by selfish reasons. But he urged his readers to support the document because it would be in *their* own interests to do so. Discuss this proposition.

## JAMES MADISON, *THE FEDERALIST,* No. 10

James Madison is sometimes described as the architect of the American political system. In this vein, *The Federalist,* No. 10 can be viewed as his blueprint.

Madison tried to design a popularly-based political system that would avoid both minority and majority tyranny. He also confronted the fact that prior democracies had been short-lived as they deteriorated into mob rule. As such, stability was an important goal. Further, Madison was particularly concerned with the problem of factions. He feared that citizens pursuing their selfish interests might band together and use their collective strength to deprive minorities of their interests and rights. In this letter, Madison proposed some solutions to such problems.

\* \* \* \* \* \* \* \* \* \* \* \* \* \* \* \* \* \* \* \* \* \* \* \* \* \*

Among the numerous advantages promised by a well constructed Union, none deserves to be more accurately developed than its tendency to break and control the violence of faction. The friend of popular governments, never finds himself so much alarmed for their character and fate, as when he contemplates their propensity to this dangerous vice. He will not fail, therefore, to set a due value on any plan which, without violating the principles to which he is attached, provides a proper cure for it. The instability, injustice and confusion introduced into the public councils, have, in truth, been the mortal diseases under which popular governments have everywhere perished; as they continue to be the favorite and fruitful topics from which the adversaries to liberty derive their most specious declamations. The valuable improvements made by the American constitutions on the popular models, both ancient and modern, cannot certainly be too much admired; but it would be an unwarrantable partiality, to contend that they have as effectually obviated the danger on this side, as was wished and expected. Complaints are everywhere heard from our most considerate and virtuous citizens . . . that our governments are too unstable, that the public good is disregarded in the conflicts of rival parties, and that measures are too often decided, not according to the rules of justice and the rights of the minor party, but by the superior force of an interested and overbearing majority. However anxiously we may wish that these complaints had no foundation, the evidence, of known facts will not permit us to deny that they are in some degree true . . . [P]revailing and increasing distrust of public engagements, and alarm for private rights, which are echoed from one end of the continent to the other . . . must be chiefly, if not wholly, effects of the unsteadiness and injustice with which a factious spirit has tainted our public administrations.

By a faction, I understand a number of citizens, whether amounting to a majority or minority of the whole, who are united and actuated by some common impulse of passion, or of interest, adverse to the rights of other citizens, or to the permanent and aggregate interests of the community.

There are two methods of curing the mischiefs of faction. The one, by removing its causes; the other, by controlling its effects.

There are again two methods of removing the causes of faction. The one, by destroying the liberty which is essential to its existence; the other, by giving every citizen the same options, the same passions, and the same interests.

It could never be more truly said, that of the first remedy, that it was worse than the disease. Liberty is to faction what air is to fire, an aliment, without which it instantly expires. But it would not be less a folly to abolish liberty, which is essential to political life because it nourishes faction, than it would be to wish the annihilation of air, which is essential to animal life, because it imparts to fire its destructive agency.

The second expedient is as impracticable, as the first would be unwise. As long as the reason of man continues to be fallible, and he is at liberty to exercise it, different opinions will be formed. . . .

The latent causes of faction are thus sown in the nature of man; and we see them everywhere brought into different degrees of activity, according to the different circumstances of civil society. A zeal for different opinions ... divided mankind into parties, inflamed them with mutual animosity, and rendered them much more disposed to vex and oppress each other, than to co-operate for their common good. So strong is this propensity of mankind, to fall into mutual animosities, that where no substantial occasion presents itself, the most frivolous and fanciful distinctions have been sufficient to kindle their unfriendly passions, and excite their most violent conflicts. But the most common and durable source of factions has been the various and unequal distribution of property. Those who hold, and those who are without property, have ever formed distinct interests in society. . . . The regulation of these various and interfering interest forms the principle task of modern legislation. . . .

The inference to which we are brought is, that the *causes* of faction cannot be removed; and that relief is only to be sought in the means of controlling its *effects*.

If a faction consists of less than a majority, relief is supplied by the republican principle, which enables the majority to defeat its sinister views, by regular vote. . . . When a majority is included in a faction, the form of popular government, on the other hand, enables it to sacrifice to its ruling passions or interest, both the public good and the rights of other citizens. To secure the public good, and private rights, against the danger of such a faction, and at the same time to preserve the spirit and the form of popular government, is then the great object to which our inquiries are directed. . . .

By what means is this object attainable? Evidently by one of two only. Either the existence of the same passion or interest in a majority, at the same time must be prevented; or the majority, having such coexistent passion or interest, must be rendered, by their number and local situation, unable to concert and carry into effect schemes of oppression. If the impulse and the opportunity be suffered to coincide . . . neither moral nor religious motives can be relied on as an adequate control. . . .

From this view of the subject, it may be concluded, that a pure democracy, by which I mean a society consisting of a small number of citizens, who assemble and administer the government in person, can admit of no cure from the mischief of faction. A common passion or interest will, in almost every case, be felt by a majority . . . and there is nothing to check the inducements to sacrifice the weaker party, or an obnoxious individual. Hence it is, that such democracies have ever been spectacles of turbulence and contention; have ever been found incompatible with personal security, or the rights of property; and have, in general, been as short in their lives, as they have been violent in their deaths. . . .

A republic, by which I mean a government in which the scheme of representation takes place, opens a different prospect, and promises the cure for which we are seeking. . . .

The two great points of difference, between a democracy and a republic, are, first, the delegation of the government, in the latter, to a small number of citizens, and greater sphere of country, over which the latter may be extended.

The effect of the first difference is, on the one hand, to refine and enlarge the public views by passing them through the medium of a chosen body of citizens, whose wisdom may best discern the true interest of their community, and whose patriotism and love of justice, will be least likely to sacrifice it to temporary or partial considerations. Under such a regulation, it may well happen, that the public voice, pronounced by the representatives of the people, will be more consonant to the public good, than if pronounced by the people themselves, convened for the purpose. . . .

The other point of difference is, the greater number of citizens, and the extent of territory, which may be brought within the compass of republican, than of democratic government; and it is this circumstance principally which renders factious combinations less to be dreaded in the former, than in the latter. The smaller the society, the fewer probably will be the distinct parties and interests composing it; the fewer the distinct parties and interests, the more frequently will a majority be found of the same party; and the smaller the number of individuals composing a majority, and the smaller the compass within which they are placed, the more easily will they concert and execute their plans of oppression. Extend the sphere, and you take in a greater variety of parties and interests; you make it less probable that a majority of the whole will have a common motive to invade the rights of other citizens; or if such a common motive exists, it will be more difficult for all who feel it to discover their own strength, and act in unison with each other. . . .

Hence, it clearly appears, that the same advantage, which a republic has over a democracy, in controlling the effects of faction, is enjoyed by a large over a small republic—is enjoyed by the union over the states composing it. Does this advantage consist in the substitution of representatives, whose enlightened views and virtuous sentiments render them superior to local prejudices, and to schemes of injustice? It will not be denied, that the representation of the union will be most likely to possess these requisite endowments. Does it consist in the greater security afforded by a greater variety of parties, against the event of any one party being able to outnumber and oppress the rest? In an equal degree does the increased variety of parties, comprised within the union, increase this security? Does it, in fine, consist in the greater obstacles opposed to the concert and accomplishment of the secret wishes of an unjust and interested majority? Here, again, the extent of the union gives it the most palpable advantage.

The influence of factious leaders may kindle a flame within their particular states, but will be unable to spread a general conflagration through the other states. . . .

* * * * * * * * * * * * * * * * * * * * * * * * * * * * * * *

*Discussion Points:*

1. Discuss Madison's views on the instability of prior forms of popular government.
2. How did Madison define "faction"? How could the *causes* of faction be removed? How did the idea that man is naturally disposed to "vex and oppress" his fellows influence Madison in this regard?
3. How could the *effects* of faction be controlled?
4. Why did Madison believe that a pure democracy could not survive the mischiefs of faction?
5. Discuss Madison's support for a republican form of government. Why would the Madisonian representative not simply reflect the demands of his constituents? Why did Madison advocate a large or an extended republic?
6. Critics have charged that Madison not only made it difficult for a tyrannical majority to form; he made it difficult for *any* majority—even legitimate ones—to form and challenge the status quo. As such, the system has been seen as fortifying the then-entrenched economic elite. Comment on this viewpoint.

## JAMES MADISON, *THE FEDERALIST,* NO. 51

In this selection, Madison again addressed the possibility that political power might be abused. Especially instructive was his pessimistic view of human nature: "If men were angels, no government would be necessary." To prevent the abuse of governmental power by men over men, he advocated that the various departments be given separate powers. Stating that "[a]mbition must be made to counteract ambition," he also argued that each department should have sufficient power to resist encroachments from the others. That is, he called for a system of structural checks and balances.

\* \* \* \* \* \* \* \* \* \* \* \* \* \* \* \* \* \* \* \* \* \* \* \* \* \* \* \*

In order to lay a due foundation for that separate and distinct exercise of the different powers of government, which to a certain extent is admitted on all hands to be essential to the preservation of liberty, it is evident that each department should have a will of its own; and consequently should be so constituted that the members of each should have as little agency as possible in the appointment of the members of the others. Were this principle rigorously adhered to, it would require that all the appointments for the supreme executive, legislative, and judiciary magistracies should be drawn from the same fountain of authority, the people, through channels having no communication whatever with one another. Perhaps such a plan of constructing the several departments would be less difficult in practice than it may in contemplation appear. Some difficulties, however, and some additional expense would attend the execution of it. Some deviations, therefore, from the principle must be admitted. In the constitution of the judiciary department in particular, it might be inexpedient to insist rigorously on the principle: first, because peculiar qualifications being essential in the members, the primary consideration ought to be to select that mode of choice which best secures these qualifications; secondly, because the permanent tenure by which the appointments are held in that department, must soon destroy all sense of dependence on the authority conferring them.

It is equally evident that the members of each department should be as little dependent as possible on those of the others, for the emoluments annexed to their offices. Were the executive magistrate, or the judges, not independent of the legislature in this particular, their independence in every other would be merely nominal.

But the great security against a gradual concentration of the several powers in the same department, consists in giving to those who administer each department the necessary constitutional means and personal motives to resist encroachments of the others. The provision for defense must in this, as in all other cases, be made commensurate to the danger of the attack. Ambition must be made to counteract ambition. The interest of the man must be connected with the constitutional rights of the place. It may be a reflection on human nature, that such devices should be necessary to control the abuses of government. But what is government itself, but the greatest of all reflections on human nature? If men were angels, no government would be necessary. If angels were to govern men, neither external nor internal controls on government would be necessary. In framing a government which is to be administered by men over men, the great difficulty lies in this: you must first enable the government to control the governed; and in the next place oblige it to control itself. A dependence on the people is, no doubt, the primary control on the government; but experience has taught mankind the necessity of auxiliary precautions. . . .

* * * * * * * * * * * * * * * * * * * * * * * * * * * * * *

*Discussion Points:*

1. Madison suggested that public officials should be selected by the people, but he made an exception for the judiciary. Why?
2. Discuss Madison's views on separation of powers and checks and balances. He could have designed a more streamlined and efficient system. Why did he prefer such a checked-and-balanced one?
3. Discuss Madison's views on human nature and their implications for framing a governmental system.

## JAMES MADISON, *THE FEDERALIST,* NO. 57

The Framers decided to establish a bicameral legislature. In this letter, Madison discussed the relationship between members of the House of Representatives and their constituents.

* * * * * * * * * * * * * * * * * * * * * * * * * * * * * *

. . . The House of Representatives is so constituted as to support in the members an habitual recollection of their dependence of the people. Before the sentiments impressed on their minds by the mode of their elevation, can be effaced by the exercise of power, they will be compelled to anticipate the moment when their power is to cease, when their exercise of it is to be reviewed, and when they must descend to the level from which they were raised; there for ever to remain unless a faithful discharge of their trust shall have established their title to a renewal of it.

I will add, as a . . . circumstance in the situation of the House of Representatives, restraining them from oppressive measures, that they can make no law which will not have its full operation on themselves and their friends, as well as on the great mass of the society. This has always been deemed one of the strongest bonds by which human policy can connect the rulers and the people together. It creates between them that communion of interest, and sympathy of sentiments, of which few governments have furnished examples; but without which every government degenerates into tyranny. If it be asked, what is to restrain the House of Representatives from making legal discriminations in favor of themselves, and a particular class of society? I answer, the genius of the whole system; the nature of just and constitutional laws; and, above all, the vigilant and manly spirit which actuates the people of America; a spirit which nourishes freedom, and in return is nourished by it.

If this spirit shall ever be so far debased as to tolerate a law not obligatory on the legislature, as well as on the people, the people will be prepared to tolerate anything but liberty.

Such will be the relation between the House of Representatives and their constituents. Duty, gratitude, interest, ambition itself, are the cords by which they will be bound to fidelity and sympathy with the great mass of the people. It is possible that these may all be insufficient to control the caprice and wickedness of men. But are they not all that government will admit, and that human prudence can devise? Are they not the genuine, and the characteristic means, by which republican government provides for the liberty and happiness of the people? . . .

\* \* \* \* \* \* \* \* \* \* \* \* \* \* \* \* \* \* \* \* \* \* \* \* \* \* \* \* \* \*

*Discussion Points:*

1. Discuss Madison's view that short terms would help ensure that Representatives would remain accountable to the masses.
2. Why did Madison think it was important that legislation apply to the legislators themselves as well as to the general public?
3. "What is to restrain the House of Representatives from making legal discriminations in favor of themselves?"

## JAMES MADISON, *THE FEDERALIST*, NO. 62

In this letter, Madison turned his attention to the Senate. Among other things, he discussed the qualifications of senators, their appointment, the length of their terms, and their powers.

\* \* \* \* \* \* \* \* \* \* \* \* \* \* \* \* \* \* \* \* \* \* \* \* \* \* \* \* \*

Having examined the constitution of the House of Representatives . . . I enter next on the examination of the Senate.

The heads under which this member of the government may be considered are—I. The qualifications of senators; II. The appointment of them by the state legislatures; III. The equality of representation in the Senate; IV. The number of senators, and the term for which they are to be elected; V. The powers vested in the Senate.

I. The qualifications proposed for senators, as distinguished from those of representatives, consist in a more advanced age and a longer period of citizenship. A senator must be thirty years of age at least; as a representative must be twenty-five. And the former must have been a citizen nine years, as seven years are required for the latter. The propriety of these distinctions is explained by the nature of the senatorial trust; which, requiring greater extent of information and stability of character, requires at the same time, that the senator should have reached a period of life most likely to supply these advantages. . . .

II. It is equally unnecessary to dilate on the appointment of senators by the state legislators. Among the various modes which might have been devised for constituting this branch . . . that which has been proposed . . . is probably the most congenial with public opinion. It is recommended by the double advantage of favoring a select appointment, and of giving the state governments such an agency in the formation of the federal government, as must secure the authority of the former, and may form a convenient link between the two systems.

III. The equality of representation in the Senate is another point, which, being evidently the result of compromise between . . . the large and the small states, does not call for much discussion. If indeed it be right, that among a people thoroughly incorporated into one nation, every district ought to have a *proportional* share in the government: and that among independent and sovereign states bound together by a simple league, the parties, however unequal in size, ought to have an *equal* share in the common councils, it does not appear to be without some reason, that in a compound republic, partaking of both the national and federal character, the government ought to be founded on a mixture of the principles of proportional [as found in the House] and equal representation [as found in the Senate]. . . .

. . . [T]he equal vote allowed to each state, is at once a constitutional recognition of the portion of sovereignty remaining in the individual states, and an instrument for preserving that residuary sovereignty. . . .

Another advantage accruing from this ingredient in the constitution of the Senate is, the additional impediment it must prove against improper acts of legislation. No law or resolution can now be passed without the concurrence, first, of a majority of the people, and then, of a majority of the states. . . .

IV. The number of senators, and the duration of their appointment, come next to be considered. In order to form an accurate judgment on both these points, it will be proper to inquire into the purposes which are to be answered by the Senate; and, in order to ascertain these, it will be necessary to review the inconveniences which the republic must suffer from the want of such an institution.

First . . . [T]hose who administer [republican governments] may forget their obligations to their constituents, and prove unfaithful to their important trust. In this point of view, a senate, as a second branch of the legislative assembly, distinct from and dividing the power with, a first, must be in all cases a salutary check on the government. It doubles the security to the people by requiring the concurrence of two distinct bodies in schemes of usurpation or perfidy, where the ambition or corruption of one would otherwise be sufficient. . . .

Second. The necessity of a senate is not less indicated by the propensity of all single and numerous assemblies, to yield to the impulse of sudden and violent passions, and to be seduced by factious leaders into intemperate and pernicious resolutions. Examples on this subject might be cited without number. . . . All that need be remarked is, that a body which is to correct this infirmity ought itself to be free from it, and consequently ought to be less numerous. It ought, moreover, to possess great firmness, and . . . hold its authority by a tenure of considerable duration.

Third. Another defect to be supplied by a senate lies in a want of due acquaintance with the objects and principles of legislation. It is not possible that an assembly of men, called, for the most part, from pursuits of a private nature, continued in appointments for a short time, and led by no permanent motive to devote the intervals of public occupation to a study of the laws, the affairs, and the comprehensive interests of their country, should, if left wholly to themselves, escape a variety of important errors in the exercise of their legislative trust. . . .

Fourth. The mutability in the public councils, arising from a rapid succession of new members, however qualified they may be, points out . . . the necessity of some stable institution in the government. Every new election in the states is found to change one-half of the representatives. From this change of men must proceed a change of opinions; and from a change of opinions, a change of measures. But a continual change even of good measures is inconsistent with every rule of prudence, and every prospect of success. . . .

\* \* \* \* \* \* \* \* \* \* \* \* \* \* \* \* \* \* \* \* \* \* \* \* \* \* \* \* \* \*

*Discussion Points:*

1. Compare and contrast the qualifications of representatives and senators.
2. Why did Madison favor the selection of senators by state legislators?
3. Why did Madison favor the decision to give small and large states the same number of seats in the Senate?
4. What did Madison think of the arrangement that laws would require the approval of both the House and the Senate?
5. Why did Madison favor a relatively lengthy term for senators?
6. In your opinion, would high congressional turnover rates be good or bad? Why?

## ALEXANDER HAMILTON, *THE FEDERALIST*, NO. 69

Alexander Hamilton wrote this letter in response to a charge from George Clinton, an Anti-Federalist, that the president would resemble an American king. Hamilton contrasted the limited powers of the elected president with the virtually unlimited powers of the British monarch in an attempt to refute Clinton's claims. In fact, Hamilton suggested that presidential powers would more closely resemble those of the New York governor.

\* \* \* \* \* \* \* \* \* \* \* \* \* \* \* \* \* \* \* \* \* \* \* \* \* \* \* \* \* \*

I proceed now to trace the real characters of the proposed executive, as they are marked out in the plan of the convention. This will serve to place in a strong light the unfairness of the representations which have been made in regard to it.

The first thing which strikes our attention is that the executive authority, with few exceptions, is to be vested in a single magistrate. This will scarcely, however, be considered as a point upon which any comparison can be grounded; for if, in this particular, there be a resemblance to the king of Great Britain, there is not less a resemblance to the Grand Seignior, to the khan of Tartary, to the Man of the Seven Mountains, or to the governor of New York.

That magistrate is to be elected for four years; and is to be re-eligible as often as the people of the United States shall think him worthy of their confidence. In these circumstances there is a total dissimilitude between him and the king . . . who is an hereditary monarch, possessing the crown as a patrimony descendible to his heirs forever; but there is a close analogy between him and a governor of New York, who is elected for three years, and is re-eligible without limitation or intermission. If we consider how much less time would be requisite for establishing a dangerous influence in a single state than for establishing a like influence throughout the United States, we must conclude that a duration of four years for the chief magistrate of the Union is a degree of permanency far less to be dreaded in that office, than a duration of three years for a corresponding office in a single state.

The president . . . would be liable to be impeached, tried, and, upon conviction of treason, bribery, or other high crimes or misdemeanors, removed from office; and would afterwards be liable to prosecution and punishment in the ordinary course of law. The . . . king . . . is sacred and inviolable; there is no constitutional tribunal to which he is amenable; no punishment to which he can be subjected without involving the crisis of a national revolution. In this delicate and important circumstance of personal responsibility, the president . . . would stand upon no better ground than a governor of New York, and upon worse ground than the governors of Virginia and Delaware.

The president . . . is to have power to return a bill, which shall have passed the two branches of legislature, for reconsideration; but the bill so returned is not to become a law unless, upon that reconsideration, it be approved by two-thirds of both houses. The king . . . has an absolute negative upon the acts of the two houses of Parliament. . . . The qualified negative of the president differs widely from this absolute negative of the British sovereign and tallies exactly with the revisionary authority of the council of revision of this state, of which the governor is a constituent part. . . .

The president is to be the

commander-in-chief of the army and navy of the United States, and of the militia of the several States, when called into the actual services of the United States. He is to have power to grant reprieves and pardons for offenses against the United States, except in cases of impeachment; to recommend to the consideration of Congress such measures as he shall judge necessary and expedient; to convene, on extraordinary occasions, both houses of the legislature, or either of them, and, in case of disagreement between them with respect to the time of adjournment, to adjourn them to such time as he shall think proper; to take care that the laws be faithfully executed; and to commission all officers of the United States.

In most of these particulars, the power of the president will resemble equally that of the king of Great Britain and of the governor of New York. The most material points of difference are these:

First. The president will have only the occasional command of such part of the militia of the nation as by legislative provision may be called into the actual service of the Union. The king . . . and the governor of New York have at all times the entire command of all the militia within their several jurisdictions. In this article, therefore, the power of the president would be inferior to that of either the monarch or the governor.

Second. The president is to be commander-in-chief of the army and navy of the United States. In this respect his authority would be nominally the same with that of the king of Great Britain, but in substance much inferior to it. It would amount to nothing more than the supreme command and direction of the military and naval forces, as first general and admiral of the Confederacy; while that of the British king extends to the declaring of war and to the raising and regulating of fleets and armies—all which, by the Constitution under consideration, would appertain to the legislature. The governor of New York, on the other hand, if by the constitution of the state vested only with the command of its militia and navy. But the constitutions of several of the states expressly declare their governors to be commanders-in-chief, as well of the army as navy; and it may well be a question whether those of New Hampshire and Massachusetts . . . do not, in this instance, confer larger powers upon their respective governors than could be claimed by a president. . . .

Third. The power of the president, in respect to pardons, would extend to all cases, except those of impeachment. The governor of New York may pardon in all cases, even in those of impeachment, except for treason and murder. Is not the power of the governor . . . on a calculation of political consequences, greater than that of the president? All conspiracies and plots against the government which have not been matured into actual treason may be screened from punishment of every kind by . . . pardoning. If a governor of New York, therefore, should be at the head of any such conspiracy . . . he could insure his accomplices and adherents an entire impunity. A president . . . on the other hand, though he may even pardon treason

. . . could shelter no offender . . . from the effects of impeachment and conviction. . . .

Fourth. The president can only adjourn the national legislature in the single case of disagreement about the time of adjournment. The British monarch may prorogue or even dissolve the Parliament. The governor of New York may also prorogue the legislature of this state for a limited time; a power which, in certain situations, may be employed to very important purposes.

The president is to have power, with the advise and consent of the Senate, to make treaties, provided two-thirds of the senators present concur. The king . . . is the sole and absolute representative of the nation in all foreign transactions. He can of his own accord make treaties of peace, commerce, alliance, and of every other description. . . . In this respect, therefore, there is no comparison between the intended power of the president and the actual power of the British sovereign. The one can perform alone what the other can only do with the concurrence of a branch of the legislature. It must be admitted that in this instance the power of the federal executive would exceed that of any state executive. But this arises naturally from the exclusive possession by the Union of that part of the sovereign power which relates to treaties. If the Confederacy were to be dissolved, it would become a question whether the executives of the several states were not solely invested with that delicate and important prerogative.

The president is also to be authorized to receive ambassadors and other public ministers. This, though it has been a rich theme of declamation, is more a matter of dignity than of authority. It is a circumstance which will be without consequence in the administration of the government; and it was far more convenient that it should be arranged in this manner than that there should be a necessity of convening the legislature, or one of its branches, upon every arrival of a foreign minister. . . .

The president is to nominate, and, with the advice and consent of the Senate, to appoint ambassadors and other public ministers, judges of the Supreme Court, and in general all officers of the United States established by law, and whose appointments are not otherwise provided for by the Constitution. The king . . . is emphatically and truly styled the fountain of honor. He not only appoints to all offices, but can create offices. He can confer titles of nobility at pleasure, and has the disposal of an immense number of church preferments. There is evidently a great inferiority in the power of the president . . . to that of the British king; nor is it equal to that of the governor of New York. . . .

The power of appointment is with us lodged in a council, composed of the governor and four members of the senate, chosen by the assembly. The governor claims, and has frequently exercised, the right of nomination, and is entitled to a casting vote in the appointment. If he really has the right of nominating, his authority is in this respect equal to that of the president, and exceeds it in the article of the casting vote. In the national government, if the Senate should be divided, no appointment could be made; in . . . New York, if the council should be divided, the governor can turn the scale and confirm his own nomination. . . . [T]he power of the chief magistrate of this state, in the disposition of offices, must, in practice, be greatly superior to that of the chief magistrate of the Union.

Hence it appears that, except as to the concurrent authority of the president in the article of treaties, it would be difficult to determine whether that magistrate would, in the aggregate, possess more or less power than the governor of New York. And it appears yet more unequivocally that there is no pretense for the parallel which has been attempted between him and the king. . . . But to render the contrast . . . still more striking, it may be of use to throw the principal circumstances of dissimilitude into a closer group.

The president . . . would be an officer elected by the people for four years; the king . . . is a perpetual and hereditary prince. The one would be amenable to personal punishment and disgrace; the person of the other is sacred and inviolable. The one would have a qualified negative upon the acts of the legislative body; the other has an absolute negative. The one would have a right to command the military and naval forces of the nation; the other, in addition to this right, possesses that of declaring war, and of raising and regulating fleets and armies by his own authority. The one would have a concurrent power with a branch of the legislature in the formation of treaties; the other is the sole possessor of the power of making treaties. The one would have a like concurrent authority in appointing of offices; the other is the sole author of all appointments. The one can confer no privileges whatever; the other can make denizens of aliens, noblemen of commoners; can erect corporations with all the rights incident to corporate bodies. The one can prescribe no rules concerning the commerce or currency of the nation; the other is in several respects the arbiter of commerce, and in this capacity can establish markets and fairs, can regulate weights and measures, can lay embargoes for a limited time, can coin money, can authorize or prohibit the circulation of foreign coin. The one has no particle of spiritual jurisdiction; the other is the supreme head and governor of the national church! What answer shall we give to those who would persuade us that things so unlike resemble each other? The same that ought to be given to those who tell us that a government, the whole power of which would be in the hands of the elective and periodical servants of the people is an aristocracy, a monarchy, and a despotism.

\* \* \* \* \* \* \* \* \* \* \* \* \* \* \* \* \* \* \* \* \* \* \* \* \* \* \* \* \* \*

*Discussion Points:*

1. Make a chart comparing and contrasting the respective powers of the governor of New York, the president of the United States, and the king of Great Britain.
2. In responding to the above, pay particular attention to the following points:
   a. term length and re-eligibility
   b. impeachment
   c. veto power
   d. commander-in-chief responsibilities
   e. reprieves and pardons
   f. convening and adjourning the legislature
   g. treaties
   h. receiving ambassadors and public ministers
   i. appointment powers
   j. commerce and currency matters
   k. spiritual jurisdiction.

## ALEXANDER HAMILTON, *THE FEDERALIST,* NO. 70

Some advocated a plural executive on grounds that such an arrangement would provide protection against tyranny. In this selection, Hamilton disagreed and discussed the merits of a single executive. He believed that a single and vigorous executive could provide the leadership needed for a successful republican government. On the other hand, he maintained that such leadership could not be supplied by a committee or council and that such arrangements could produce dangers of their own.

\* \* \* \* \* \* \* \* \* \* \* \* \* \* \* \* \* \* \* \* \* \* \* \* \* \* \* \* \* \*

There is an idea, which is not without its advocates, that a vigorous Executive is inconsistent with the genius of republican government. The enlightened well-wishers to this species of government must at least hope that the supposition is destitute of foundation; since they can never admit its truth, without at the same time admitting the condemnation of their own principles. Energy in the Executive is a leading character in the definition of good government. It is essential to the protection of the community against foreign attacks; it is not less essential to the steady administration of the laws; to the protection of property against those irregular and high-handed combinations which sometimes interrupt the ordinary course of justice; to the security of liberty against the enterprises and assaults of ambition, of faction, and of anarchy. Every man the least conversant in Roman story, knows how often that republic was obliged to take refuge in the absolute power of a single man, under the formidable title of Dictator, as well against the intrigues of ambitious individuals who aspired to the tyranny, and the seditions of whole classes of the community whose conduct threatened the existence of all government, as against the invasions of external enemies who menaced the conquest and destruction of Rome.

There can be no need, however, to multiply arguments or examples on this head. A feeble Executive implies a feeble execution of the government. A feeble execution is but another phrase for a bad execution; and a government ill executed, whatever it may be in theory, must be, in practice, a bad government.

Taking it for granted, therefore, that all men of sense will agree in the necessity of an energetic Executive, it will only remain to inquire, what are the ingredients which constitute this energy? How far can they be combined with those other ingredients which constitute safety in the republican sense? And how far does this combination characterize the plan which has been reported by the convention?

The ingredients which constitute energy in the Executive are, first, unity; secondly, duration; thirdly, an adequate provision for its support; fourthly, competent powers.

The ingredients which constitute safety in the republican sense are, first, a due dependence on the people, and secondly, a due responsibility.

Those politicians and statesmen who have been the most celebrated for the soundness of their principles and for the justice of their views, have declared in favor of a single Executive and a numerous legislature. They have with great propriety, considered energy as the most necessary qualification of the former, and have regarded this as most applicable to power in a single hand, while they have, with equal propriety, considered the latter as best adapted to deliberation and wisdom, and best calculated to conciliate the confidence of the people and to secure their privileges and interests. . . .

But one of the weightiest objections to a plurality in the Executive, and which lies as much against the last as the first plan, is, that it tends to conceal faults and destroy responsibility. Responsibility is of two kinds—to censure and to punishment. The first is the more important of the two, especially in an elective office. Man, in public trust, will much oftener act in such a manner as to render him unworthy of being any longer trusted, than in such a manner as to make him obnoxious to legal punishment. But the multiplication of the Executive adds to the difficulty of detection in either case. It often becomes impossible amidst mutual accusations, to determine on whom the blame or the punishment of a pernicious measure, or series of pernicious measures, ought really to fall. It is shifted from one to another with so much dexterity, and under such plausible appearances, that the public opinion is left in suspense about the real author. The circumstances which may have led to any national miscarriage or misfortune are sometimes so complicated that, where there are a number of actors who may have had different degrees and kinds of agency, though we may clearly see upon the whole that there has been mismanagement, yet it may be impracticable to pronounce to whose account the evil which may have been incurred is truly chargeable. . . .

A little consideration will satisfy us, that the species of security sought for in the multiplication of the Executive, is unattainable. Numbers must be so great as to render combination difficult, or they are rather a source of danger than of security. The united credit and influence of several individuals must be more formidable to liberty, than the credit and influence of either of them separately. When power, therefore, is placed in the hands of so small a number of men, as to admit of their interest and views being easily combined in a common enterprise, by an artful leader, it becomes more liable to abuse, and more dangerous when abused, than if it belodged in the hands of one man; who, from the very circumstance of his being alone, will be more narrowly watched and more readily suspected, and who cannot unite so great a mass of influence as when he is associated with others. The Decemvirs of Rome, whose name denotes their number, were more to be dreaded in their usurpation than any ONE of them would have been. No person would think of proposing an Executive much more numerous than that body; from six to a dozen have been suggested for the number of the council. The extreme of these numbers, is not too great for an easy combination; and from such a combination America would have more to fear, than from the ambition of any single individual. A council to a magistrate, who is himself responsible for what he does, are generally nothing better than a clog upon his good intentions, are often the instruments and accomplices of his bad and are almost always a cloak to his faults.

\* \* \* \* \* \* \* \* \* \* \* \* \* \* \* \* \* \* \* \* \* \* \* \* \* \* \* \* \* \* \*

*Discussion Points:*

1. Discuss Hamilton's observation that, "A feeble executive implies a feeble execution of the government . . . and a government ill executed . . . must be, in practice, a bad government."
2. Discuss the ingredients that provide energy in the executive.
3. Discuss the ingredients that provide safety in the executive.
4. Discuss the dangers associated with a plural executive. Pay particular attention to difficulties involved in attempting to affix responsibility for particular actions.


## ALEXANDER HAMILTON, *THE FEDERALIST,* NO. 78

In this letter, Hamilton predicted that the judiciary would be the "least dangerous" branch of the national government. He rejected the idea that federal judges should be elected and that they should serve limited terms. Instead, he argued that they should enjoy permanent tenure. Further, in light of the need for judicial independence under a "limited Constitution," he advised against the popular election of judges.

\* \* \* \* \* \* \* \* \* \* \* \* \* \* \* \* \* \* \* \* \* \* \* \* \* \* \* \* \* \*

We proceed now to an examination of the judiciary department of the proposed government.

In unfolding the defects of the existing Confederation, the utility and necessity of a federal judicature have been clearly pointed out . . . [T]he propriety of the institution in the abstract is not disputed; the only questions which have been raised being relative to the manner of constituting it, and to its extent. To these points, therefore, our observations shall be confined. . . .

Whoever attentively considers the different departments of power must perceive, that, in a government in which they are separated from each other, the judiciary, from the nature of its function, will always be the least dangerous to the political rights of the Constitution; because it will be least in a capacity to annoy or injure them. The Executive not only dispenses the honors, but holds the sword of the community. The legislature not only commands the purse, but prescribes the rules by which the duties and rights of every citizen are to be regulated. The judiciary, on the contrary, has no influence over either the sword or the purse; no direction either of strength or of the wealth of the society; and can take no active resolution whatever. It may truly be said to have neither FORCE nor WILL, but merely judgment; and must ultimately depend upon the aid of the executive arm even for the efficacy of its judgments.

This simple view of the matter suggests several important consequences. It proves incontestably, that the judiciary is beyond comparison the weakest of the three departments of power; that it can never attack with success either of the other two; and that all possible care is requisite to enable it to defend itself against their attacks. . . . It equally proves, that though individual oppression may now and then proceed from the courts of justice, the general liberty of the people can never be endangered from that quarter. . . . [F]rom the natural feebleness of the judiciary, it is in continual jeopardy of being overpowered, awed, or influenced, by its co-ordinate branches; and that as nothing can contribute so much to its firmness and independence as permanency in office, this quality may therefore be justly regarded as an indispensable ingredient in its constitution, and, in a great measure, as the citadel of the public justice and the public security.

The complete independence of the courts of justice is peculiarly essential in a limited Constitution. By a limited Constitution, I understand one which contains certain specified exceptions to the legislative authority; such, for instance, as that it shall pass no bills of attainder, no *ex-post-facto* laws, and the like. Limitations of this kind can be preserved in practice no other way than through the medium of courts of justice, whose duty it must be to declare all acts contrary to the manifest tenor of the Constitution void. Without this, all the reservations of particular rights or privileges would amount to nothing. . . .

There is no position which depends on clearer principles than that every act of a delegated authority, contrary to the tenor of the commission under which it is exercised, is void. No legislative act, therefore, contrary to the Constitution, can be valid. . . .

If it be said that the legislative body are themselves the constitutional judges of their own powers, and that the construction they put upon them is conclusive upon the other departments, it may be answered, that this cannot be the natural presumption, where it is not to be collected from any particular provisions in the Constitution. It is not otherwise to be supposed that the Constitution could intend to enable the representatives of the people to substitute their *will* to that of their constituents. It is far more rational to suppose that the courts were designed to be an intermediate body between the people and the legislature, in order, among other things, to keep the latter within the limits assigned to their authority. The interpretation of the laws is the proper and peculiar province of the courts. A constitution is, in fact, and must be, regarded by the judges as a fundamental law. It must therefore belong to them to ascertain its meaning, as well as the meaning of any particular act proceeding from the legislative body. If there should happen to be an irreconcilable variance between the two, that which has the superior obligation and validity ought, of course, to be preferred; in other words, the Constitution ought to be preferred to the statute, the intention of the people to the intention of their agents.

Nor does the conclusion by any means suppose a superiority of the judicial to the legislative power. It only supposes that the power of the people is superior to both; and that where the will of the legislature declared in its statutes, stands in opposition to that of the people declared in the Constitution, the judges ought to be governed by the latter, rather than the former. They ought to regulate their decisions by the fundamental laws, rather than by those which are not fundamental. . . .

If, then, the courts of justice are to be considered as the bulwarks of a limited Constitution against legislative encroachments, this consideration will afford a strong argument for the permanent tenure of judicial offices, since nothing will contribute so much as this to that independent spirit in the judges which must be essential to the faithful performances of so arduous a duty. . . .

That inflexible and uniform adherence to the rights of the Constitution, and of individuals, which we perceive to be indispensable in the courts of justice, can certainly not be expected from judges who hold their offices by a temporary commission. Periodical appointments, however regulated, or by whomsoever made, would, in some way or other, be fatal to their necessary independence. If the power of making them was committed either to the Executive or legislature, there would be danger of improper complaisance to the branch which possessed it; if to both, there would be an unwillingness to hazard the displeasure of either; if to the people, or the persons chosen by them for the special purpose, there would be too great disposition to consult popularity, to justify a reliance that nothing would be consulted but the Constitution and the laws.

There is yet further and a weightier reason for the permanency of the judicial offices, which is deducible from the nature of the qualifications they require. It has been frequently remarked, with great propriety, that a voluminous code of laws is one of the inconveniences necessarily connected with the advantages of a free government. To avoid an arbitrary discretion in the courts, it is indispensable that they should be bound down by strict rules and precedents, which serve to define and point out their duty in every particular case that comes before them; and it will readily be conceived from the variety of controversies which grow out of the folly and wickedness of mankind, that the records of those precedents must unavoidable swell to a very considerable bulk, and must demand long and laborious study to acquire a competent knowledge of them. Hence it is, that there can be but few men in the society who will have sufficient skill in the laws to qualify them for the stations of judges. And making the proper deductions for the ordinary depravity of human nature, the number must be still smaller of those who unite the requisite integrity with the requisite knowledge. These considerations apprise us, that the government can have no great option between fit character; and that a temporary duration in office, which would naturally discourage such characters from quitting a lucrative line of practice to accept a seat on the bench, would have a tendency to throw the administration of justice into hands less able, and less well-qualified, to conduct it with utility and dignity. In the present circumstances of this country, and in those in which it is likely to be for a long time to come, the disadvantages on this score would be greater than they may at first sight appear; but it must be confessed, that they are far inferior to those which present themselves under the other aspects of the subject.

\* \* \* \* \* \* \* \* \* \* \* \* \* \* \* \* \* \* \* \* \* \* \* \* \* \* \* \* \* \*

*Discussion Points:*

1. Why did Hamilton see the judiciary as the "least dangerous" branch?
2. Why did Hamilton think that federal judges needed permanent tenure in office?
3. What is a "limited Constitution"? Why is judicial independence essential in such a system?
4. Did Hamilton suggest that he supported the power of judicial review? Explain.
5. How did Hamilton think federal judges should be selected? What were his objections to their selection by way of a popular vote?

6. What did Hamilton say about the requisite qualifications of federal judges? How did these ideas relate to his views on how these judges should be selected?
7. In *The Federalist,* No. 51, Madison also addressed the selection and tenure of federal judges. Compare his views to Hamilton's.

## ALEXANDER HAMILTON, *THE FEDERALIST,* NO. 84

In this letter, Hamilton argued against the need for a written bill of rights. He contended that the Constitution already provided adequate protection for civil rights and liberties. Additionally, he suggested that such a bill of rights might even prove dangerous.

\* \* \* \* \* \* \* \* \* \* \* \* \* \* \* \* \* \* \* \* \* \* \* \* \* \* \*

The most considerable of the remaining objections is, that the plan of the convention contains no bill of rights. Among other answers given to this, it has been upon different occasions remarked, that the constitutions of several of the states are in a similar predicament. I add, that New York is of the number. And yet the persons who in the state oppose the new system . . . are among the most intemperate partisans of a bill of rights. To justify their zeal in this matter they allege two things: one is, that though the constitution of New York has no bill of rights prefixed to it, yet it contains in the body of it, various provisions in favor of particular privileges and rights, which, in substance, amount to the same thing; the other is, that the Constitution adopts, in their full extent, the common and statute law of Great Britain, by which many other rights, not expressed, are equally secured.

To the first I answer, that the Constitution offered by the convention contains, as well as the constitution of this state, a number of such provisions.

Independent of those which relate to the structure of the government, we find the following: Article I, section 3, clause 7. "Judgment in cases of impeachment shall not extend further than to removal from office, and disqualification to hold and enjoy any office of honor, trust, or profit under the United States; but the party convicted shall, nevertheless, be liable and subject to indictment, trial, judgment, and punishment, according to law." Section 9 of the same article, clause 2. "The privilege of the writ of *habeas corpus* shall not be suspended, unless when in cases of rebellion or invasion the public safety may require it." Clause 3. "No bill of attainder or *ex post facto* law shall be passed."

Clause 7. "No title of nobility shall be granted by the United States; and no person holding any office of profit or trust under them, shall, without the consent of the congress, accept of any present, emolument, office, or title, of any kind whatever, from any king, prince, or foreign states." Article III, section 2, clause 3. "The trial of all crimes, except in cases of impeachment, shall be by jury; and such trial shall be held in the state where the said crimes shall have been committed; but when not committed within any state, the trial shall be at such place or places as the congress may by law have directed." Section 3 of the same article. "Treason against the United States shall consist only in levying war against them, or in adhering to their enemies, giving them aid and comfort. No person shall be convicted of treason, unless on the testimony of two witnesses to the same overt act, or on confession in open court." And clause 3 of the same section. "The congress shall have power to declare the punishment of treason; but no attainder of treason shall work corruption of blood, or forfeiture, except during the life of the person attained."

It may well be a question, whether these are not, upon the whole, of equal importance with any which are to be found in the constitution of this state. The establishment of the writ of *habeas corpus,* the prohibition of *ex post facto* laws, and of titles of nobility, *to which we have no corresponding provisions in our constitution,* are perhaps greater securities to liberty than any it contains. The creation of crimes after the commission of the fact, or, in other words, the subjecting of men to punishment for things which, when they are done, were breaches of no law; and the practice of arbitrary imprisonments have been, in all ages, the favorite and most formidable instruments of tyranny. . . .

To the second, that is, to the pretended establishment of the common and statute law by the Constitution, I answer, that they are expressly made subject "to such alterations and provisions as the legislature shall from time to time make concerning the same." They are therefore at any moment liable to repeal by the ordinary legislative power, and of course have no constitutional sanction. The only use of the declaration was to recognize the ancient law, and to remove doubts which might have been occasioned by the revolution. This consequently can be considered as no part of a declaration of rights; which under our constitutions must be intended to limit the power of the government itself.

It has been several times truly remarked, that bills of rights are . . . reservations of rights not surrendered to the prince. . . . Here, in strictness, the people surrender nothing; and as they retain everything, they have no need of particular reservations. "We the people of the United

States, to secure the blessings of liberty to ourselves and our posterity do *ordain* and *establish* this constitution for the United States of America"; This is a better recognition of popular rights, than volumes of those aphorisms, which make the principal figure in several of our state bills of rights, and which would sound much better in a treatise of ethics, than in a constitution of government.

But a minute detail of particular rights is certainly far less applicable to a Constitution like that under consideration, which is merely intended to regulate the general political interests of the nation, than to one which has the regulation of every species of personal and private concerns. If therefore the loud clamors against the plan of the convention, on this score, are well founded, no epithets of reprobation will be too strong for the constitution of this state. But the truth is, that both of them contain all which, in relation to their objects, is reasonably to be desired.

I go further, and affirm, that bills of rights . . . are not only unnecessary in the proposed Constitution, but would even be dangerous. They would contain various exceptions to powers not granted, and on this very account would afford a colorable pretext to claim more than were granted. For why declare that things shall not be done which there is no power to do? Why, for instance, should it be said, that the liberty of the press shall not be restrained, when no power is given by which restrictions may be imposed? I will not contend that such a provision would confer a regulating power; but it is evident that it would furnish, to men disposed to usurp, a plausible pretense for claiming that power. They might urge with a semblance of reason that the Constitution ought not to be charged with the absurdity of providing against the abuse of an authority, which was not given, and that the provision against restraining the liberty of the press afforded a clear implication, that a right to prescribe proper regulations concerning it, was intended to be vested in the national government. This may serve as a specimen of the numerous handles which would be given to the doctrine of constructive powers, by the indulgence of an injudicious zeal for bills of rights. . . .

There remains but one other view of this matter to conclude the point. The truth is . . . that the Constitution is itself . . . a bill of rights. . . . Is it one object of a bill of rights to declare and specify the political privileges of the citizens in the structure and administration of the government? This is done in the most ample and precise manner in the plan of the convention; comprehending various precautions for the public security, which are not to be found in any of the state constitutions. Is another object of a bill of rights to define certain immunities and modes of proceeding, which are relative to personal and private concerns? This we have seen has been attended to, in a variety of cases, in the same plan. Advertising therefore to the substantial meaning of a bill of rights, it is absurd to allege that it is not to be found in the work of the convention. It may be said that it does not go far enough, though it will not be easy to make this appear; but it can with no propriety be contended that there is no such thing. It certainly must be immaterial what mode is observed as to the order of declaring the rights of the citizens, if they are provided for in any part of the instrument which establishes the government. Whence it must be apparent that much of what has been said on this subject rests merely on verbal and nominal distinctions, entirely foreign to the substance of the thing. . . .

\* \* \* \* \* \* \* \* \* \* \* \* \* \* \* \* \* \* \* \* \* \* \* \* \* \* \* \* \* \* \* \*

*Discussion Points:*

1. Hamilton claimed that the New York constitution contained no bill of rights, yet some New Yorkers criticized the proposed national Constitution for its failure to include an explicit bill of rights. How did such critics "justify their zeal"?
2. What examples did Hamilton give of rights protected by the proposed Constitution? Some of these rights were not protected by the New York constitution. Discuss his claim that related practices have constituted some of the "most formidable instruments of tyranny."
3. Why did Hamilton think that no explicit bill of rights was necessary in the United States Constitution?
4. Why did Hamilton think that inclusion of an explicit bill of rights in the United States Constitution might prove dangerous?

# CHAPTER 10

# THE ANTI-FEDERALISTS (1787–1788)

During the ratification debates of 1787 and 1788, opponents of the proposed Constitution argued that it would establish a political system that would too closely resemble Great Britain's. Known as the Anti-Federalists, they were suspicious of centralized power and championed the rights and powers of people at the state level. They wanted to preserve the Articles of Confederation and tried to persuade their listeners and readers to reject the Constitution. Like the authors of *The Federalist* papers, they too put their views in writing.

\* \* \* \* \* \* \* \* \* \* \* \* \* \* \* \* \* \* \* \* \* \* \* \* \* \* \* \* \*

## THE FEDERAL FARMER

In his "Observations Leading to A Fair Examination of the System of Government Proposed by the Late Convention," the Federal Farmer struck at the root of the Federalist approach. Ascribed by some scholars to Richard Henry Lee, the work is among the ablest of the Anti-Federalist pieces, raising fundamental questions about the consequences of consolidating the states. The second essay, written in letter form, typified his arguments. He concluded with the prediction that another revolution would ensue if the proposed plan were adopted.

\* \* \* \* \* \* \* \* \* \* \* \* \* \* \* \* \* \* \* \* \* \* \* \* \* \* \* \* \*

... The general government will consist of a new species of executive, a small senate, and a very small house of representatives. As many citizens will be more than three hundred miles from the seat of this government as will be nearer to it, its judges and officers cannot be very numerous without making our governments very expensive. Thus will stand the state and the general governments, should the constitution be adopted without any alterations in their organization; but as to powers, the general government will possess all essential ones, at least on paper, and those of the states a mere shadow of power. And therefore, unless the people shall make some great exertions to restore to the state governments their powers in matters of internal police; as the powers tolay and collect, exclusively, internal taxes, to govern the militia, and to hold the decisions of their own judicial courts upon their own laws final, the balance cannot possibly continue long; but the state governments must be annihilated, or continue to exist for no purpose.

It is however to be observed, that many of the essential powers given the national government are not exclusively given; and the general government may have prudence enough to forbear the exercise of those which may still be exercised by the respective states. But this cannot justify the impropriety of giving powers, the exercise of which prudent men will not attempt and imprudent men will, or probably can, exercise only in a manner destructive of free government. . . . Though we cannot have now a complete idea of what will be the operations of the proposed system, we may, allowing things to have their common course, have a very tolerable one. The powers lodged in the general government, if exercised by it, must intimately affect the internal police of the states, as well as external concerns; and there is no reason to expect the numerous state governments, and their connections, will be very friendly to the execution of federal laws in those internal affairs, which hitherto have been under their own immediate management. There is more reason to believe, that the general government, far removed from the people, and none of its members elected oftener than once in two years, will be forgot or neglected, and its laws in many cases disregarded, unless a multitude of officers and military force be continually kept in view, and employed to enforce the execution of the laws, and to make the government feared and respected. No position can be truer than this, that in this country either neglected laws, or a military execution of them, must lead to a revolution, and to the destruction of freedom. Neglected laws must first lead to anarchy and confusion; and a military execution of laws is only a shorter way to the same point—despotic government.

Yours, &c.<br>The Federal Farmer

* * * * * * * * * * * * * * * * * * * * * * * * * * * * * * * *

*Discussion Points:*

1. In his discussion of federalism, the Federal Farmer claimed that

the proposed Constitution would lead to the annihilation of state governments. Why?
2. Discuss the Federal Farmer's prediction that ratification of the new Constitution would lead to another revolution.


## THE CENTINEL

The most prolific of the Anti-Federalists was the Centinel, whose essays appeared in various Philadelphia papers. The fourth essay, from which excerpts appear below, carried the Centinel's argument that, instead of faulting the Articles of Confederation for the present difficulties of the United States, it would be more reasonable to blame problems associated with financing the revolutionary war effort.

* * * * * * * * * * * * * * * * * * * * * * * * * * * * *

To the People of Pennsylvania.
Friends, Countrymen and fellow Citizens.
That the present confederation is inadequate to the objects of the union seems to be universally allowed. The only question is, what additional powers are wanting to give due energy to the federal government? We should, however, be careful in forming our opinion on this subject, not to impute the temporary and extraordinary difficulties that [have] hitherto impeded the execution of the confederation, to defects in the system itself. Taxation is in every government, a very delicate and difficult subject; hence it has been the policy of all wise statesmen, as far as circumstances permitted to lead the people by small beginnings and almost imperceptible degrees, into the habits of taxation; where the contrary conduct has been pursued, it has ever failed of full success, not unfrequently proving the ruin of the projectors. . . .
I am persuaded that a due consideration, will evince, that the present inefficacy of the requisitions of Congress, is not owing to a defect in the confederation, but the peculiar circumstances of the times. . . .
It is to be lamented that the interested and designing have availed themselves so successfully of the present crisis, and under the specious pretence of having discovered a panacea for all the ills of the people, they are about establishing a system of government, that will prove more destructive to them, than the wooden horse filled with soldiers did in ancient times to the city of Troy; this horse was intro-

duced by their hostile enemy the Grecians, by a prostitution of the sacred rites of their religion; in like manner, my fellow citizens[,] are aspiring despots among yourselves prostituting the name of a Washington to cloak their designs upon your liberties. . . .

A transfer to Congress of the power of imposing imposts on commerce and the unlimited regulation of trade, I believe is all that is wanting to render America as prosperous as it is in the power of any form of government to render her; this properly understood would meet the views of all the honest and well meaning. . . .

After so recent a triumph over British despots, after such torrents of blood and treasure have been spent, after involving ourselves in the distresses of an arduous war, and incurring such a debt, for the express purpose of asserting the rights of humanity, it is truly astonishing that a set of men among ourselves, should have the effrontery to attempt the destruction of our liberties. But in this enlightened age to hope to dupe the people by the arts they are practising, is still more extraordinary. . . .

That the powers of Congress ought to be strengthened, all allow, but is this a conclusive proof of the necessity to adopt the proposed plan; is it a proof that because the late convention, in the first essay upon so arduous and difficult a subject, harmonised in their ideas, that a future convention will not, or that after a full investigation and mature consideration of the objections, they will not plan a better government and one more agreeable to the sentiments of America, or is it any proof that they can never again agree in any plan? The late convention must indeed have been inspired, as some of its advocates have asserted, to admit the truth of these positions, or even to admit the possibility of the proposed government, being such a one as America ought to adopt; for this body went upon original ground, foreign from their intentions or powers, they must therefore have been wholly uninformed of the sentiments of their constituents in respect to this form of government, as it was not in their contemplation when the convention was appointed to erect a new government, but to strengthen the old one. Indeed they seem to have been determined to monopolize the exclusive merit of the discovery, or rather as if darkness was essential to its success they precluded all communication with the people, by closing their doors; thus the well disposed members unassisted by public information and opinion, were induced by those arts that are now practising on the people, to give their sanction to this system of despotism.

Is there any reason to presume that a new convention will not agree upon a better plan of government? Quite the contrary, for perhaps there never was such a coincidence on any occasion as on the present[;] the opponents to the proposed plan, at the same time in every part of the continent, harmonised in the same objections; such an uniformity of opposition is without example and affords the strongest demonstration of its solidity. Their objections too are not local, are not confined to the interests of any one particular state to the prejudice of the rest, but with a philanthropy and liberality that reflects lustre on humanity, that dignifies the character of America, they embrace the interests and happiness of the whole union[;] they do not even condescend to minute blemishes, but show that the main pillars of the fabric are bad, that the essential principles of liberty and safety are not to be found in it, that despotism will be the necessary and inevitable consequences of its establishment.

Centinel

\* \* \* \* \* \* \* \* \* \* \* \* \* \* \* \* \* \* \* \* \* \* \* \* \* \* \* \* \* \* \* \*

*Discussion Points:*

1. Discuss the Centinel's comments on taxation.
2. The Centinel compared the advocates of the proposed Constitution to the soldiers inside the wooden horse that threatened Troy. What was his point?
3. The Centinel agreed that congressional powers to regulate trade and commerce needed to be enhanced. Did he support any additional changes?
4. The Centinel claimed that the delegates to the Philadelphia Convention met in secrecy and exceeded their charge to revise the Articles of Confederation. Discuss this claim.
5. The Centinel proposed another convention. Why did he think that the critics of the proposed Constitution would be able to transcend local interests and look toward "the happiness of the whole union"?

# BRUTUS

The essays of Brutus are among the most important of the Anti-Federalist papers. In the selection below, Brutus attacked the Federalists for empowering a national government without specifying detailed limits to those powers. He argued forcefully for the adoption of an explicit bill of rights. While Brutus was not the only Anti-Federalist to voice such concerns, his letter is an especially lucid example of such sentiment. The eventual addition of a written bill of rights to the United States Constitution—in the form of the first ten amendments—is testimony to the power of these arguments.

* * * * * * * * * * * * * * * * * * * * * * * * * * * * *

... So far it is from being true, that a bill of rights is less necessary in the general constitution than in those of the states, the contrary is evidently the fact. —This system, if it is possible for the people of America to accede to it, will be an original compact; and being the last, will, in the nature of things, vacate every former agreement inconsistent with it. For it being a plan of government received and ratified by the whole people, all other forms, which are in existence at the time of its adoption, must yield to it. This is expressed in positive and unequivocal terms, in the 6th article. "That this constitution and the laws of the United States, which shall be made in pursuance thereof, and all treaties made, or which shall be made, under the authority of the United States, shall be the supreme law of the land: and the judges in every state shall be bound thereby, any thing in the *constitution,* or laws of any state, *to the contrary* notwithstanding."

"The senators and representatives before-mentioned, and the members of the several legislatures, and all executive and judicial officers, both of the United States, and of the several states, shall be bound, by oath or affirmation, to support this constitution."

It is therefore not only necessarily implied thereby, but positively expressed, that the different state constitutions are repealed and entirely done away, so far as they are inconsistent with this, with the laws which shall be made in pursuance thereof, or with treaties made, or which shall be made, under the authority of the United States; of what avail will the constitutions of the respective states be to preserve the rights of its citizens? Should they be plead, the answer would be, the constitution of the United States, and the laws made in pursuance thereof, is the supreme law, and all legislatures and judicial officers, whether of the general or state governments, are bound by the state oath to support it. No priviledge, reserved by the bills of rights, or secured by the state government, can limit the power granted by this, or restrain any laws made in pursuance of it. It stands therefore on its own bottom, and must receive a construction by itself without any reference to any other—And hence it was of the highest importance, that the most precise and express declarations and reservations of rights should have been made.

This will appear the more necessary, when it is considered, that not only the constitution and laws made in pursuance thereof, but all treaties made, or which shall be made, under the authority of the United States, are the supreme law of the land, and supersede the constitutions of all the states. The power to make treaties, is vested in the president, by and with the advice and consent of two thirds of the senate. I do not find any limitation, or restriction, to the exercise of this power. The most important article in any constitution may therefore be repealed, even without a legislative act. Ought not a government, vested with such extensive and indefinite authority, to have been restricted by a declaration of rights? It certainly ought.

So clear a point is this, that I cannot help suspecting, that persons who attempt to persuade people, that such reservations were less necessary under this constitution than under those of the states, are willfully endeavoring to deceive, and to lead you into an absolute state of vassalage.

Brutus

\* \* \* \* \* \* \* \* \* \* \* \* \* \* \* \* \* \* \* \* \* \* \* \* \* \* \* \* \* \*

*Discussion Points:*

1. Why did Brutus think that a written bill of rights was more necessary in the national Constitution than in the constitutions of the states?
2. Why did Brutus contend that individuals could not rely on their state constitutions to protect them against the national government? What did he say about Article VI in this regard? What did he say about treaties?
3. Compare and contrast Brutus's advocacy of an explicit bill of rights with Hamilton's opposition to the same in *The Federalist,* No. 84. Whom do you find more persuasive? Why?

## GEORGE CLINTON

George Clinton was New York's first post-Independence governor. At the time, most states made governors subordinate to their legislative branches in various ways. For example, governors were often elected by state legislatures, their salaries could be cut by legislative action, and they served short terms. By contrast, New York established a relatively powerful governorship and Clinton used his powers vigorously.

Clinton was a dedicated Anti-Federalist. He argued forcefully against adoption of the Constitution in "The Letters of Cato." In the selection below, "To the Citizens of the State of New York," he maintained that there was little resemblance between his office and the proposed presidency. In fact, he argued, the president would become an American king.

As noted previously, Alexander Hamilton wrote *The Federalist,* No. 69 in response to Clinton's charges. Hamilton likened the president's powers to those of the New York governor. The fact that Clinton was himself the governor in question added credibility to his rejection of Hamilton's defenses of Article II. On the other hand, if the Constitution were ratified, Clinton's office would be relatively diminished in stature. As such, some regarded his objections as self-serving.

* * * * * * * * * * * * * * * * * * * * * * * * * * * *

. . . . The executive power as described in the 2d article, consists of a president and vice-president, who are to hold their offices during the term of four years; the same article has marked the manner and time of their election, and established the qualifications of the president; it also provides against the removal, death, or inability of the president and vice-president—regulates the salary of the president, delineates his duties and powers; and, lastly, declares the causes for which the president and vice-president shall be removed from office.

. . . [T]he construction of the first paragraph of the first section of the second article is vague and inexplicit, and leaves the mind in doubt as to the election of a president and vice-president, after the expiration . . . [of] the first term of four years . . . [T]his inexplicitness perhaps may lead to an establishment for life.

It is remarked by Montesquieu, in treating of republics, that in all magistracies, the greatness of the power must be compensated by the brevity of the duration, and that a longer time than a year would be dangerous . . . [P]ower connected with considerable duration may be dangerous to the liberties of a republic . . . [T]his tempts his ambition, which . . . is . . . pernicious and the duration of his office for any considerable time favors his views, gives him the means and time to perfect and execute his designs, he therefore fancies that he may be great and glorious by oppressing his fellow citizens, and raising himself to permanent grandeur on the ruins of his country . . . [H]is power of nomination and influence on all appointments, . . . and garrisoned by troops under his direction, . . . the unrestrained power of granting pardons for treason, which may be used to screen from punishment those whom he had secretly instigated to commit the crime, and thereby prevent a discovery of his own guilt, his duration in office for four years: these, and various other principles evidently prove the truth of the position, that if the president is possessed of ambition, he has power and time sufficient to ruin his country. . . .

The establishment of a vice-president is as unnecessary as it is dangerous. This officer, for want of other employment, is made president of the senate, thereby blending the executive and legislative powers, besides always giving to some one state, from which he is to come, an unjust pre-eminence.

It is a maxim in republics that the representative of the people should be of their immediate choice; but by the manner in which the president is chosen, he arrives to this office at the fourth or fifth hand, nor does the highest vote, in the way he is elected, determine the choice. . . .

. . . . [W]herein does this president, invested with his powers and prerogatives, essentially differ from the king of Great Britain (save as to name, the creation of nobility, and some immaterial incidents, the offspring of absurdity and locality). . . .

You must . . . beware that the advocates of this new system do not deceive you by a fallacious resemblance between it and your own state government which you so much prize; and, if you examine, you will perceive that the chief magistrate of this state is your immediate choice, controlled and checked by . . . the people, divested of the prerogative of influencing war and peace, making treaties, receiving and sending embassies, and commanding standing armies and navies, which belong to the power of the confederation, and will be convinced that this government is no more like a true picture of your own than an Angel of Darkness resembles an Angel of Light.

November 22, 1787

. . . . I cannot help remarking that inexplicitness seems to pervade this whole political fabric . . . Before the existence of express political compacts it was reasonably implied that the magistrate should govern with wisdom and justice; but mere implication was too feeble to restrain the unbridled ambition of a bad man, or afford security against negligence, cruelty or any other defect of mind. . . . Therefore, a general presumption that rulers will govern well is not a sufficient security. You are then under a sacred obligation to provide for the safety of your posterity. . . . It is a duty you owe likewise to your own reputation, for you have a great name to lose; you are characterized as cautious, prudent and jealous in politics; whence is it therefore that you are about to precipitate yourselves into a sea of uncertainty, and adopt a system so vague, and which has discarded so many of your valuable rights? Is it because you do not believe that an American can be a tyrant? If this be the case, you rest on a weak basis: Americans are like other men in similar situations, when the manners and opinions of the community are changed . . . and your political compact inexplicit, your posterity will find that great power connected with ambition, luxury and flattery, will as readily produce a Caesar, Caligula, Nero and Domitain in America, as the same causes did in the Roman Empire.

\* \* \* \* \* \* \* \* \* \* \* \* \* \* \* \* \* \* \* \* \* \* \* \* \* \* \* \* \* \*

*Discussion Points:*

1. Why did Clinton object to the idea that the president would be eligible for re-election without limit?
2. Discuss Clinton's view that the president's powers over troops, appointments and pardons would enable him to "ruin his country."
3. Why did Clinton regard the vice-presidency as an "unnecessary" and "dangerous" office? Do you agree? Why or why not?
4. What were Clinton's objections to the manner in which the president would be selected?
5. An "Angel of Darkness." Caligula. Nero. Clinton predicted dire consequences if the Constitution were ratified. Were his criticisms plausible? Which of his arguments were the strongest?
6. Clinton told his readers that they should not be deceived by apparent similarities between the presidency and the New York governorship. Instead, he claimed that the presidency "differs but very immaterially from the establishment of monarchy in Great Britain." As noted, Hamilton in *The Federalist,* No. 69, responded to Clinton's charges and rejected the proposition that Article II would create an "American king." Compare and contrast Clinton's and Hamilton's views on this matter. With the benefit of historical hindsight, assess the strength of their respective arguments.

# PART IV
# EARLY EFFORTS TO INTERPRET AND APPLY THE CONSTITUTION

# CHAPTER 11

# HAMILTON'S OPINION ON THE CONSTITUTIONALITY OF THE BANK (1790)

Hamilton's advocacy of a strong central government has already been mentioned. As a means to this end, Hamilton—as Secretary of the Treasury under President Washington—recommended to Congress on December 14, 1790 the establishment of a national bank. Congress passed his plan on February 8, 1791. Washington was unsure of the constitutionality of the measure. He requested opinions from Hamilton and Jefferson. Hamilton based his response on Article I, section 8, clause 18 of the Constitution: the necessary and proper or "elastic" clause. His view was that this provision provided Congress with certain implied powers which extended to the incorporation of a national bank.

\* \* \* \* \* \* \* \* \* \* \* \* \* \* \* \* \* \* \* \* \* \* \* \* \* \* \* \*

... Now it appears to the Secretary of the Treasury that this general principle is inherent in the very definition of government, and essential to every step of the progress to be made by that of the United States, namely:

That every power vested in a government is in its nature *sovereign,* and includes, by *force* of the *term* a right to employ all the *means* requisite and fairly applicable to the attainment of the ends of such power, and which are not precluded by restrictions and exceptions specified in the Constitution, or not immoral, or not contrary to the *essential ends* of political society. . . .

It is not denied that there are *implied* as well as *express powers,* and that the *former* are as effectually delegated as the *latter.* And for the sake of accuracy it shall be mentioned, that there is another class of powers, which may be properly denominated, *resulting powers.* . . .

It is conceded that *implied powers* are to be considered as delegated

95

equally with *express ones.* Then it follows, that as a power of erecting a corporation may as well be *implied* as any other thing, it may as well be employed as an *instrument* or *mean* of carrying into execution any of the specified powers, as any other *instrument* or *mean* whatever. The only question must be . . . whether the mean to be employed, or in this instance, the corporation to be erected, has a natural relation to any of the acknowledged objects or lawful ends of the government. . . .

. . . [I]t was the intent of the Convention . . . to give a liberal latitude to the exercise of the specified powers. The expressions have peculiar comprehensiveness. They are "to make all *laws* necessary and proper for *carrying into execution* the *foregoing powers,* and *all other powers,* vested by the Constitution in the *government* of the United States, or in any department or *officer* thereof. . . .

. . . [T]he powers contained in a constitution of government, especially those which concern the general administration of the affairs of a country, its finances, trade, defense &c., ought to be construed liberally in advancement of the public good. . . . The means by which national exigencies are to be provided for, national inconveniences obviated, national prosperity promoted, are of such infinite variety, extent, and complexity, that there must of necessity be great latitude of discretion on the selection and application of those means. Hence . . . the necessity and propriety of exercising the authorities intrusted to a government on principles of liberal construction. . . .

It is presumed to have been satisfactorily shown in the course of the preceding observation:

1. That the power of the government, as to the objects intrusted to its management, is, in its nature, sovereign.
2. That the right of erecting corporations is one inherent in, and inseparable from, the idea of sovereign power.
3. That the position, that the government of the United States can exercise no power but such as is delegated to it by the Constitution, does not militate against this principle.
4. That the word *necessary,* in the general clause, can have no *restrictive* operation derogating from the force of this principle; indeed, that the degree in which a measure is or is not *necessary,* cannot be a test of *constitutional right,* but of *expediency only.*
5. That the power to erect corporations is not to be considered as an *independent* or *substantive* power, but as an *incidental* and *auxiliary* one, and was therefore more properly left to implication than expressly granted.
6. That the principle in question does not extend the power of the

government beyond the prescribed limits, because it only affirms a power to *incorporate* for purposes *within the sphere* of the *specified powers.*

And lastly, that the right to exercise such a power in certain cases is unequivocally granted in the most *positive* and *comprehensive* terms. . . .

A hope is entertained that it has, by this time, been made to appear, to the satisfaction of the President, that a bank has a natural relation to the power of collecting taxes—to that of regulating trade—to that of providing for the common defence—and that, as the bill under consideration contemplates the government in the light of a joint proprietor of the stock of the bank, it brings the case within the provision of the Constitution which immediately respects the property of the United States.

Under a conviction that such a relation subsists, the Secretary of the Treasury, with all deference, conceives, that it will result as a necessary consequence from the position, that all the specified powers of government are sovereign, as to the proper objects; that the incorporation of a bank is a constitutional measure; and that the objections taken to the bill, in this respect, are ill-founded. . . .

\* \* \* \* \* \* \* \* \* \* \* \* \* \* \* \* \* \* \* \* \* \* \* \* \* \* \* \* \* \* \*

*Discussion Points:*

1. The Constitution does not explicitly authorize Congress to establish a bank but Hamilton "found" such authorization. Discuss his claim that "there are implied as well as express powers."
2. Hamilton relied upon the necessary and proper clause in arguing that Congress had the power to establish a national bank. Discuss his views on the subject. Explain his interpretation of the word "necessary."

# CHAPTER 12

# JEFFERSON'S OPINION ON THE CONSTITUTIONALITY OF THE BANK (1790)

Thomas Jefferson contended that the proposal to establish a bank fell outside the powers of Congress. He read the necessary and proper clause more restrictively than did Hamilton. Jefferson also relied on the Tenth Amendment in fashioning his argument. After careful consideration of these conflicting opinions, President Washington endorsed Hamilton's plan.

\* \* \* \* \* \* \* \* \* \* \* \* \* \* \* \* \* \* \* \* \* \* \* \* \* \* \* \* \*

.... I consider the foundation of the Constitution as laid on this ground—that *all powers not delegated to the United States, by the Constitution, nor prohibited by it to the states, are reserved to the states, or the people* (10th amendment). To take a single step beyond the boundaries thus specially drawn around the powers of Congress, is to take possession of a boundless field of power, no longer susceptible of any definition.

The incorporation of a bank, and the powers assumed by this bill, have not, in my opinion, been delegated to the United States by the Constitution.

I. *They are not among the powers specially enumerated. For these are,—*

1. A power to lay taxes for the purpose of paying the debts of the United States....
2. To "borrow money"....
3. "To regulate commerce with foreign nations, and among the states, and with the Indian tribes"....

   Still less are these powers covered by any other of the special enumerations.

II. Nor are they within either of the general phrases, which are the two following:—

1. "To lay taxes to provide for the general welfare of the United States". . . Congress are not to lay taxes *ad libitum, for any purpose they please;* but only to *pay the debts,* or *provide for the welfare, of the Union.* In like manner, they are not *to do anything they please,* to provide for the general welfare, but only to lay *taxes* for that purpose. . . .

2. The second general phrase is, "to make all laws *necessary* and proper for carrying into execution the enumerated powers." But they can all be carried into execution without a bank. A bank, therefore, is not necessary, and consequently not authorized by this phrase.

It has been argued that a bank will give great facility or convenience in the collection of taxes. Suppose this were true; yet the Constitution allows only the means which are "necessary," not those which are merely "convenient," for effecting the enumerated powers. If such a latitude of construction be allowed to this phrase as to give any non-enumerated power, it will go to every one; for there is no one which ingenuity may not torture into a *convenience, in some way or other, to some one* of so long a list of enumerated powers. It would swallow up all the delegated powers, and reduce the whole to one phrase. . . that is to say, to those means without which the grant of the power would be nugatory.

Perhaps bank bills may be a more convenient vehicle than treasury orders. But a little *difference* in the degree of convenience cannot constitute the necessity which the Constitution makes the ground for assuming any non-enumerated power. . . .

Can it be thought that the Constitution intended that, for a shade or two of *convenience* . . . Congress should be authorized to break down the most ancient and fundamental laws of the several states. . . .

Nothing but a necessity invincible by other means, can justify such a prostration of laws, which constitute the pillars of our whole system of jurisprudence. Will Congress be too strait-laced to carry the Constitution into honest effect, unless they may pass over the foundation laws of the state governments, for the slightest convenience to theirs?

The negative of the president is the shield provided by the Constitution to protect, against the invasions of the legislature, 1. *The rights of the executive;* 2. *Of the judiciary;* 3. *Of the states and state legislatures.* The present is the case of a right remaining exclusively with the states, and is, consequently, one of those intended by the Constitution to be placed under his protection.

It must be added, however, that, unless the President's mind, on a view of everything which is urged for and against this bill, is tolerably clear that it is unauthorized by the Constitution, if the *pro* and the *con* hang so evenly as to balance his judgment, a just respect for the wisdom of the legislature would naturally decide the balance in favor of their opinion. It is chiefly for cases where they are clearly misled by error, ambition, or interest, that the Constitution has placed a check in the negative of the President.

* * * * * * * * * * * * * * * * * * * * * * * * * * * * * *

*Discussion Points:*

1. What did Jefferson say about the Tenth Amendment? Hamilton, in effect, argued that while the Constitution did not expressly authorize Congress to establish a national bank, the power *was* implicitly delegated as a means necessary and proper for collecting taxes, regulating trade, and so on. Discuss Jefferson's and Hamilton's respective positions.
2. How did Jefferson interpret the word "necessary"? Compare and contrast his interpretation with Hamilton's.
3. What did Jefferson say about the President's "negative" or veto power?

# CHAPTER 13

## *MARBURY V. MADISON*
### 1 Cranch 137; 2 L.Ed. 60 (1803)

In the November 1800 elections, Jefferson defeated Adams for the presidency and the Republicans took control of Congress from the Federalists. But Adams and his Federalist associates did not have to leave office until inauguration day—March 4, 1801. They decided to make the most of their remaining time in power.

Congress passed the Judiciary Act of 1801, which established a number of new judgeships. In the waning days of his administration, Adams tried to fill these newly-created vacancies with loyal Federalists. He was still signing such commissions into the eve of Jefferson's inauguration—hence the phrase, "midnight judges." One of Adams's late appointments was that of John Marshall, his secretary of state and a strong Federalist, to serve as Chief Justice of the United States Supreme Court.

William Marbury was another of Adams's late appointees. He was named a justice of the peace for the District of Columbia. Adams signed Marbury's commission and Marshall countersigned it on March 3, 1801, but Marshall failed to deliver it. When Jefferson assumed office, he instructed his secretary of state, James Madison, to withhold Marbury's undelivered commission.

The Republicans went on to repeal the Judiciary Act of 1801. They also turned the impeachment power against some sitting Federalist judges. Marbury still wanted his commission and he filed suit asking the Supreme Court to issue a writ of mandamus to force Madison to deliver the commission. Section 13 of the Judiciary Act of 1789 authorized the Supreme Court to issue such writs on original jurisdiction. On the basis of this legislation, Marbury brought his case to the Supreme Court.

It was clear that Jefferson would refuse to comply with a decision ordering him to give Marbury the commission. Further, it was generally assumed that if the Court issued such an order, the Republicans would try to impeach the new Chief Justice, John Marshall. On the other hand, if the young Court appeared to back down in the face of such political forces, it might never recover its credibility.

Marshall ruled that the Supreme Court lacked jurisdiction over the case because Section 13 of the 1789 Judiciary Act unconstitutionally enlarged the Court's original jurisdiction. Lower federal courts had previously held congressional legislation invalid. A number of state cases reflected the principle that courts can review legislation. In *The Federalist,* No. 78, Hamilton supported this practice. There is also evidence that public opinion regarded such judicial power as appropriate. But this was the first time that the Supreme Court clearly reviewed and invalidated an act of Congress on grounds that it violated the Constitution. As such, this landmark case is remembered for establishing this power of judicial review.

* * * * * * * * * * * * * * * * * * * * * * * * * * * * *

Mr. Chief Justice Marshall delivered the opinion of the Court, saying in part:

. . . [T]he following questions have been considered and decided.

1st. Has the applicant a right to the commission he demands? . . . [The Court finds that he has.]

2nd. If he has a right, and that right has been violated, do the laws of his country afford him a remedy? . . . [The Court finds that they do.]

3rd. If they do afford him a remedy, is it a mandamus issuing from this court? . . .

[Section 13 of the Judiciary Act of 1789] authorizes the Supreme Court "to issue writs of mandamus in cases warranted by the principles and usages of law, to any courts appointed, or persons holding office, under the authority of the United States."

The Secretary of State, being a person holding [such] an office . . . , is precisely within the letter of the description, and if this court is not authorized to issue a writ of mandamus to such an officer, it must be because the law is unconstitutional, and therefore absolutely incapable of conferring the authority, and assigning the duties which its words purport to confer and assign.

The Constitution vests the whole judicial power of the United States in one Supreme Court, and in such inferior courts as Congress shall, from time to time, ordain and establish. . . .

In the distribution of this power it is declared that "the Supreme Court shall have original jurisdiction in all cases affecting ambassadors, other public ministers and consuls, and those in which a state shall be a party. In all other cases, the Supreme Court shall have appellate jurisdiction.". . . .

To enable this court, then, to issue a mandamus, it must be shown to be an exercise of appellate jurisdiction, or be necessary to enable them to exercise appellate jurisdiction. . .

It is the essential criterion of appellate jurisdiction, that it revises and corrects the proceedings in a cause already instituted, and does not create that cause. . .

The authority, therefore, given to the Supreme Court, by the Act establishing the judicial courts of the United States, to issue writs of mandamus to public officers, appears not to be warranted by the Constitution; and it becomes necessary to inquire whether a jurisdiction so conferred can be exercised.

The question, whether an Act, repugnant to the Constitution can become the law of the land, is a question deeply interesting to the United States. . . .

That the people have an original right to establish, for their future government, such principles as, in their opinion, shall most conduce to their happiness, is the basis upon which the whole American fabric has been erected. The exercise of this original right is a very great exertion; nor can it, nor ought it, to be frequently repeated. The principles, therefore, so established, are deemed fundamental. And as the authority from which they proceed is supreme, and can seldom act, they are designed to be permanent. . . .

This original and supreme will organizes the government, and assigns to different departments their respective powers. It may either stop here, or establish certain limits not to be transcended by those departments.

The government of the United States is of the latter description. The powers of the legislature are defined and limited; and that those limits may not be mistaken, or forgotten, the Constitution is written. . . . It is a proposition too plain to be contested, that the Constitution controls any legislative act repugnant to it; or, that the legislature may alter the Constitution by an ordinary act.

Between these alternatives there is no middle ground. The Constitution is either a superior paramount law, unchangeable by ordinary means, or it is on a level with ordinary legislative acts, and, like other acts, is alterable when the legislature shall please to alter it.

If the former part of the alternative be true, then a legislative act contrary to the Constitution is not law; if the latter part be true, then written constitutions are absurd attempts on the part of the people to limit a power in its own nature illimitable.

Certainly all those who have framed written constitutions contemplate them as forming the fundamental and paramount law of the nation, and consequently, the theory of every such government must be, that an act of the legislature, repugnant to the constitution, is void. . . .

If an act of the legislature, repugnant to the Constitution, is void, does it, notwithstanding its invalidity, bind the courts, and oblige them to give it effect? Or, in other words, though it be not law, does it constitute a rule as operative as if it was a law? . . .

It is emphatically the province and duty of the judicial department to say what the law is. Those who apply the rule to particular cases must, of necessity, expound and interpret that rule. If two laws conflict with each other, the courts must decide on the operation of each.

So if a law be in opposition to the Constitution; if both the law and the Constitution apply to a particular case, so that the court must either decide that case conformably to the law, disregarding the Constitution; or conformably to the Constitution, disregarding the law; the court must determine which of these conflicting rules governs the case. This is of the very essence of judicial duty.

If, then, the courts are to regard the Constitution, and the Constitution is superior to any ordinary act of the legislature, the Constitution, and not such ordinary act, must govern the case to which they both apply.

Those, then, who controvert the principle that the Constitution is to be considered, in court, as a paramount law, are reduced to the necessity of maintaining that courts must close their eyes on the Constitution and see only the law.

This doctrine would subvert the very foundation of all written constitutions. It would declare that an act which, according to the principles and theory of our government, is entirely void, is yet, in practice, completely obligatory. It would declare that if the legislature shall do what is expressly forbidden, such act, notwithstanding the express prohibition, is in reality effectual. . . .

That . . . would of itself be sufficient, in America, where written constitutions have been viewed with so much reverence, for rejecting the construction. But the peculiar expressions of the Constitution of the United States furnish additional arguments in favor of its rejection.

The judicial power of the United States is extended to all cases arising under the Constitution.

Could it be the intention of those who gave this power, to say that in using it the Constitution should not be looked into? That a case arising under the Constitution should be decided without examining the instrument under which it arises?

This is too extravagant to be maintained.

In some cases, then, the Constitution must be looked into by the judges. And if they can open it at all, what part of it are they forbidden to read or obey?

There are many other parts of the Constitution which serve to illustrate this subject.

It is declared that "no tax or duty shall be laid on articles exported from any state." Suppose a duty on the export of cotton, of tobacco, or of flour; and a suit instituted to recover it. . . . Ought the judges to close their eyes on the Constitution, and only see the law?

The Constitution declares "that no bill of attainder or ex post facto law shall be passed."

If, however, such a bill should be passed, and a person should be prosecuted under it, must the court condemn to death those victims whom the Constitution endeavors to preserve?

"No person," says the Constitution, "shall be convicted of treason unless on the testimony of two witnesses to the same overt act, or on confession in open court."

Here the language of the Constitution is addressed especially to the courts. It prescribes, directly for them, a rule of evidence not to be departed from. If the legislature should change that rule, and declare one witness, or a confession out of court, sufficient for conviction, must the constitutional principle yield to the legislative Act?

From these, and many other selections which might be made, it is apparent, that the framers of the Constitution contemplated the instrument as a rule for the government of courts, as well as of the legislature.

Why otherwise does it direct the judges to take an oath to support it? . . .

Why does a judge swear to discharge his duties agreeably to the Constitution of the United States if that Constitution forms no rule for his government—if it is closed upon him, and cannot be inspected by him? . . .

It is also not entirely unworthy of observation that in declaring what shall be the supreme law of the land, the Constitution itself is first mentioned; and not the laws of the United States generally, but those only which shall be made in pursuance of the Constitution, have that rank.

Thus the particular phraseology of the Constitution . . . confirms and strengthens the principle, supposed to be essential to all written constitutions, that a law repugnant to the Constitution is void; and that courts, as well as other departments, are bound by that instrument.

The rule must be discharged.

\* \* \* \* \* \* \* \* \* \* \* \* \* \* \* \* \* \* \* \* \* \* \* \* \* \* \* \* \*

*Discussion Points:*

1. Review Hamilton's comments on judicial review in *The Federalist,* No. 78.
2. Why did Marshall rule that the Court lacked jurisdiction to issue the writ? What specific constitutional provision did Congress violate? How did Marshall use the "supremacy clause" of Article VI in reaching his decision?
3. Could Congress have authorized the Court to issue such writs on appellate jurisdiction? What must be done to modify the Court's original jurisdiction?
4. Marshall managed to establish the Court's power of judicial review while avoiding a direct showdown with Jefferson. Since it was Marshall himself who failed to deliver Marbury's commission in the first place, critics thought he should have disqualified himself from participating in the case. What do you think?
5. Marshall noted that judges take an oath to uphold the Constitution. But the president and congressmen take such oaths too. Critics argued that judges were just as likely to violate the Constitution as were presidents and congressmen. Should a judge's interpretation of the Constitution be superior to a president's or congressman's interpretation?
6. Courts at various levels might have occasion to interpret the Constitution, but the United States Supreme Court is the highest court in the land. As a result of this case, the Supreme Court has the last word on matters of constitutional interpretation (unless the document is amended to, in effect, overturn a Supreme Court decision). In light of the aforementioned stipulation that the Constitution is the "supreme law of the land," how important is it that the Constitution be interpreted and applied consistently in all the states?

# CHAPTER 14

## *MCCULLOCH V. MARYLAND*
### 4 Wheaton 316; 4 L.Ed. 579 (1819)

In 1791, Congress established the First Bank of the United States. Alexander Hamilton was one of the Bank's strongest advocates. As noted previously, in contrast to Thomas Jefferson, Hamilton argued that Congress had the implied power to incorporate the Bank as a means "necessary and proper" to the execution of enumerated powers. The First Bank's charter expired in 1811.

Financial conditions following the War of 1812 convinced some that a national bank should be reestablished. Congress established the Second Bank of the United States in 1816. It provoked much controversy. Some still questioned Congress's constitutional authority to create such an institution. Others attacked the Bank on financial grounds, claiming that it was a *source* of much financial distress. Several states restricted the activities of the Bank and imposed heavy burdens on it. A law passed by the Maryland legislature was at issue in this case.

In 1812, Maryland passed a law that required banks not chartered by the State to pay either a tax on each issuance of bank notes, or an annual fee of $15,000. A $500 penalty was imposed for each offense. In the case of the Baltimore branch of the Bank of the United States, the total penalty could have amounted to millions of dollars. McCulloch, cashier for the Baltimore branch, issued notes without complying with the Maryland law. The State brought an action to recover the revenue in dispute.

* * * * * * * * * * * * * * * * * * * * * * * * * * * * * * * *

Mr. Chief Justice Marshall delivered the opinion of the Court, saying in part:

In the case now to be determined, the defendant, a sovereign State, denies the obligation of a law enacted by the legislature of the Union, and the plaintiff, on his part, contests the validity of an act which has been passed by the legislature of that State. The Constitution of our country, in its most interesting and vital parts, is to be considered; the conflicting powers of the government of the Union and of its members, as marked in that Constitution, are to be discussed. . . .

. . . the government of the Union, though limited in its powers, is supreme within its sphere of action. This would seem to result necessarily from its nature. It is the government of all; its powers are delegated by all; it represents all, and acts for all. Though any one state may be willing to control its operations, no State is willing to allow others to control them. The nation, on those subjects on which it can act, must necessarily bind its component parts. But this question is not left to mere reason: the people have, in express terms, decided it, by saying, "this Constitution, and the laws of the United States, which shall be made in pursuance thereof, shall be the supreme law of the land," and by requiring that the members of the State legislatures and the officers of the executive and judicial departments of the states, shall take the oath of fidelity of it.

The government of the United States, then, though limited in its powers, is supreme; and its laws, when made in pursuance of the Constitution, form the supreme law of the land, "any thing in the Constitution or laws of any State to the contrary notwithstanding."

Among the enumerated powers, we do not find that of establishing a bank or creating a corporation. But there is no phrase in the instrument which, like the Articles of Confederation, excludes incidental or implied powers; and which requires that every thing granted shall be expressly and minutely described. Even the Tenth Amendment, which was framed for the purpose of quieting the excessive jealousies which had been excited, omits the word "expressly," and declares only that the powers "not delegated to the United States, nor prohibited to the States, are reserved to the States or to the people"; thus leaving the question, whether the particular power which may become the subject of contest has been delegated to the one government, or prohibited to the other, to depend on a fair construction of the whole instrument.

Although, among the enumerated powers of government, we do not find the word "bank" or "incorporation," we find the great powers to lay and collect taxes; to borrow money; to regulate commerce; to declare and conduct a war; and to raise and support armies and navies. The sword and the purse, all the external relations, and no inconsiderable portion of the industry of the nation, are entrusted to its government. . . . But it may with great reason be contended that a government, entrusted with such ample powers, on the due execution of which the happiness and prosperity of the nation so vitally depends, must also be entrusted with ample means for their execution. The power being given, it is the interest of the nation to facilitate its execution. . . .the Constitution. . . does not profess to enumerate the means by which the powers it confers may be executed; nor does it prohibit the creation of a corporation if the existence of such a being be essential to the beneficial exercise of those powers. It is, then, the subject of fair inquiry, how far such means may be employed.

. . . the Constitution of the United States has not left the right of Congress to employ the necessary means for the execution of the powers conferred on the government to general reasoning. To its enumeration of powers is added that of making "all laws which shall be necessary and proper, by this Constitution, in the government of the United States, or in any department thereof". . . .

The result of the most careful and attentive consideration bestowed upon this clause is, that if it does not enlarge, it cannot be construed to restrain the powers of Congress, or to impair the right of the legislature to exercise its best judgment in the selection of measures to carry into execution the constitutional powers of the government. . . .

We admit, as all must admit, that the powers of the government are limited, and that its limits are not to be transcended. But we think the sound construction of the Constitution must allow to the national legislature that discretion, with respect to the means by which the powers it confers are to be carried into execution, which will enable that body to perform the high duties assigned to it, in the manner most beneficial to the people. Let the end be legitimate, let it be within the scope of the Constitution, and all means which are appropriate, which are plainly adapted to that end, which are not prohibited, but consist with the letter and spirit of the Constitution, are constitutional. . . .

After the most deliberate consideration, it is the unanimous and decided opinion of this Court that the act to incorporate the Bank of the United States is a law made in pursuance of the Constitution, and is a part of the supreme law of the land.

The branches, proceeding from the same stock, and being conducive to the complete accomplishment of the object, are equally constitutional. . . .

. . .we proceed to inquire. . .Whether the State of Maryland may, without violating the Constitution, tax that branch? . . .

. . .That the power to tax involves the power to destroy; that the power to destroy may defeat and render useless the power to create; that there is a plain repugnance in conferring on one government a power to control the constitutional measure of another, which other, with respect to those very measures, is declared to be supreme over that which exerts the control, are propositions not to be denied. . . .

If the States may tax one instrument employed by the government in the execution of its powers, they may tax any and every other instrument. They may tax the mail; they may tax the mint; they may tax patent rights; they may tax the papers of the custom-house; they may tax judicial process; they may tax all the means employed by the government to an excess which would defeat all the ends of government. This was not intended by the American people. They did not design to make their government dependent on the States. . . .

. . . The question is, in truth, a question of supremacy; and, if the right of the States to tax the means employed by the general government be conceded, the declaration that the Constitution, and the laws made in pursuance thereof, shall be the supreme law of the land, is empty and unmeaning declamation. . . .

. . . The people of all the States have created the general government, and have conferred upon it the general power of taxation. The people of all the States, and the States themselves, are represented in Congress, and, by their representatives, exercise this power. When they tax the chartered institutions of the States, they tax their constituents; and these taxes must be uniform. But when a State taxes the operations of the government of the United States, it acts upon institutions created, not by their own constituents, but by people over whom they claim no control. It acts upon the measure of a government created by others as well as themselves, for the benefit of others in common with themselves. The difference is that which always exists, and always must exist, between the action of the whole on a part, and the action of a part on the whole—between the laws of a government declared to be supreme, and those of a government which, when in opposition to those laws, is not supreme. . . .

. . . The result is a conviction that the States have no power, by taxation or otherwise, to retard, impede, burden or in any manner control, the operations of the constitutional laws enacted by Congress to carry into execution the powers vested in the general government. That is, we think, the unavoidable consequence of that supremacy which the Constitution has declared.

We are unanimously of the opinion, that the law passed by the legislature of Maryland, imposing a tax on the Bank of the United States, in unconstitutional and void. . . .

* * * * * * * * * * * * * * * * * * * * * * * * * * * * * * * *

*Discussion Points:*

1. Compare and contrast Marshall's opinion in *McCulloch* with

Hamilton's and Jefferson's respective arguments about the constitutionality of the Bank of the United States.

2. In arguing that the Constitution confers certain implied powers upon Congress, what did Marshall say about the Tenth Amendment?

3. Do you agree with Marshall's observation that "the power to tax involves the power to destroy"? Why or why not?

4. Compare and contrast Marshall's use of the supremacy clause (Article VI) in *Marbury* and *McCulloch*.

# CHAPTER 15

## *GIBBONS V. OGDEN*

### 9 Wheaton 1; 6 L.Ed. 23 (1824)

A major question facing the Supreme Court concerned the application of the "Commerce Clause" (Article I, section 8, clause 3) to a developing nation. That Clause, which empowers the national government to regulate commerce between states, was a response to problems experienced when individual states erected trade barriers under the Articles of Confederation. This was the first Commerce-Clause case to reach the Supreme Court.

In 1808, the New York legislature gave Robert Livingston and Robert Fulton a thirty-year franchise to operate steamboats in New York waters. The monopoly provided that no one would be allowed to navigate in New York waters by steam without a license from Livingston and Fulton. This arrangement hampered Livingston and Fulton's would-be competitors and neighboring states began to pass retaliatory laws.

Aaron Ogden had received a license from Livingston and Fulton. He operated boats between New York and New Jersey. His former partner, Thomas Gibbons, was also operating steamboats in these waters. Gibbons did not have a license from Livingston and Fulton. Instead, he operated under a coasting license obtained from the United States government. Ogden obtained an injunction from a New York court enjoining Gibbons from operating without a New York license. Gibbons appealed to the U.S. Supreme Court.

Chief Justice Marshall wrote the opinion for the Court. He first considered the definition of the "commerce" that Congress could regulate. Gibbons carried passengers, not goods and products. Nevertheless, Marshall construed "commerce" broadly to cover various forms of intercourse. Second, Congress was authorized to regulate interstate commerce. Was this commerce of a purely internal or intrastate nature and, thus, beyond congressional reach? Marshall held that commerce "among the states" cannot stop at the external borders of a state, but may be "introduced into the interior." That being the case here, he ruled that Congress could "follow" relevant activities into New York to regulate them. Finally, he addressed the conflict between Gibbons's federal coasting license and Ogden's state license. Once again, he relied on the supremacy clause of Article VI in ruling in favor of the federal enactment.

* * * * * * * * * * * * * * * * * * * * * * * * * * *

Mr. Chief Justice Marshall delivered the opinion of the Court, saying in part:

The appellant contends that this decree is erroneous, because the laws which purport to give the exclusive privilege it sustains, are repugnant to the Constitution and the laws of the United States.

They are said to be repugnant:

1. To that clause in the Constitution which authorizes Congress to regulate commerce. . . .

This instrument contains an enumeration of powers expressly granted by the people to their government. It has been said that these powers ought to be construed strictly. . . . What do gentlemen mean by a strict construction? If they contend only against that enlarged construction which would extend words beyond their natural and obvious import, we might question the application of the term, but should not controvert the principle. If they contend for that narrow construction which, in support of some theory not to be found in the Constitution, would deny to the government those powers which the words of the grant, as usually understood, import, and which are consistent with the general views and objects of the instrument; for that narrow construction, which would cripple the government, and render it unequal to the objects for which it is declared to be instituted, and to which the powers given, as fairly understood, render it competent; then we cannot perceive the propriety of this strict construction, nor adopt it as the rule by which the Constitution is to be expounded. . . . We know of no rule for construing the extent of such powers, other than is given by the language of the instrument which confers them, taken in connection with the purposes for which they were conferred.

The words are, "Congress shall have power to regulate commerce with foreign nations, and among the several States, and with the Indian tribes."

The subject to be regulated is commerce; and our Constitution being, as was aptly said at the bar, one of enumeration and not of definition, to ascertain the extent of the power it becomes necessary to settle the meaning of the word. The counsel for the appellee would limit it to traffic, to buying and selling, or the interchange of commodities, and do not admit that it comprehends navigation. This would restrict a general term, applicable to many objects, to one of its significations. Commerce, undoubtedly, is traffic but it is something more; it is intercourse. It describes the commercial intercourse between nations, and parts of nations, in all its branches, and is regulated by prescribing rules for carrying on that intercourse. The mind can scarcely conceive a system for regulating commerce between nations which shall exclude all laws concerning navigation, which shall be silent on the admission of the vessels of one nation into the ports of the other, and be confined to prescribing rules for the conduct of individuals in the actual employment of buying or selling, or of barter. . . .

. . .The word used in the Constitution, then, comprehends, and has been always understood to comprehend, navigation within its meaning; and a power to regulate navigation is as expressly granted as if that term had been added to the word *commerce.*

To what commerce does this power extend? The Constitution informs us, to commerce "with the foreign nations, and among the several States, and with the Indian tribes."

It has, we believe, been universally admitted, that these words comprehend every species of commercial intercourse between the United States and foreign nations. No sort of trade can be carried on between this country and any other, to which this power does not extend . . . .

The subject to which the power is next applied is to commerce "among the several States." The word *among* means intermingled with. A thing which is among others is intermingled with them. Commerce among the States cannot stop at the external boundary line of each State, but may be introduced into the interior.

It is not intended to say that these words comprehend that commerce which is completely internal, which is carried on between man and man in a State, or between different parts of the same State, and which does not extend to or affect other states. . . .

. . .The completely internal commerce of a State, then, may be considered as reserved for the State itself.

But, in regulating commerce with foreign nations, the power of Congress does not stop at the jurisdictional lines of the several States. . . . If it exists within the States, if a foreign voyage may commence or terminate at a port within a State, then the power of Congress may be exercised within a State.

This principle is, if possible, still more clear when applied to commerce "among the several States." They either join each other, in which case they are separated by a mathematical line, or they are remote from each other, in which case other States lie between them. . . . Commerce among the States, must of necessity, be commerce with the States. . . . The power of Congress, then, whatever it may be, must be exercised within the territorial jurisdiction of the several States.

. . .We are now arrived at the inquiry—What is the power?

It is the power to regulate; that is, to prescribe the rule by which commerce is to be governed. This power, like all others vested in Congress, is complete in itself, may be exercised to its utmost extent, and acknowledges not limitations other than are prescribed in the Constitution. . . .

The power of Congress, then, comprehends navigation within the limits of every State in the Union; so far as the navigation may be, in any manner, connected with "commerce with foreign nations, or among the several States, or with the Indian tribes." It may, of consequence, pass the jurisdictional line of New York, and act upon the very waters to which the prohibition now under consideration applies.

But it has been urged with great earnestness that, although the power of Congress to regulate commerce with foreign nations, and among the several States, be co-extensive with the subject itself, and have no other limits than are prescribed in the Constitution, yet the States may severally exercise the same power within their respective jurisdictions. . . .

The sole question is, can a State regulate commerce with foreign nations and among the States, while Congress is regulating it? . . .

. . .the Court will enter upon the inquiry, whether the laws of New York, as expounded by the highest tribunal of that State, have, in their application to this case, come into collision with an act of Congress, and deprived a citizen of a right to which that act entitles him. Should this collision exist, it will be immaterial whether those laws were passed in virtue of a concurrent power "to regulate commerce with foreign nations and among the several States" or in virtue of a power to regulate their domestic trade and police. In one case and the other, the acts of New York must yield to the law of Congress; and the decision sustaining the privilege they confer, against a right given by a law of the Union, must be erroneous.

This opinion has been frequently expressed in this Court, and is founded as well on the nature of the government as on the words of the Constitution. In argument, however, it has been contended that if a law passed by a State, in the exercise of its acknowledged sovereignty, comes into conflict with a law passed by Congress in pursuance of the Constitution, they affect the subject, and each other, like equal opposing powers.

But the framers of our Constitution foresaw this state of things, and provided for it by declaring the supremacy not only of itself, but of the laws made in pursuance of it. . . . In every such case, the act of Congress, or the treaty, is supreme; and the law of the State, though enacted in the exercise of powers not controverted, must yield to it.

. . ."An act [of Congress] for the enrolling and licensing of steamboats" . . . authorizes a steamboat employed, or intended to be employed, only in a river or bay of the United States, owned wholly or in part by an alien, resident within the United States, to be enrolled and licensed as if the same belonged to a citizen of the United States.

This act demonstrates the opinion of Congress that steamboats may be enrolled and licensed in common with vessels using sails. They are, of course, entitled to the same privileges, and can no more be restrained from navigating waters, and entering ports which are free to such vessels, than if they were wafted on their voyage by winds instead of being propelled by the agency of fire. The one element may be as legitimately used as the other for every commercial purpose authorized by the law of the Union; and the act of a State inhibiting the use of either to any vessel having a license under the act of Congress comes, we think, in direct collision with the act.

\* \* \* \* \* \* \* \* \* \* \* \* \* \* \* \* \* \* \* \* \* \* \* \* \* \* \* \* \* \* \*

*Discussion Points:*

1. How did Marshall define "commerce"?
2. How did Marshall respond to the contention that New York was regulating internal rather than interstate commerce?
3. Compare and contrast Marshall's use of the supremacy clause in *Marbury, McCulloch,* and *Gibbons* respectively.
4. On the basis of his opinions in these cases, discuss Marshall's general beliefs regarding the power of the national government vis a vis the power of state governments.

# CHAPTER 16

## BARRON V. BALTIMORE
### 7 Peters 243; 8 L.Ed. 672 (1833)

A written Bill of Rights that restricted governmental power on behalf of individual liberty was added to the Constitution shortly after its ratification. But did these limitations apply only against the national government or against state and local governmental actions too?

The First Amendment specifies that *Congress* shall make no law abridging freedom of religion, speech, press, or assembly. Likewise, additional limitations fail to make explicit reference to state and local governments. Furthermore, historical evidence suggests that the Framers concentrated on limiting the powers of the national government.

While paving its streets, the City of Baltimore diverted some streams from their natural courses. As a result, deposits of sand and gravel built up near Barron's Wharf, rendering the water shallow and the wharf useless. Barron sued for damages on the Fifth-Amendment ground that he had been deprived of his property for public use without just compensation.

In this, his last constitutional decision, Chief Justice Marshall agreed that Barron had been denied effective use of his property without just compensation. But he held that the Fifth Amendment affords this protection against the national government alone.

Thirty-five years later, the Fourteenth Amendment was adopted. It says that no *State* shall "deprive any person of life, liberty, or property, without due process of law. A process of "selective incorporation" has taken place by which rights and liberties deemed essential to due process of law are absorbed into the Fourteenth Amendment and protected against state encroachment. While *Barron v. Baltimore* has not been overruled, today Barron could bring his case under the Fourteenth Amendment's due process clause. In this way, the Court can now review state and local denials of the kinds of liberties that are protected by the Bill of Rights at the national level.

\* \* \* \* \* \* \* \* \* \* \* \* \* \* \* \* \* \* \* \* \* \* \* \* \* \* \* \*

.... [T]he fifth amendment must be understood as restraining the power of the general government, not as applicable to the States. In their several constitutions they have imposed such restrictions on their respective governments as their own wisdom suggested ... It is a subject on which they judge exclusively....

.... Had the framers of these amendments intended them to be limitations on the powers of the State governments they would have imitated the framers of the original Constitution, and have expressed that intention. Had Congress engaged in the extraordinary occupation of improving the constitutions of the several States by affording the people additional protection from the exercise of power by their own governments in matters which concerned themselves alone, they would have declared this purpose in plain and intelligible language.

.... In almost every convention by which the Constitution was adopted, amendments to guard against the abuse of power were recommended. These amendments demanded security against the apprehended encroachments of the general government—not against those of the local government.

.... These amendments contain no expression indicating an intention to apply them to the State governments. This Court cannot so apply them.

We are of the opinion that the provision in the fifth amendment ... declaring that private property shall not be taken for public use without just compensation, is intended solely as a limitation on the exercise of power by the government of the United States, and is not applicable to the legislation of the States. We are therefore of the opinion that there is no repugnancy between the several acts of the General Assembly of Maryland ... and the Constitution of the United States....

\* \* \* \* \* \* \* \* \* \* \* \* \* \* \* \* \* \* \* \* \* \* \* \* \* \* \* \* \*

*Discussion Points:*

1. Why did Marshall refuse to apply the Bill of Rights to state and local governments?
2. Compare and contrast Marshall's arguments about the Bill of Rights with points raised by Brutus and by Hamilton in *The Federalist,* No. 84.
3. If Barron did enjoy a right to compensation from his State, where would he have to find it?

# PART V:
# THE CONSTITUTION IN THE
# SECOND HALF OF THE
# NINETEENTH CENTURY

# CHAPTER 17

## *DRED SCOTT V. SANFORD*
### 19 Howard 393, 15 L.Ed. 691 (1857)

The second time the Supreme Court declared a congressional statute unconstitutional was in *Dred Scott v. Sanford*. The case dealt with the constitutional implications of slavery in the territories at a time when political debate over the issue was growing increasingly heated. The Court's decision only intensified the controversy and damaged the Court's reputation in the process.

In 1834, Dred Scott, a Negro slave owned by Dr. Emerson, was taken by Emerson from Missouri to Illinois, where slavery was prohibited. Later, Scott was taken to Fort Snelling in the Louisiana Territory, an area where slavery was prohibited by the Missouri Compromise of 1820. Subsequently, Scott was brought back to the slave state of Missouri. Scott claimed that he became a free man when he entered the free territories and that he remained free. Scott had been sold to John Sanford of New York and, as such, he sued Sanford for his freedom.

By a seven-to-two vote, the Supreme Court held that Scott was not a citizen. As a result, he had no standing in federal court under the Constitution's diversity-of-citizenship provision. Further, the Court ruled that the Missouri Compromise unconstitutionally deprived a master of his "property" without due process of law. The practical effect of this decision was reversed with the ratification of the Fourteenth Amendment.

\* \* \* \* \* \* \* \* \* \* \* \* \* \* \* \* \* \* \* \* \* \* \* \* \* \* \* \*

Mr. Chief Justice Taney delivered the opinion of the Court.

... The question is simply this: Can a Negro, whose ancestors were imported into this country and sold as slaves, become a member of the political community formed and brought into existence by the Constitution ... and as such become entitled to all the rights, and privileges, and immunities guarantied (sic) by that instrument to the citizen? One of which rights is the privilege of suing in a court of the United States in the cases specified in the Constitution.

We think . . . [negroes] . . . are not included, and were not intended to be included, under the word "citizens" in the Constitution, and can therefore claim none of the rights and privileges which that instrument provides for and secures to citizens of the United States. On the contrary, they were at that time considered as a subordinate and inferior class of being, who had been subjugated by the dominant race, and, whether emancipated or not, yet remained subject to their authority, and had no rights or privileges but such as those who held the power of the Government might choose to grant them. . . .

The question then arises, whether the provisions of the Constitution, in relation to the personal rights and privileges to which the citizen of a State should be entitled, embraced the negro African race, at that time in this country, or who might afterwards be imported, who had then or should afterwards be made free in any State; and to put it in the power of a single State to make him a citizen of the United States, and endue him with the full rights of citizenship in every other State without their consent? . . .

The court thinks the affirmative of these propositions cannot be maintained. . . .

In the opinion of the court, the legislation and histories of the times, and the language used in the Declaration of Independence, show, that neither the class of persons who had been imported as slaves, nor their descendants, whether they had become free or not, were then acknowledged as part of the people, nor intended to be included in the general words used in that memorable instrument. . . .

They had for more than a century before been regarded as beings of an inferior order, and altogether unfit to associate with the white race, either in social or political relations; and so far inferior, that they had no rights which the white man was bound to respect; and that the negro might justly and lawfully be reduced to slavery for his benefit. He was bought and sold, and treated as an ordinary article of merchandise and traffic, whenever a profit could be made by it. This opinion was at that time fixed and universal in the civilized portion of the white race. . . .

The only two provisions [of the Constitution] which point to them and include them [Article I, Section 9 and Article IV, Section 2] treat them as property, and make it the duty of the Government to protect it. . . .

The act of Congress, upon which the plaintiff relies, declares that slavery and involuntary servitude, except as a punishment for crime, shall be forever prohibited in . . . [the Louisiana Territory] . . . And the

... [question] is whether Congress was authorized to pass this law under any of the powers granted to it by the Constitution; for if the authority is not given by that instrument, it is the duty of this court to declare it void and inoperative, and incapable of conferring freedom upon any one who is held as a slave under the laws of any one of the States.

. . . . [A]n Act of Congress which deprives a citizen of the United States of his liberty or property, merely because he came himself or brought his property into a particular Territory . . . and who had committed no offenses against the laws, could hardly be dignified with the name due process of law.

The powers over person and property of which we speak are not only not granted to Congress, but are in express terms denied [by the Fifth Amendment], and they are forbidden to exercise them. . . .

Upon these considerations, it is the opinion of the court that the act of Congress which prohibited a citizen from holding and owning property of this kind in [the Louisiana Territory] . . . is not warranted by the Constitution, and is therefore void; and that neither Dred Scott himself, nor any of his family, were made free by being carried into this territory; even if they had been carried there by the owner, with the intention of becoming a permanent resident. . . .

Mr. Justice McLean and Mr. Justice Curtis dissented.

\* \* \* \* \* \* \* \* \* \* \* \* \* \* \* \* \* \* \* \* \* \* \* \* \* \* \* \* \*

*Discussion Points:*

1. Why did Taney find the Missouri Compromise unconstitutional? Why was Dred Scott considered a piece of "property" and not a citizen?
2. How did the Fourteenth Amendment reverse the effect of this decision?
3. Taney relied heavily upon the intent of the Constitution's Framers. Discuss some of the implications and problems associated with this mode of constitutional interpretation.

# CHAPTER 18

# LINCOLN'S MESSAGE TO THE SPECIAL SESSION OF CONGRESS (1861)

During the Civil War period, President Lincoln took some steps that were of questionable constitutionality. For example, in 1863 he announced that all slaves in areas under Confederate control would be "forever free" and he authorized the enlistment of freed slaves into the Union army. Critics challenged his authority to do this. In an April 4, 1864 letter to Albert G. Hodges, editor of the Frankfort, Kentucky *Commonwealth*, Lincoln explained that he was trying to preserve the nation itself:

... Was it possible to lose the nation and yet preserve the Constitution? By general law, life and limb must be protected, yet often a limb must be amputated to save a life; but a life is never wisely given to save a limb. I felt that measures otherwise unconstitutional might become lawful by becoming indispensable to the preservation of the Constitution through the preservation of the nation. ...

Back in April of 1861, General Beauregard fired on Fort Sumter and the fighting started. Congress was not in session at the time, but Lincoln acted quickly and boldly. He expanded the army and advanced public funds to private parties without prior congressional authorization. Especially controversial was his declaration of martial law on April 27, 1861. This order enabled military authorities to arrest civilians suspected of assisting the enemy and suspended *habeus corpus* rights in certain sections of the country. In September 1862, he extended his order to all parts of the country where "disloyal" elements were active.

A writ of *habeus corpus* is a court order that directs a jailer to bring a prisoner into court to determine whether there are sufficient grounds to continue to hold the prisoner in custody. This protects individuals against being imprisoned illegally. Article I, Section 9, Clause 2 guarantees this right, stating that, "The privilege of the writ of *habeus corpus* shall not be suspended, unless when in cases of rebellion or invasion, the public safety may require it."

Although the Constitution permits the suspension of *habeus corpus*, a question arises: *who* shall issue the suspension order? In *Ex Parte Merryman* (17 Fed. Cas. 144, 1861), the Supreme Court noted that Article I is the legislative article and ruled that a president cannot suspend *habeus corpus*, even in an emergency. This power rests with Congress. Congress did eventually give Lincoln retroactive authorization to exercise the powers that he had assumed. In *Ex Parte Milligan* (4 Wall 2, 1866), the Supreme Court faced related issues. With congressional approval, Lincoln authorized military arrests of persons who interfered with the war effort and provided for trials before military commissions. The Court held that the authorization of such military trials of civilians away from the theater of war, and where civil courts were operating, was a denial of the right to a jury trial. It is important to point out, however, that this case was decided *after* the military crisis had passed.

The following passage concerns Lincoln's original decision to suspend *habeus corpus* while Congress was not in session. When Congress reconvened for a special session in July 1861, he sought approval of his actions and offered his explanations.

* * * * * * * * * * * * * * * * * * * * * * * * * * * *

Fellow-Citizens of the Senate and House of Representatives:

Having been convened on an extraordinary occasion, as authorized by the Constitution, your attention is not called to any ordinary subject of legislation.

At the beginning of the present Presidential term, four months ago, the functions of the Federal Government were found to be generally suspended within the several states of South Carolina, Georgia, Alabama, Mississippi, Louisiana, and Florida, excepting only those of the Post-Office Department. . . .

Finding this condition of things and believing it to be an imperative duty upon the incoming Executive to prevent, if possible, the consummation of such attempt to destroy the Federal Union, a choice of means to that end became indispensable. . . .

. . . [T]his issue embraces more than the fate of these United States. It presents to the whole family of man the question whether a constitutional republic, or democracy—a government of the people by the same people—can or can not maintain its territorial integrity against its own domestic foes. It presents the question whether discontented individuals, too few in numbers to control administration . . . can always . . . break up their government, and thus practically put an end to free government upon the earth. It forces us to ask, Is there in all republics this inherent and fatal weakness? Must a government of necessity be too strong for the liberties of its own people, or too weak to maintain its own existence?

So viewing the issue, no choice was left but to call out the war power of the Government and so to resist force employed for its destruction by force for its preservation.

The call was made, and the response of the country was most gratifying, surpassing in unanimity and spirit the most sanguine expectation. . . .

Other calls were made for volunteers to serve three years unless sooner discharged, and also for large additions to the Regular Army and Navy. These measures, whether strictly legal or not, were ventured upon under what appeared to be a popular demand and a public necessity, trusting then, as now, that Congress would readily ratify them. It is believed that nothing has been done beyond the constitutional competency of Congress.

Soon after the first call for militia it was considered a duty to authorize the Commanding General in proper cases, according to his discretion, to suspend the privilege of the writ of *habeus corpus*, or, in other words to arrest and detain without resort to the ordinary processes and forms of law such individuals as he might deem dangerous to the public safety. This authority has purposely been exercised but very sparingly. Nevertheless, the legality and propriety of what has been done under it are questioned, and the attention of the country has been called to the proposition that one who is sworn to "take care that the laws be faithfully executed" should not himself violate them. Of course some consideration was given to the questions of power and propriety before this matter was acted upon. The whole of the laws which were required to be faithfully executed were being resisted and failing of execution in nearly one-third of the States. Must they be allowed to finally fail of execution, even had it been perfectly clear that by the use of the means necessary to their execution some single law, made in such extreme tenderness of the citizen's liberty that practically it relieves more of the guilty than of the innocent, should to a very limited extent be violated? To state the question more directly, Are all the laws but one to go unexecuted, and the Government itself go to pieces lest that one be violated? Even in such a case, would not the official oath be broken if the Government should be overthrown when it was believed that disregarding the single law would tend to preserve it? But it was not believed that this question was presented. It was not believed that any law was violated. The provision of the Constitution that "the privilege of the writ of *habeus corpus* shall not be suspended unless when, in cases of rebellion or invasion, the public safety may require it" is equivalent to a provision—is a provision—that such privilege may be suspended when, in cases of rebellion or invasion, the public safety does require it. It was decided that we have a case of rebellion and that the public safety does require the qualified suspension of the privilege of the writ which was authorized to be made. Now it is insisted that Congress, and not the Executive, is vested with this power; but the Constitution itself is silent as to which or who is to exercise the power; and as the provision was plainly made for a dangerous emergency, it can not be believed the framers of the instrument intended that in every case the danger should run its course until Congress could be called together, the very assembling of which might be prevented, as was intended in this case, by the rebellion.

No more extended argument is now offered, as an opinion at some length will probably be presented by the Attorney-General. Whether there shall be any legislation upon the subject, and, if any, what, is submitted entirely to the better judgment of Congress. . . .

* * * * * * * * * * * * * * * * * * * * * * * * * * * * * * * *

*Discussion Points:*

1. How did Lincoln justify his actions? Do you find his arguments persuasive? Why or why not?
2. "Must a government of necessity be too strong for the liberties of its own people, or too weak to maintain its own existence?" What does Lincoln's question mean and what do you think about it?
3. It was argued that the president, who is charged with taking care that the laws are "faithfully executed," should not himself violate them. How did Lincoln respond? Is his response convincing?
4. Lincoln claimed that the Constitution is silent about whether the president or Congress has the authority to suspend *habeus corpus*. Do you agree with him or do you agree with the Supreme Court in *Merryman* that this power is legislative? Why?

# CHAPTER 19

# THE GETTYSBURG ADDRESS (1863)

As noted, Lincoln believed that a president was justified in taking extra-constitutional steps if such actions were necessary to preserve the nation. In his memorable Gettysburg Address, he defended the enormous sacrifices made during the Civil War on similar grounds. He delivered this short speech on November 19, 1863 at a ceremony to dedicate part of the Gettysburg battlefield as a national cemetery for those who were killed in this battle.

\* \* \* \* \* \* \* \* \* \* \* \* \* \* \* \* \* \* \* \* \* \* \* \* \* \* \*

Four score and seven years ago our fathers brought forth on this continent a new nation, conceived in liberty and dedicated to the proposition that all men are created equal.

Now we are engaged in a great civil war, testing whether that nation or any nation so conceived and so dedicated can long endure. We are met on a great battlefield of that war. We have come to dedicate a portion of that field as a final resting place for those who here gave their lives that that nation might live. It is altogether fitting and proper that we should do this.

But, in a larger sense, we cannot dedicate—we cannot consecrate—we cannot hallow—this ground. The brave men, living and dead, who struggled here have consecrated it far above our poor power to add or detract. The world will little note nor long remember what we say here, but it can never forget what they did here. It is for us, the living, rather, to be dedicated here to the unfinished work which they who fought here have thus far so nobly advanced.

It is rather for us to be here dedicated to the great task remaining before us—that from these honored dead we take increased devotion to that cause for which they gave the last full measure of devotion; that we here highly resolve that these dead shall not have died in vain; that this nation, under God, shall have a new birth of freedom; and that government of the people, by the people, for the people shall not perish from the earth.

\* \* \* \* \* \* \* \* \* \* \* \* \* \* \* \* \* \* \* \* \* \* \* \* \* \* \* \* \* \*

*Discussion Points:*

1. In stating that "[t]he world will little note nor long remember what we say here," Lincoln proved to be a poor prophet. How was he as a historian? Discuss his remark that this nation was "dedicated to the proposition that all men are created equal."
2. In 1776, the American colonists withdrew their consent from the King and declared their independence from England. Compare and contrast this action with the attempt by the Confederate states to secede from the Union.
3. Discuss some of the implications associated with the view that a president can take steps not authorized by the Constitution if he regards such steps as necessary to the preservation of the nation. If you are supportive of Lincoln's position, consider whether you would be equally supportive if similar arguments were advanced by a president whom you hold in relatively lower esteem.

# CHAPTER 20

# THE TENURE OF OFFICE ACT CONTROVERSY (1867)

Separation of powers has led to numerous clashes between and among the branches of the federal government. One such struggle developed after the Civil War when President Andrew Johnson and Radical Republicans in Congress fought for control of Reconstruction policy.

After the military defeat of the South, the problem of how to reconstruct the Union was a tremendous challenge. The Constitution provided no explicit guidance. Further, what should the national government do to secure the civil rights of freed slaves? Some, including President Johnson, advocated a quick restoration of the Union with no protection for former slaves beyond the legal prohibition of slavery. Others wanted readmission of Southern states to depend on guarantees that loyal Unionists would hold power and that freed slaves would acquire the basic rights of American citizenship. This more radical position was endorsed by many congressional Republicans.

Early in 1866, Congress approved a bill extending the life of the Freedmen's Bureau—an agency that provided educational, employment, and legal aid to freed slaves. Congress also approved a civil rights bill to provide some legal safeguards for blacks. Although the bills were considered relatively moderate—and enjoyed wide Republican support—President Johnson vetoed them. Congress overrode his veto of the Civil Rights Act, but some feared Johnson would not enforce such legislation. As such, congressional Republicans drafted the Fourteenth Amendment, which expanded "citizenship" and guaranteed equal protection of the laws. Johnson argued that the Amendment gave the central government too much power over state affairs and twelve Southern and border states opposed it as well. Nevertheless, the Amendment was ratified in July 1868.

In 1867, Congress passed the First Reconstruction Act. Again, Congress had to override a presidential veto. The Act placed the South under military rule for a time and offered to readmit any state that ratified a new constitution providing for black suffrage. Johnson tried to thwart congressional will by dismissing officeholders who supported the Act and by countermanding the orders of generals who were enforcing it in the Southern military districts.

Congress responded by passing the Tenure of Office Act. It required the President to get Senate approval to remove federal officials whose appointments had needed Senate consent. Congress also passed the Command of the Army Act, limiting Johnson's ability to give orders to the military commanders. Johnson objected that these laws violated the principle of separation of powers.

The Constitution outlines the president's power to appoint federal officials with the consent of the Senate (Article II, Section 2). But the Framers did not specify how such officials would be removed. In later years, the Supreme Court ruled that a president can unilaterally remove purely executive officials, even if their appointment required senatorial consent, so that he can "faithfully execute" the laws (*Myers v. U.S.*, 272 U.S. 52, 1926). The Court has also held, however, that if the official performs quasi-legislative or quasi-judicial duties and is not a purely executive officer, the president cannot remove him/her unilaterally without a demonstration of cause (*Humphrey's Executor (Rathbun) v. U.S.*, 295 U.S. 602, 1935 and *Wiener v. U.S.*, 357 U.S. 349, 1958). But the issue was unresolved at the time of Johnson's clash with Congress.

Below are excerpts from the Tenure of Office Act, Johnson's veto of this Act (his veto was overridden), and the Command of the Army Act. Johnson did not veto the latter Act because it was attached as a rider to an army appropriations bill that he wanted. He did, however, protest against those sections that restricted his command of the army.

\* \* \* \* \* \* \* \* \* \* \* \* \* \* \* \* \* \* \* \* \* \* \* \* \* \* \* \*

*Tenure of Office Act*
*Be it enacted,* That every person holding any civil office to which he has been appointed by and with the advice and consent of the Senate, and every person who shall hereafter be appointed to any such office, and shall become duly qualified to act therein, is, and shall be entitled to hold such office until a successor shall have been in like manner appointed and duly qualified . . . *Provided,* That the Secretaries of State, of the Treasury, of War, of the Navy, and of the Interior, the Postmaster-General, and the Attorney-General, shall hold their office respectively for and during the term of the President by whom they may

have been appointed and for one month thereafter, subject to removal by and with the advice and consent of the Senate. . . .

Section 3. That the President shall have power to fill all vacancies which may happen during the recess of the Senate, by reason of death or resignation, by granting commissions which shall expire at the end of their next session thereafter. . . .

Section 5. That if any person shall, contrary to the provisions of this act, accept any appointment to or employment in any office, or shall hold or exercise or attempt to hold or exercise, any such office or employment, he shall be deemed, and is hereby declared to be, guilty of a high misdemeanor, and, upon trial and conviction thereof, he shall be punished therefor by a fine not exceeding ten thousand dollars, or by imprisonment not exceeding five years, or both said punishments, in the discretion of the court.

Section 6. That every removal, appointment, or employment, made, had, or exercised, contrary to the provisions of this act. . . .are hereby declared to be, high misdemeanors, and, upon trial and conviction thereof, every person guilty thereof shall be punished by a fine not exceeding ten thousand dollars, or by imprisonment not exceeding five years, or both. . . .

## Veto of Tenure of Office Act

. . . In effect the bill provides that the President shall not remove from their places any of the civil officers whose terms of service are not limited by law without the advice and consent of the Senate of the United States. The bill in this respect conflicts, in my judgment, with the Constitution of the United States. The question, as Congress is aware, is by no means a new one. That the power of removal is constitutionally vested in the President of the United States is a principle which has been not more distinctly declared by judicial authority and judicial commentators than it has been uniformly practiced. . . .

The question has often been raised in subsequent times of high excitement, and the practice of the Government has, nevertheless, conformed in all cases to the decision thus early made. . . .

Thus has the important question presented by this bill been settled, in the language of the late Daniel Webster . . . by construction, settled by precedent, settled by the practice of the Government, and settled by statute. The events of the last war furnished a practical confirmation of the wisdom of the Constitution as it has hitherto been maintained in many of its parts, including that which is now the subject of consideration. When the war broke out, rebel enemies, traitors, abettors, and sympathizers were found in every Department of the Government, as well as in the affairs. Upon which probable suspicion they were promptly displaced by my predecessor, so far as they held their offices under executive authority, and their duties were confided to new and loyal successors. No complaints against that power or doubts of its wisdom were entertained in any quarter. I sincerely trust and believe that no such civil war is likely to occur again. I can not doubt, however, that in whatever form and on whatever occasion sedition can raise an effort to hinder or embarrass or defeat the legitimate action of this Government. . . .

### Command of the Army Act

. . . *And be it further enacted,* That the headquarters of the General of the army of the United States shall be at the city of Washington, and all orders and instructions relating to military operations issued by the President or Secretary of War shall be issued through the General of the army, and, in case of his inability, through the next in rank. The General of the army shall not be removed, suspended, or relieved from command, or assigned to duty elsewhere than at said headquarters, except at his own request, without the previous approval of the Senate; and any orders or instructions relating to military operations issued contrary to the requirements of this section shall be null and void; and any officer who shall issue orders or instructions contrary to the provisions of this section shall be deemed guilty of a misdemeanor in office; and any officer of the army who shall transmit, convey, or obey any orders or instructions so issued contrary to the provisions of this section, knowing that such orders were so issued, shall be liable to imprisonment for not less than two nor more than twenty years, upon conviction thereof in any court of competent jurisdiction. . . .

* * * * * * * * * * * * * * * * * * * * * * * * * * * * *

*Discussion Points:*

1. Explain Johnson's argument that the Tenure of Office Act conflicted with the Constitution. He claimed that the removal power "is constitutionally vested in the president." Do you agree? Why or why not?
2. Do you think the Command of the Army Act was constitutional? Did it interfere with the President's powers as commander-in-chief of the armed forces? Explain.

# CHAPTER 21

# THE IMPEACHMENT OF PRESIDENT JOHNSON (1868)

Disagreements between President Johnson and Congress over the Command of the Army Act and the Tenure of Office Act culminated in Johnson's impeachment. He had tried to discharge Secretary of War, Edwin Stanton. Stanton enjoyed support from Radical Republicans in Congress. On February 24, 1868, the House voted to impeach Johnson for violating the Tenure of Office Act. He was then placed on trial before the Senate. The Constitution specifies that conviction and removal from office requires a two-thirds Senate vote. Johnson avoided conviction and removal by a single vote when 35 senators voted guilty and 19 voted not guilty.

The failed impeachment effort proved somewhat embarrassing for congressional Republicans, but the attempt helped them prevail on the broader Reconstruction issue. During the trial, Johnson promised to enforce the Reconstruction Acts if he remained in office. He fulfilled this pledge.

This was the only impeachment trial in history for an American president. The question did not arise again seriously until 1974.

\* \* \* \* \* \* \* \* \* \* \* \* \* \* \* \* \* \* \* \* \* \* \* \* \* \* \* \* \* \* \*

ARTICLES EXHIBITED BY THE HOUSE OF REPRESENTATIVES OF THE UNITED STATES, IN THE NAME OF THEMSELVES AND ALL THE PEOPLE OF THE UNITED STATES, AGAINST ANDREW JOHNSON, PRESIDENT OF THE UNITED STATES, IN MAINTENANCE AND SUPPORT OF THEIR IMPEACHMENT AGAINST HIM FOR HIGH CRIMES AND MISDEMEANORS IN OFFICE.

ARTICLE I. That said Andrew Johnson President of the United States, on the 21st day of February . . . 1868, . . . unmindful of the high duties of his office, of his oath of office, and of the requirement of the Constitution that he should take care that the laws be faithfully executed, did unlawfully and in violation of the Constitution and laws of the United States issue an order in writing for the removal of Edwin M. Stanton from the Office of Secretary for the Department of War, said Edwin M. Stanton having been theretofore duly appointed and commissioned, by and with the advice and consent of the Senate of the United States, as such Secretary; and said Andrew Johnson, . . . on the 12th day of August . . . 1867, and during the recess of said Senate, having suspended by his order Edwin M. Stanton from said office, and within twenty days after the first day of the next meeting of said Senate—that is to say, on the 12th day of December, in the year last aforesaid—having reported to said Senate such suspension with the evidence and reasons for his action in the case and the name of the person designated to perform the duties of such office temporarily until the next meeting of the Senate; and said Senate thereafterwards, on the 13th day of January, A.D. 1868, having duly considered the evidence and reasons reported by said Andrew Johnson for said suspension, and having refused to concur in said suspension, whereby and by force of the provisions of an act entitled "An act regulating the tenure of certain civil offices," passed March 2, 1867, said Edwin M. Stanton did forthwith resume the functions of his office, whereof the said Andrew Johnson had then and there due notice; and said Edwin M. Stanton, by reason of the premises, on said 21st day of February, being lawfully entitled to hold said office of Secretary for the Department of War; which said order for the removal of said Edwin M. Stanton is in substance as follows; that is to say:

> Executive Mansion,
> Washington, D.C.
> February 21, 1868.

Hon. Edwin M. Stanton
Washington, D.C.

Sir: By virtue of the power and authority vested in me as President by the Constitution and laws of the United States, you are hereby removed from office as Secretary for the Department of War, and your functions as such will terminate upon receipt of this communication.

You will transfer to Brevet Major-General Lorenzo Thomas, Adjutant-General of the Army, who has this day been authorized and empowered to act as Secretary of War ad interim, all records, books, papers, and other public property now in your custody and charge.

> Respectfully, yours,
> Andrew Johnson.

which order was unlawfully issued with intent ... to violate the [Tenure of Office Act] ... whereby said Andrew Johnson, President of the United States, did then and there commit and was guilty of a high misdemeanor in office....

### March 3, 1868

The following additional articles of impeachment were agreed to viz:

Article X. That said Andrew Johnson, President of the United States, unmindful of the high duties of his office and the dignity and proprieties thereof, and of the harmony and courtesies which ought to exist and be maintained between the executive and legislative branches of the Government of the United States, ... did attempt to bring into disgrace, ridicule, hatred, contempt, and reproach the Congress of the United States and the several branches thereof, to impair and destroy the regard and respect of all the good people of the United States for the Congress and legislative power thereof (which all officers of the Government ought inviolably to preserve and maintain), and to excite the odium and resentment of all the good people of the United States against Congress and the laws by it duly and constitutionally enacted....

* * * * * * * * * * * * * * * * * * * * * * * * * * * * * * *

*Discussion Points:*

1. Review Article I, Section 2, Clause 5; Article I, Section 3, Clauses 6 and 7; and Article II, Section 4 regarding impeachment. Do you think impeachment should be used more or less frequently? Should it be easier or more difficult to employ? Is the *threat* of impeachment an effective check on the abuse of presidential power?

2. What alternatives, if any, are available if substantial numbers of people think that the president's actions are misguided?

3. If a president tries to obstruct the will of Congress through frequent vetoes, has he committed an impeachable offense? What if he tries to obstruct congressional will through less-than-enthusiastic execution of legislative programs? Would this be an impeachable offense? What if the president commits no *overt* high crimes and misdemeanors, but he literally sits around all day with his feet up on his desk and does nothing? Has he committed an impeachable offense?

# CHAPTER 22

## THE CIVIL RIGHTS CASES
### 109 U.S. 3; 3 S.Ct. 18; 27 L.Ed. 835 (1883)

The Thirteenth, Fourteenth, and Fifteenth Amendments were enacted to protect the rights of freed slaves. In the closing days of the Reconstruction, however, many in Congress thought that specific laws were necessary to ensure that the rights of blacks would be respected by—and protected against—whites who were regaining control of Southern state governments. One such law was the Civil Rights Act of 1875. The Act made it both a crime and a civil wrong for any person to deny any other person "the full and equal enjoyment of any of the accommodations, advantages, facilities and privileges of inns, public conveyances on land or water, theaters and other places of public amusement" on racial grounds.

The Supreme Court's decision in this case, based on five cases that were grouped together, seriously undermined the civil rights effort of this period. The Court found the Act unconstitutional. Justice Bradley, writing for the majority, ruled that the Thirteenth Amendment did not authorize Congress to pass this law because racial discrimination is not the same as involuntary servitude. Furthermore, he claimed that the Fourteenth Amendment gave Congress the power to prevent discrimination by states, but it did not authorize Congress to prohibit discrimination by private parties.

As the sole dissenter in this case, Justice Harlan rejected the majority's view of the Thirteenth Amendment. He argued that the burdens of racial discrimination "constitute badges of slavery and servitude" and that the Act was an appropriate measure to protect former slaves against such racial injuries. Years later, in the case of *Jones v. Alfred H. Mayer, Co.* (392 U.S. 409, 1968), the Court accepted Harlan's reasoning. In *Jones*, Justice Stewart, writing for the Court, said that the Thirteenth Amendment permits Congress to prohibit private racial discrimination because the Amendment was intended to remove badges of slavery from this Nation. In Stewart's words,

.... Congress has the power under the Thirteenth Amendment rationally to determine what are the badges and the incidents of slavery and the authority to translate that determination into effective legislation. . . . [W]hen racial discrimination herds men into ghettos and makes their ability to buy property turn on the color of their skin, then it too is a relic of slavery. . . . The Thirteenth Amendment includes the right to buy whatever a white man can, the right to live wherever a white man can live. . . .

* * * * * * * * * * * * * * * * * * * * * * * * * * * * *

Mr. Justice Bradley delivered the opinion of the Court, saying in part:
. . . [T]he primary and important question in all the cases is the constitutionality of law. . . .

The essence of the law is, not to declare boldly that all persons shall be entitled to the full and equal enjoyment of the accommodation, advantages, facilities, and privileges of inns, public conveyances, and theaters; but that such enjoyment shall not be subject to any conditions applicable only to citizens of a particular race or color. . . .

Has Congress constitutional power to make such a law? Of course, no one will contend that the power to pass it was contained in the Constitution before the adoption of the last three amendments. The power is sought, first, in the Fourteenth Amendment, and the views and arguments of distinguished Senators, advanced whilst the law was under consideration, claiming authority to pass it by virtue of that amendment, are the principal arguments adduced in favor of the power. . . .

The first section of the Fourteenth Amendment . . . , after declaring who shall be citizens of the United States, and of the several States, is prohibitory in its character, and prohibitory upon the States. It declares that:

No State shall make or enforce any law which shall abridge the privileges or immunities of citizens of the United States; nor shall any State deprive any person of life, liberty, or property without due process of law; nor deny to any person within its jurisdiction the equal protection of the laws.

It is State action of a particular character that is prohibited. Individual invasion of individual rights is not the subject matter of the amendment. It has a deeper and broader scope. It nullifies and makes void all State legislation, and State action of every kind, which impairs the privileges and immunities of citizens of the United States, or which injures them in life, liberty or property without due process of law, or which denies to any of them the equal protection of the laws. It not only does this, but, in order that the national will, thus declared, may not be a mere *brutum fulmen*, the last section of the amendment invests Congress with power to enforce it by appropriate legislation. To enforce what? To enforce the prohibition. To adopt appropriate legislation for correcting the effects of such prohibited State laws and State acts, and thus to render them effectually null, void, and innocuous. This is the legislative power conferred upon Congress, and this is the whole of it. . . . Positive rights and privileges are undoubtedly secured by the Fourteenth Amendment; but they are secured by way of prohibition against State laws and State proceedings affecting those rights and privileges, and by power given to Congress to legislate for the purpose of carrying such prohibition into effect. . . .

[U]ntil some State law has been passed, or some State action through its officers or agents has been taken, adverse to the rights of citizens sought to be protected by the Fourteenth Amendment, no legislation of the United States under said amendment, nor any proceedings under such legislation, can be called into activity; for the prohibitions of the amendment are against State laws and acts done under State authority. . . . In fine, the legislation which Congress is authorized to adopt in this behalf is not general legislation upon the rights of the citizen, but corrective legislation, that is, such as may be necessary and proper for counteracting such laws as the States may adopt or enforce, and which, by the amendment, they are prohibited from making or enforcing, or such acts and proceedings as the States may commit or take, and which, by the amendment, they are prohibited from committing or taking. . . . It is sufficient for us to examine whether the law in question is of that character.

An inspection of the law shows that it makes no reference whatever to any supposed or apprehended violation of the Fourteenth Amendment on the part of the States. It is not predicated on any such view. It proceeds *ex directo* to declare that certain acts committed by individuals shall be deemed offences, and shall be prosecuted and punished by proceedings in the courts of the United States. It does not profess to be corrective of any constitutional wrong committed by the States. . . . In other words, it steps into the domain of local jurisprudence, and lays down rules for the conduct of individuals in society towards each other, and imposes sanctions for the enforcement of those rules, without referring in any manner to any supposed action of the State or its authorities.

If this legislation is appropriate for enforcing the prohibitions of the amendment, it is difficult to see where it is to stop. . . . The truth is, that the implication of a power to legislate in this manner is based upon the assumption that if the States are forbidden to legislate or act in a particular way on a particular subject, and power is conferred upon Congress to enforce the prohibition, this gives Congress power to legislate generally upon that subject, and not merely power to provide modes of redress against such State legislation or action. The assumption is certainly unsound. It is repugnant to the Tenth Amendment of the Constitution. . . .

In this connection it is proper to state that civil rights, such as are guaranteed by the Constitution against State aggression, cannot be impaired by the wrongful acts of individuals, unsupported by State authority in the shape of laws, customs, or judicial or executive proceedings. The wrongful act of an individuals, unsupported by any such authority, is simply a private wrong, or a crime of that individual. . . . An individual cannot deprive a man of his right to vote. . . ; he may, by force or fraud, interfere with the enjoyment of the right in a particular case. . . ; but unless protected in these wrongful acts by some shield of State law or State authority, he cannot destroy or injure the right; he will only render himself amenable to satisfaction or punishment; and amenable therefore to the laws of the State where the wrongful acts are committed. Hence, in all those cases where the Constitution seeks to protect the rights of the citizen against discriminative and unjust laws of the State by prohibiting such laws, it is not individual offences, but abrogation and denial of rights, which it denounces, and for which it clothes the Congress with power to provide a remedy. . . .

We have discussed the question presented by the law on the assumption that a right to enjoy equal accommodation and privileges in all inns, public conveyances, and places of public amusement, is one of the essential rights of the citizen which no State can abridge or interfere with. Whether it is such a right, or not, is a different question which . . . it is not necessary to examine. . . .

But the power of Congress to adopt direct and primary, as distinguished from corrective legislation, on the subject in hand, is sought, in the second place, from the Thirteenth Amendment. . . .

This amendment, as well as the Fourteenth, is undoubtedly self-executing without any ancillary legislation, so far as its terms are applicable to any existing state of circumstances. By its own unaided force and effect it abolished slavery, and established universal freedom. . . .

The only question under the present head, therefore, is whether the refusal to any person of the accommodations of an inn, or a public conveyance, or a place of public amusement, by an individual, and without any sanction or support from any State law or regulation, does inflict upon such persons any manner of servitude, or form of slavery, as those terms are understood in this country? . . .

It would be running the slavery argument into the ground to make it apply to every act of discrimination which a person may see fit to make as to the guests he will entertain, or as to the people he will take into his coach or cab or car, or admit to his concert or theater, or deal with in other matters of intercourse or business.

. . . We are of opinion, that no countenance of authority for the passage of the law in question can be found in either the Thirteenth or Fourteenth Amendment of the Constitution; and no other ground of authority for its passage being suggested, it must necessarily be declared void, at least so far as its operation in the several States is concerned. . . .

Mr. Justice Harlan, dissenting, said in part:

The opinion in these cases proceeds, it seems to me, upon grounds entirely too narrow and artificial. . . .

The Thirteenth Amendment, it is conceded, did something more than to prohibit slavery as an *institution*, resting upon distinctions of race, and upheld by positive law. . . . Was it the purpose of the nation simply to destroy the institution, and then remit the race, theretofore held in bondage, to the several States for such protection, in their civil rights, . . . as those States, in their discretion, might choose to provide? Were the States against whose protest the institution was destroyed, to be left free, so far as national interference was concerned, to make or allow discriminations against that race, as such, in the enjoyment of those fundamental rights which by universal concession, inhere in a state of freedom? . . . .

That there are burdens and disabilities which constitute badges of slavery and servitude, and that the power to enforce by appropriate legislation the Thirteenth Amendment may be exerted by legislation of a direct and primary character, for the eradication, not simply of the institution, but of its badges and incidents, are propositions which ought to be deemed indisputable. . . . I hold that since slavery [was] the moving or principal cause of the adoption of that amendment, and since that institution rested wholly upon the inferiority, as a race, of those held in bondage, their freedom necessarily involved immunity from, and protection against, all discrimination against them, because of their race, in respect of such civil rights as belong to freemen of other races. Congress, therefore, under its express power to enforce that amendment, by appropriate legislation, may enact laws to protect that people against the deprivation, *because of their race*, of any civil rights granted to other freemen in the same State. . . .

\* \* \* \* \* \* \* \* \* \* \* \* \* \* \* \* \* \* \* \* \* \* \* \* \* \* \* \* \*

*Discussion Points:*

1. Why did Justice Bradley rule that the Act was not an appropriate congressional enforcement of the Fourteenth Amendment? Discuss the "state action" concept fully.
2. Why did Justice Bradley rule that the Act was not an appropriate congressional enforcement of the Thirteenth Amendment?
3. Explain Justice Harlan's dissenting argument that the Act *was* an appropriate congressional enforcement of the Thirteenth Amendment.
4. Do you find Justice Bradley or Justice Harlan more persuasive? Why?

# CHAPTER 23

## *PLESSY V. FERGUSON*

### 163 U.S. 537; 16 S.Ct. 1138; 41 L.Ed. 256 (1896)

After the Reconstruction, some Southern states adopted laws that established and enforced a system of racial segregation. Separate facilities were created for blacks and whites. Separate schools, parks, bus and train accommodations, and the like were required by law. Following the Supreme Court's decision in the 1883 *Civil Rights Cases*, no party could raise a constitutional claim when discrimination was practiced by private parties. If the racial discrimination was required by law, however, state action was present and some believed that disadvantaged blacks could bring Fourteenth-Amendment based challenges.

In 1890, the Louisiana legislature passed a law requiring "that all railway companies carrying passengers in their coaches in this state shall provide equal but separate accommodations for the white and colored races. . . ." Plessy was seven-eighths Caucasian and one-eighth Negroid. He refused to vacate a seat in the white compartment of a railway car and was convicted for violating the law.

Justice Henry Brown, writing for a seven-to-one majority, held that the law violated neither the Thirteenth nor Fourteenth Amendments. In the process, the Court endorsed the principle of "separate but equal" facilities for different races. Justice Harlan once again authored a dissenting opinion. In it, he anticipated the eventual reversal of this decision in *Brown v. Board of Education of Topeka* (1954).

\* \* \* \* \* \* \* \* \* \* \* \* \* \* \* \* \* \* \* \* \* \* \* \* \* \* \* \*

Mr. Justice Brown delivered the opinion of the Court, saying in part:
. . . This case turns upon the constitutionality of an act of the general assembly of the state of Louisiana, passed in 1890, providing for separate railway carriages for the white and colored races. . . .

The constitutionality of this act is attacked upon the ground that it conflicts both with the 13th Amendment of the Constitution, abolishing slavery, and the 14th Amendment, which prohibits certain restrictive legislation on the part of the states.

1. That it does not conflict with the 13th Amendment, which abolished slavery and involuntary servitude, except as a punishment for crime, is too clear for argument. . . .

A statute which implies merely a legal distinction between the white and colored races—a distinction which is founded in the color of the two races, and which must always exist so long as white men are distinguished from the other race by color—has no tendency to destroy the legal equality of the two races, or re-establish a state of involuntary servitude. Indeed, we do not understand that the 13th Amendment is strenuously relied upon by the plaintiff in error in this connection. . . .

The object of the amendment was undoubtedly to enforce the absolute equality of the two races before the law, but in the nature of things it could not have been intended to abolish distinctions based upon color, or to enforce social, as distinguished from political, equality, or a commingling of the two races upon terms unsatisfactory to either. Laws permitting, and even requiring their separation in places where they are liable to be brought into contact do not necessarily imply the inferiority of either race to the other, and have been generally, if not universally, recognized as within the competency of the state legislatures in the exercise of their police power. The most common instance of this is connected with the establishment of separate schools for white and colored children, which have been held to be a valid exercise of the legislative power even by courts of states where the political rights of the colored race have been longest and most earnestly enforced. . . .

It is claimed by the plaintiff in error that, in any mixed community, the reputation of belonging to the dominant race, in this instance the white race is *property*, in the same sense that a right of action, or of inheritance, is property. Conceding this to be so, for the purposes of this case, we are unable to see how this statute deprives him of, or in any way affects his right to, such property. If he be a white man and assigned to a colored coach, he may have his action for damages against the company for being deprived of his so-called property. Upon the other hand, if he be a colored man and be so assigned, he has been deprived of no property, since he is not lawfully entitled to the reputation of being a white man. . . .

So far, then, as a conflict with the 14th Amendment is concerned, the case reduces itself to the question whether the statute of Louisiana is a reasonable regulation, and with respect to this there must necessarily be a large discretion on the part of the legislature. In determining the question of reasonableness it is at liberty to act with reference to the established usages, customs, and traditions of the people, and with a view to the promotion of their comfort, and the preservation of the public peace and good order. Gauged by this standard, we cannot say that a law which authorizes or even requires the separation of the two races in public conveyances is unreasonable or more obnoxious to the 14th Amendment than the acts of Congress requiring separate schools for colored children in the District of Columbia, the constitutionality of which does not seem to have been questioned, or the corresponding acts of state legislatures.

We consider the underlying fallacy of the plaintiff's argument to consist in the assumption that the enforced separation of the two races stamps the colored race with a badge of inferiority. If this be so, it is not by reason of anything found in the act, but solely because the colored race chooses to put that construction upon it. The argument necessarily assumes that if, as has been more than once the case, and is not unlikely to be so again, the colored race should become the dominant power in the state legislature, and should enact a law in precisely similar terms, it would thereby relegate the white race to an inferior position. We imagine that the white race, at least, would not acquiesce in this assumption. The argument also assumes that social prejudice may be overcome by legislation, and that equal rights cannot be secured to the Negro except by an enforced commingling of the two races. We cannot accept this proposition. If the two races are to meet on terms of social equality, it must be the result of natural affinities, a mutual appreciation of each other's merits and a voluntary consent of individuals. . . . Legislation is powerless to eradicate racial instincts or to abolish distinctions based upon physical differences, and the attempt to do so can only result in accentuating the difficulties of the present situation. If the civil and political right of both races be equal, one cannot be inferior . . . to the other civilly or politically. If one race be inferior to the other socially, the Constitution of the United States cannot put them upon the same plane.

Mr. Justice Harlan, dissenting, said in part:

. . . . In respect of civil rights, common to all citizens, the Constitution . . . does not, I think, permit any public authority to know the race of those entitled to be protected in the enjoyment of such rights. Every true man has pride of race, and under appropriate circumstances, when the rights of others, his equals before the law, are not to be affected, it is his privilege to express such pride and to take such action based upon it as to him seems proper. But I deny that any legislative body or judicial tribunal may have regard to the race of citizens when the civil rights of those citizens are involved. Indeed such legislation as that here in question is inconsistent, not only with that equality of rights which pertains to citizenship, national and state, but with the personal liberty enjoyed by every one within the United States. . . .

In my opinion, the judgment this day rendered will, in time, prove to be quite as pernicious as the decision made by this tribunal in the *Dred Scott* Case. It was adjudged in that case that the descendants of Africans who were imported into this country and sold as slaves were not included nor intended to be included under the word "citizens" in the Constitution, and could not claim any of the rights and privileges which that instrument provided for and secured to citizens of the United States; that at the time of the adoption of the Constitution they were "considered as a subordinate and inferior class of beings, who had been subjugated by the dominant race, and, whether emancipated or not, yet remained subject to their authority, and had no rights or privileges but such as those who held the power and the government might choose to grant them." The recent amendments of the Constitution, it was supposed, had eradicated these principles from our institutions. But it seems that we have yet, in some of the states, a dominant race, a superior class of citizens, which assumes to regulate the enjoyment of civil rights, common to all citizens, upon the basis of race. The present decision, it may well be apprehended, will not only stimulate aggressions, more or less brutal and irritating, upon the admitted rights of colored citizens, but will encourage the belief that it is possible, by means of state enactments, to defeat the beneficent purposes which the people of the United States had in view when they adopted the recent amendments of the Constitution, by one of which the blacks of this country were made citizens of the United States and of the states in which they respectively reside and whose privileges and immunities, as citizens, the states are forbidden to abridge. Sixty millions of whites are in no danger from the presence here of eight millions of blacks. The destinies of the two races in this country are indissolubly linked together, and the interests of both require that the common government of all shall not permit the seeds of race hate to be planted under the sanction of law. What can more certainly arouse race hate, what more certainly create and perpetuate a feeling of distrust between these races, than state enactments which in fact proceed on the ground that colored citizens are so inferior and degraded that they cannot be allowed to sit in public coaches occupied by white citizens? That, as all will admit, is the real meaning of such legislation as was enacted in Louisiana. . . .

If evils will result from the commingling of the two races upon public highways established for the benefit of all, they will be infinitely less than those that will surely come from state legislation regulating the enjoyment of civil rights upon the basis of race. We boast of the freedom enjoyed by our people above all other peoples. But it is difficult to reconcile that boast with a state of the law which, practically, puts the brand of servitude and degradation upon a large class of our fellow citizens, our equals before the law. The thin disguise of "equal" accommodations for passengers in railroad coaches will not mislead anyone, or atone for the wrong this day done. . . .

I am of opinion that the statute of Louisiana is inconsistent with the personal liberty of citizens, white and black, in that state, and hostile to both the spirit and letter of the Constitution of the United States. If laws of like character should be enacted in the several states of the Union, the effect would be in the highest degree mischievous. Slavery as an institution tolerated by law would, it is true, have disappeared from our country, but there would remain a power in the states, by sinister legislation, to interfere with the full enjoyment of the blessings of freedom; to regulate civil rights, common to all citizens, upon the basis of race; and to place in a condition of legal inferiority a large body of American citizens, now constituting a part of the political community, called the people of the United States, for whom and by whom, through representatives, our government is administered. Such a system is inconsistent with the guarantee given by the Constitution to each state of a republican form of government, and may be stricken down by Congressional action, or by the courts in the discharge of their solemn duty to maintain the supreme law of the land, anything in the Constitution or laws of any state to the contrary notwithstanding.

For the reasons stated, I am constrained to withhold my assent from the opinion and judgment of the majority.

\* \* \* \* \* \* \* \* \* \* \* \* \* \* \* \* \* \* \* \* \* \* \* \* \* \* \* \* \* \* \*

*Discussion Points:*

1. Why did Justice Brown rule that the Louisiana law did not violate the Thirteenth Amendment? Why did he hold that it did not violate the Fourteenth Amendment?
2. Discuss Justice Brown's reliance upon "the established usages, customs, and traditions of the people."
3. Discuss Justice Brown's claim that the law did not stamp blacks "with a badge of inferiority." What did Justice Harlan say on this point? Which Justice was more persuasive? Why?

4. Why did Justice Harlan contend that the law was "hostile to both the spirit and the letter of the Constitution"?
5. What do you think about the Court's conclusion that "separate but equal" facilities do not violate the Constitution?

# PART VI:
# THE CONSTITUTION IN THE
# FIRST HALF OF THE
# TWENTIETH CENTURY

# CHAPTER 24

## *SCHENCK V. UNITED STATES*
### 249 U.S. 47; 39 S.Ct. 247; 63 L.Ed. 470 (1919)

During World War I, Congress passed the Espionage Act of 1917 and the Sedition Act of 1918. The former made it a crime to circulate false statements, to interfere with military success, to attempt to cause disloyalty in the armed forces, or to attempt to obstruct recruiting. The latter made it a crime to incite resistance to the government. Clearly, these laws restricted freedom of speech. Did they violate the First Amendment? The Supreme Court, holding that such First-Amendment freedoms are not absolute, ruled that they did not in the case below.

Charles T. Schenck, general secretary of the Socialist Party, was accused of sending some 15,000 pamphlets to men who had been called to military service, urging them to resist the draft. The pamphlet contained the text of the first section of the Thirteenth Amendment and argued that the Conscription Act established an unconstitutional system of involuntary servitude. Schenck was convicted in federal court of violating the Espionage Act by attempting to cause insubordination in the armed forces and by obstructing recruitment. He maintained that his conduct was protected by the First Amendment's guarantees of freedom of speech and the press.

Writing for the unanimous Court, Justice Holmes upheld Schenck's conviction on grounds that the government can restrict speech if it presents a "clear and present danger" to the nation. Freedom of speech, Holmes suggested, is limited by the wartime demands of national security. Speech, he argued, must be evaluated in context. Here, the nature of the times conditioned the act and made it a crime.

* * * * * * * * * * * * * * * * * * * * * * * * * * * * * *

Mr. Justice Holmes delivered the opinion of the Court, saying in part:

The document in question, upon its first printed side, recited the First section of the Thirteenth Amendment, said that the idea embodied in it was violated by the Conscription Act, and that a conscript is little better than a convict. In impassioned language it intimated that conscription was despotism in its worst form and a monstrous wrong against humanity, in the interest of Wall Street's chosen few.... Of course the document would not have been sent unless it had been intended to have some effect, and we do not see what effect it could be expected to have upon persons subject to the draft except to influence them to obstruct the carrying of it out. The defendants do not deny that the jury might find against them on this point.

But it is said, suppose that that was the tendency of this circular, it is protected by the First Amendment to the Constitution. Two of the strongest expressions are said to be quoted respectively from well-known public men. It well may be that the prohibition of laws abridging the freedom of speech is not confined to previous restraints, although to prevent them may have been the main purpose.... We admit that in many places and in ordinary times the defendants, in saying all that was said in the circular, would have been within their constitutional rights. But the character of every act depends upon the circumstances in which it is done.... The most stringent protection of free speech would not protect a man in falsely shouting fire in a theater, and causing a panic.... The question in every case is whether the words used are used in such circumstances and are of such a nature as to create a clear and present danger that they will bring about the substantive evils that Congress has a right to prevent. It is a question of proximity and degree. When a nation is at war many things that might be said in time of peace are such a hindrance to its effort that their utterance will not be endured so long as men fight, and that no court could regard them as protected by any constitutional right. It seems to be admitted that if an actual obstruction of the recruiting service were proved, liability for words that produced the effect might be enforced. The Statute of 1917, in Section 4, punishes conspiracies to obstruct as well as actual obstruction. If the act (speaking, or circulating a paper), its tendency and the intent with which it is done, are the same, we perceive no ground for saying that success alone warrants making the act a crime....

\* \* \* \* \* \* \* \* \* \* \* \* \* \* \* \* \* \* \* \* \* \* \* \* \* \* \* \* \* \*

*Discussion Points:*

1. The First Amendment states, "Congress shall make no law ... abridging the freedom of speech. . ." The Espionage Act abridged Schenck's freedom of speech. A literal interpretation of the First

Amendment would have overturned Schenck's conviction. How did Justice Holmes interpret the First Amendment? Do you agree with his interpretation or do you think that free speech should be absolutely protected under the Constitution? Why?

2. How would you respond if Schenck claimed that he believed that Congress had set the Constitution on "fire" by passing the Conscription Act and that his pamphlet was designed to alert his fellow citizens to the danger?

3. Is it sensible to balance the interests of an individual in free speech against the general security interests of the nation at large? Discuss some of the implications of this balancing approach to constitutional adjudication.

# CHAPTER 25

## NEAR V. MINNESOTA
### 283 U.S. 697; 51 S.Ct. 625; 75 L.Ed. 1357 (1931)

As previously noted, in *Barron v. Baltimore* (1833), the Supreme Court held that the provisions of the Bill of Rights do no apply directly against the states. In subsequent years, however, some such protections have been applied against states by way of the Fourteenth Amendment. *Near v. Minnesota* marked the first time that the Court found a state law unconstitutional for violating the freedom of the press that is protected by the Fourteenth Amendment's due process clause.

The so-called "Minnesota press gag law" provided for shutting down any newspaper that printed "malicious, scandalous, or defamatory" materials. Such an injunction could only be lifted by the judge who issued it and s/he would have to be persuaded that the publication would be unobjectionable in the future. Critics pointed out that an injured party could sue the publication for libel after the fact, but this law imposed censorship *before* the fact; it restrained publication itself.

*The Saturday Press*, published in Minneapolis, charged various public officials with misconduct in office. The law was enforced and publication was enjoined.

By a five-to-four vote, the Supreme Court ruled that the law was an unconstitutional abridgment of press freedom as guaranteed by the Fourteenth Amendment.

\* \* \* \* \* \* \* \* \* \* \* \* \* \* \* \* \* \* \* \* \* \* \* \* \* \* \*

Mr. Chief Justice Hughes delivered the opinion of the Court, saying in part:

. . . . The statute not only operates to suppress the offending newspaper or periodical but to put the publisher under an effective censorship. When a newspaper or periodical is found to be "malicious, scandalous, and defamatory," and is suppressed as such, resumption of publication is punishable as a contempt of court by fine or imprisonment. . . .

If we cut through the mere details of procedure, the operation and effect of the statute in substance is that public authorities may bring the owner or publisher of a newspaper or periodical before a judge upon a charge of . . . publishing scandalous and defamatory matter—in particular that the matter consists of charges against public officers of official dereliction—and unless the owner or publisher is able and disposed to bring competent evidence to satisfy the judge that the charges are true and are published with good motives and for justifiable ends, his newspaper or periodical is suppressed and further publication is made punishable as a contempt. This is the essence of censorship.

. . . . But it is recognized that punishment for the abuse of the liberty accorded to the press is essential to the protection of the public, and that the common law rules that subject the libeler to responsibility for the public offense, as well as for the private injury, are not abolished by the protection extended in our constitutions. . . . In the present case, . . . [f]or whatever wrong the appellant has committed or may commit, by his publications, the state appropriately affords both public and private redress by its libel laws. . . [T]he statute in question does not deal with punishments; it provides for no punishment, except in case of contempt for violation of the court's order, but for suppression and injunction, that is, for restraint upon publication. . . .

The fact that the liberty of the press may be abused by miscreant purveyors of scandal does not make any the less necessary the immunity of the press from previous restraint in dealing with official misconduct. Subsequent punishment for such abuses as may exist is the appropriate remedy, consistent with constitutional privilege. . . .

For these reasons we hold the statute . . . to be an infringement of the liberty of the press guaranteed by the 14th Amendment. . . .

\* \* \* \* \* \* \* \* \* \* \* \* \* \* \* \* \* \* \* \* \* \* \* \* \* \* \* \* \* \*

*Reflections and Suggestions:*

1. Why did Hughes find the law unconstitutional? In light of *Barron*, how did Hughes conclude that freedom of the press is guaranteed at the *state* level?
2. According to Hughes, what is the appropriate remedy available to a party who is injured by a publication?
3. Recall Holmes's clear-and-present danger test (see *Schenck*). If the nation were at war and if the publication posed a clear and present danger to national security, should the Court interpret the Constitution so as to permit the government to restrain publication before the fact? Why or why not?

# CHAPTER 26

# *SCHECHTER POULTRY CORPORATION V. UNITED STATES*

## 295 U.S. 495; 55 S.Ct. 837; 79 L.Ed. 1570 (1935)

Article I, Section 8, Clause 3 gives Congress the power "[t]o regulate commerce . . . among the several states. . . ." As previously discussed, Chief Justice Marshall interpreted this clause broadly in *Gibbons v. Ogden* (1824). The clause authorizes Congress to regulate *interstate* commerce. Commercial activities that are purely internal to a state are beyond congressional reach; such activities could be regulated by the state in question. But what if commercial activities occur inside a state and have a significant impact on commerce beyond the state's borders? What if apparently local activities substantially affect interstate commerce? Can Congress regulate such activities? Two distinct lines of precedent developed over the years.

In a series of cases, the Supreme Court ruled that Congress could not reach such "intrastate" commercial activities. In *U.S. v. E. C. Knight* (156 U.S. 1, 1895), and *Carter v. Carter Coal Co.* (298 U.S. 238, 1936), the Court held that sugar manufacturing and mining, respectively, had no direct effects on interstate commerce and, as such, were beyond the reach of Congress. In *Hammer v. Dagenhart* (247 U.S. 251, 1918), the Court invalidated congressional labor regulations, again, on grounds that the commercial activities at issue exerted no direct effects on interstate commerce. Such precedents obstructed congressional efforts to regulate labor-management relations and other economic matters.

But several other important cases were decided differently. In *The Shreveport Case (Houston East & West Texas Ry. Co. v. U.S.)* (234 U.S. 342, 1914), the Court upheld congressional regulation of railway rates in Texas on grounds that the rates had a "substantial effect" on interstate commerce. Also, in *Stafford v. Wallace* (259 U.S. 495, 1922), the Court upheld congressional regulation of stockyards on grounds that these points were "throats" through which the "stream of commerce" flows. Unregulated activities here could impede the "free flow" of commerce. These precedents supported congressional attempts to regulate economic matters. The existence of such conflicting precedents generated uncertainty about Congress's commerce powers.

Franklin Delano Roosevelt took the oath of office on March 4, 1933 in the midst of the Great Depression. The financial crisis was so severe that the governors of New York and Illinois had declared bank holidays. Roosevelt immediately called Congress into session, and during what became known as "The Hundred Days," Congress passed a number of bills to combat pressing economic problems. At the heart of the program for industrial recovery was the National Industrial Recovery Act. The Act gave virtual control of the nation's industries to the federal government through the use of codes of conduct for specific industries.

The NIRA tried to eliminate unfair competition, improve working conditions, provide higher wages and shorter hours, eliminate child labor, conserve natural resources, and fight unemployment. Industry representatives and government officials were to draft codes of fair competition for each industry. The codes would require presidential approval. If an industry failed to develop its own code, the President was authorized to draft one for it. The Schechter brothers, poultry dealers in Brooklyn, were charged with violating the "Live Poultry Code."

Chief Justice Hughes delivered the opinion for the unanimous Supreme Court. He found the NIRA unconstitutional for two main reasons. First, the Act was an illegal delegation of legislative power to the President; Congress left him too much discretion regarding the codes. Second, the Schechters' activities were intrastate in nature and, hence, beyond congressional reach.

President Roosevelt was bitterly disappointed with the Court's decision. Over the next few years, the Court dealt him additional setbacks as it found other pieces of New Deal legislation unconstitutional as well. Following his overwhelming reelection in November of 1936, he made plans to strike back at the Court before it dismantled his entire New Deal program. On February 5, 1937, he sent Congress a plan calling for the addition of a new justice to the Court for every justice over the age of seventy. If adopted, the plan would have enabled Roosevelt to appoint six new justices of his own choosing. Although the New Deal programs were popular and the Court's decisions were not, Roosevelt's "Court-packing plan" aroused public and congressional opposition. It threatened judicial independence and was ultimately rejected. Shortly thereafter, however, the Court began to uphold some of

Roosevelt's programs. In this sense, some speak of the "Judicial Revolution of 1937" as a point when the Court's approach to congressional economic regulations shifted.

\* \* \* \* \* \* \* \* \* \* \* \* \* \* \* \* \* \* \* \* \* \* \* \* \* \* \* \* \* \* \*

Mr. Chief Justice Hughes delivered the opinion of the Court, saying in part:

... We are told that the provision of the statute authorizing the adoption of codes must be viewed in the light of the grave national crisis with which Congress was confronted. Undoubtedly, the conditions to which power is addressed are always to be considered when the exercise of power is challenged. Extraordinary conditions may call for extraordinary remedies. But the argument necessarily stops short of an attempt to justify action which lies outside the sphere of constitutional authority. Extraordinary conditions do not create or enlarge constitutional power. The Constitution established a national government with powers deemed to be adequate, as they have proved to be both in war and peace, but these powers of the national government are limited by the constitutional grants. Those who act under these grants are not at liberty to transcend the imposed limits because they believe that more or different power is necessary. Such assertions of extraconstitutional authority were anticipated and precluded by the explicit terms of the Tenth Amendment—"The powers not delegated to the United States by the Constitution, nor prohibited by it to the States, are reserved to the States respectively, or to the people..."

... The Constitution provides that "All legislative powers herein granted shall be vested in a Congress of the United States, which shall consist of a Senate and House of Representatives." Article I, Section 1. And the Congress is authorized "To make all laws which shall be necessary and proper for carrying into execution" its general powers. Article I, Section 8, par. 18. The Congress is not permitted to abdicate or to transfer to others the essential legislative functions with which it is thus vested. . . .

Accordingly, we look to the statute to see whether Congress has overstepped these limitations—whether Congress in authorizing "codes of fair competition" has itself established the standards of legal obligation, thus performing its essential legislative function, or, by the failure to enact such standards, has attempted to transfer that function to others. . . .

The Government urges that the codes will "consist of rules of competition deemed fair for each industry by representative members of that industry—by the persons most vitally concerned and most familiar with its problems".... Such a delegation of legislative power is unknown to our law and is utterly inconsistent with the constitutional prerogatives and duties of Congress.

The question, then, turns upon the authority which Section 3 of the Recovery Act vests in the President to approve or prescribe. If the codes have standing as penal statutes, this must be due to the effect of the executive action. But Congress cannot delegate legislative power to the President to exercise an unfettered discretion to make whatever laws he thinks may be needed or advisable.... For the legislative undertaking, Section 3 sets up no standards, aside from the statement of the general aims of rehabilitation, correction, and expansion described in Section 1. In view of the scope of that broad declaration, and of the nature of the few restrictions that are imposed, the discretion of the President in approving or prescribing codes, and thus enacting laws for the government of trade and industry throughout the country, is virtually unfettered. We think that the code-making authority thus conferred is an unconstitutional delegation of legislative power....

This aspect of the case presents the question whether the particular provisions of the Live Poultry Code, which the defendants were convicted for violating and for having conspired to violate, were within the regulating power of Congress.

These provisions relate to the hours and wages of those employed by defendants in their slaughterhouses in Brooklyn and to the sales there made to retail dealers and butchers.

(1) Were these transactions "*in*" interstate commerce? Much is made of the fact that almost all the poultry coming to New York is sent there from other States. But the code provisions, as here applied, do not concern the transportation of the poultry from other States to New York, or the transactions of the commission men or others to whom it is consigned, or the sales made by such consigners to defendants. When defendants had made their purchases, whether at the West Washington Market in New York City or at the railroad terminals serving the City, or elsewhere, the poultry was trucked to their slaughterhouses in Brooklyn for local disposition. The interstate transactions in relation to that poultry then ended. Defendants held the poultry at their slaughterhouse markets for slaughter and local sale to retail dealers and butchers, who in turn sold directly to consumers. Neither the slaughtering nor the sales by defendants were transactions in interstate commerce....

The undisputed facts thus afford no warrant for the argument that the poultry handled by defendants at their slaughterhouse markets was in a "*current*" or "*flow*" of interstate commerce and was thus subject to congressional regulation. The mere fact that there may be a constant flow of commodities into a State does not mean that the flow continues after the property has arrived and has become commingled with the mass of property within the State and is there held solely for local disposition and use. So far as the poultry here in question is concerned, the flow in interstate commerce had ceased. The poultry had come to a permanent rest within the State. . . .

(2) Did the defendants' transactions directly "*affect*" interstate commerce so as to be subject to federal regulation? The power of Congress extends not only to the regulation of transactions which are part of interstate commerce, but to the protection of that commerce from injury. . . .

In determining how far the federal government may go in controlling intrastate transactions upon the ground that they "affect" interstate commerce, there is a necessary and well-established distinction between direct and indirect effects. . . .

But where the effect of intrastate transactions upon interstate commerce is merely indirect, such transactions remain with the domain of state power. If the commerce clause were construed to reach all enterprises and transactions which could be said to have an indirect effect upon interstate commerce, the federal authority would embrace practically all the activities of the people, and the authority of the State over its domestic concerns would exist only by sufferance of the federal government.

We are of the opinion that the attempt through the provisions of the Code to fix the hours and wages of employees of defendants in their intrastate business was not a valid exercise of federal power.

On both the grounds we have discussed, the attempted delegation of legislative power, and the attempted regulation of intrastate transactions which affect interstate commerce only indirectly, we hold the code provisions here in question to be invalid and that the judgment of conviction must be reversed. . . .

\* \* \* \* \* \* \* \* \* \* \* \* \* \* \* \* \* \* \* \* \* \* \* \* \* \* \* \* \* \*

*Discussion Points:*

1. Why did Hughes rule that the NIRA unconstitutionally delegated legislative power to the President? Why did he think Congress overstepped the reach of its commerce powers in trying to regulate the activities in question?
2. In *Schenck,* Holmes said that individual rights must be evaluated

in light of prevailing circumstances. In *Schechter*, Hughes said that "while [e]xtraordinary conditions may call for extraordinary remedies . . . . [e]xtraordinary conditions do not create or enlarge constitutional power." Compare and contrast these two positions.

# CHAPTER 27

## *UNITED STATES V. CURTISS-WRIGHT EXPORT CORPORATION*

### 299 U.S. 304; 57 S.Ct. 216; 81 L.Ed. 255 (1936)

In 1934, Congress passed a joint resolution authorizing the President to forbid the sale of arms to warring countries in the Chaco region (Paraguay and Bolivia) if he thought such an embargo would help bring about peace. Congress did not limit the President's discretion as it delegated this power to him. Violations of such presidential orders would be treated as criminal offenses. The President decided to impose such an embargo and Curtiss-Wright Export Corporation was charged with violating the order by selling guns to Bolivia. The Corporation challenged the legality of this delegation of legislative power to the President. Writing for a seven-to-one majority, Justice Sutherland found that presidential powers in the field of international relations are so extensive that his actions would be justified even without a joint resolution.

\* \* \* \* \* \* \* \* \* \* \* \* \* \* \* \* \* \* \* \* \* \* \* \* \* \* \* \* \* \*

Mr. Justice Sutherland delivered the opinion of the Court, saying in part:

.... Whether, if the Joint Resolution had related solely to internal affairs, it would be open to the challenge that it constituted an unlawful delegation of legislative power to the Executive, we find it unnecessary to determine. The whole aim of the resolution is to affect a situation entirely external to the United States, and falling within the category of foreign affairs....

.... In this vast external realm, with its important, complicated, delicate and manifold problems, the President alone has the power to speak or listen as a representative of the nation. He *makes* treaties with the advice and consent of the Senate; but he alone negotiates. Into the field of negotiation the Senate cannot intrude; and Congress itself is powerless to invade it. . . .

It is important to bear in mind that we are here dealing not alone with an authority vested in the President by an exertion of legislative power, but with such an authority plus the very delicate plenary and exclusive power of the President as the sole organ of the Federal government in the field of international relations—a power which does not require as a basis for its exercise an act of Congress. . . It is quite apparent that if, in the maintenance of our international relations, embarrassment . . . is to be avoided and success for our aims achieved, congressional legislation . . . within the international field must often accord to the President a degree of discretion and freedom from statutory restriction which would not be admissable were domestic affairs alone involved. Moreover, he, not Congress, has the better opportunity of knowing the conditions which prevail in foreign countries, and especially is this true in time of war. . . .

Practically every volume of the United States Statutes contains one or more acts or joint resolutions of Congress authorizing action by the President in . . . foreign relations which either leave the exercise of the power to his unrestricted judgment, or provide a standard far more general than that which has always been considered requisite with regard to domestic affairs. . . .

. . . A legislative practice such as we have here, evidenced . . . by the movement of a steady stream for a century and a half of time . . . [proves] the presence of unassailable ground for the constitutionality of the practice, to be found in the origin and history of the power involved, or in its nature, or in both combined. . . .

\* \* \* \* \* \* \* \* \* \* \* \* \* \* \* \* \* \* \* \* \* \* \* \* \* \* \* \* \* \* \*

*Discussion Points:*

1. Discuss the distinction that Justice Sutherland makes between presidential power in domestic and foreign affairs. Do you agree with him? Why or why not?
2. Do you agree with Sutherland regarding the "exclusive power" of the President as the "sole organ of the Federal government in the field of international relations?" What powers, if any, does the Constitution assign to Congress in the international field?

# CHAPTER 28

## NLRB V. JONES & LAUGHLIN STEEL CORPORATION

### 301 U.S. 1; 57 S.Ct. 615; 81 L.Ed. 893 (1937)

Shortly after the Court invalidated the NIRA in *Schechter*, Congress passed the National Labor Relations Act (Wagner Act). The Act dealt with labor-management relations. It defined a series of seven or eight unfair labor practices and applied to all labor disputes that obstructed interstate commerce. The Act also established the National Labor Relations Board. This independent commission was authorized to investigate complaints and to issue cease-and-desist orders against those engaging in unfair labor practices. In this way, the Act was designed to ensure the right of collective bargaining for American workers.

In this case, the NLRB had found that the Jones & Laughlin Steel Corporation had engaged in unfair labor practices. The Corporation had discriminated against union members, was intimidating employees to prevent them from organizing, and had fired some employees because of their union activities. The NLRB ordered the fired men reinstated. The Corporation refused to comply. The Circuit Court of Appeals refused to enforce the NLRB order and the case was appealed to the Supreme Court.

The Wagner Act extended to labor relations at manufacturing sites. In view of previous Court decisions holding that manufacturing was not interstate commerce (see *E. C. Knight, Carter, Hammer*, and *Schechter*), it was expected by some that the Court would invalidate this Act. Instead, the Court abandoned its earlier distinction between manufacturing and interstate commerce and upheld the Act on the theory that the Corporation's far-flung activities depended upon and exerted a close and substantial impact upon interstate commerce. Therefore, the Court concluded, the commerce clause enabled Congress to regulate in this area.

It is interesting to note that Chief Justice Hughes, who also authored the *Schechter* decision, wrote the opinion for the Court's five-to-four majority in this case. The *Jones & Laughlin* decision reflected a change in the Court's handling of New Deal legislation. It may be regarded as one of the products of the aforementioned judicial revolution of 1937.

\* \* \* \* \* \* \* \* \* \* \* \* \* \* \* \* \* \* \* \* \* \* \* \* \* \* \*

Mr. Chief Justice Hughes delivered the opinion of the Court, saying in part:

. . . The facts as to the nature and scope of the business of the Jones & Laughlin Steel Corporation have been found by the Labor Board. . . .

Summarizing these operations, the Labor Board concluded that the works in Pittsburgh and Aliquippa "might be likened to the heart of a self-contained, highly integrated body. They draw in the raw materials from Michigan, Minnesota, West Virginia, Pennsylvania in part through arteries and by means controlled by the respondent; they transform the materials and then pump them out to all parts of the nation through the vast mechanism which the respondent has elaborated. . . ."

*The Scope of the Act.* The Act is challenged in its entirety as an attempt to regulate all industry, thus invading the reserved powers of the States over their local concerns. . . .

We think it clear that the National Labor Relations Act may be construed so as to operate within the sphere of constitutional authority. The jurisdiction conferred upon the Board, and invoked in this instance, is found in Section 10(a), which provides: "Section 10(a), the Board is empowered, as hereinafter provided, to prevent any person from engaging in any unfair labor practice (listed in Section 8) affecting commerce."

The critical words of this provision, prescribing the limits of the Board's authority in dealing with the labor practices, are "affecting commerce. . . ."

There can be no question that the commerce thus contemplated by the Act (aside from that within a Territory or the District of Columbia) is interstate and foreign commerce in the constitutional sense. The Act also defines the term "affecting commerce" Section 2(7):

"The term *affecting commerce* means in commerce, or burdening or obstructing commerce or the free flow of commerce, or having led or tending to lead to a labor dispute burdening or obstructing commerce or the free flow of commerce."

This definition is one of exclusion as well as inclusion. The grant of authority to the Board does not purport to extend to the relationship between all industrial employees and employers. . . . It purports to reach only what may be deemed to burden or obstruct that commerce and, thus qualified, it must be construed as contemplating the exercise of control within constitutional bounds. It is a familiar principle that acts which directly burden or obstruct interstate or foreign commerce, or its free flow, are within the reach of the congressional power. Acts having that effect are not rendered immune because they grow out of labor disputes. . . . It is the effect upon commerce, not the source of the injury, which is the criterion.

. . . Respondent says that whatever may be said of employees engaged in interstate commerce, the industrial relations and activities in the manufacturing department of respondent's enterprise are not subject to Federal regulation. The argument rests upon the proposition that manufacturing in itself is not commerce. . . .

Although activities may be interstate in character when separately considered, if they have such a close and substantial relation to interstate commerce that their control is essential or appropriate to protect that commerce from burdens and obstructions, Congress cannot be denied the power to exercise that control. . . .

Giving full weight to respondent's contention with respect to a break in the complete continuity of the "stream of commerce" by reason of respondent's manufacturing operations, the fact remains that the stoppage of those operations by industrial strife would have a most serious effect upon interstate commerce. In view of the respondent's far-flung activities, it is idle to say that the effect would be indirect or remote. It is obvious that it would be immediate and might be catastrophic. We are asked to shut our eyes to the plainest facts of our national life and to deal with the question of direct and indirect effects in an intellectual vacuum. Because there may be but direct and remote effects upon interstate commerce in connection with a host of local enterprises throughout the country, it does not follow that other industrial activities do not have such a close and intimate relation to interstate commerce as to make the presence of industrial strife a matter of the most urgent national concern. When industries organize themselves on a national scale, making their relation to interstate commerce the dominant factor in their activities, how can it be maintained that their industrial labor relations constitute a forbidden field into which Congress may not enter when it is necessary to protect interstate commerce from the paralyzing effects of industrial war? We have often said that interstate commerce itself is a practical conception. It is equally true that interferences with that commerce must be appraised by a judgment that does not ignore actual experience.

Experience has abundantly demonstrated that the recognition of the right of employees to self-organization and to have representatives of their own choosing for ... collective bargaining is often an essential condition of industrial peace. Refusal to confer and negotiate has been one of the most prolific causes of strife. ...

... [R]espondent's enterprise ... presents in a most striking way the close and intimate relation which a manufacturing industry may have to interstate commerce, and we have no doubt that Congress had constitutional authority to safeguard the right of respondent's employees to self-organization and freedom in the choice of representatives for collective bargaining. ...

Our conclusion is that the order of the Board was within its competency and that the Act is valid as here applied. ...

* * * * * * * * * * * * * * * * * * * * * * * * * * * * * * *

*Discussion Points:*

1. How did the Corporation's argument that the Wagner Act was unconstitutional relate to the Court's decision in *Schechter*?
2. How did Hughes conclude that the Wagner Act was a constitutional expression of Congress's power to regulate interstate commerce?
3. Compare and contrast Hughes's opinion in *Schechter* with his opinion in this case. In what sense do his opinions seem inconsistent? In what sense might they be construed as compatible after all?

# CHAPTER 29

## WEST VIRGINIA STATE BOARD OF EDUCATION V. BARNETTE

### 319 U.S. 624; 63 S.Ct. 1178; 87 L.Ed. 1628 (1943)

Freedom of religion, like freedom of speech and press, is not absolute. In such cases, the Court frequently assesses the relative weights of competing societal and individual interests. The issue of compulsory flag salutes illustrates this point.

A number of states passed laws requiring school children to salute the flag. Children who refused to comply could be expelled. In *Minersville School District v. Gobitis* (310 U.S. 586, 1940), the Court, in an opinion by Justice Frankfurter, upheld such a law. There the child of Jehovah's Witnesses refused to salute the flag on grounds that to do so would violate their religious belief that the laws of God are superior to those of government. Frankfurter balanced individual interests in religious freedom against societal interests in promoting national unity and security. The Court allowed the Board's judgment, that the compulsory flag salute would advance national unity, to prevail. Justice Stone wrote a sharply-critical dissenting opinion.

Shortly thereafter, the West Virginia legislature passed a law requiring all schools to offer courses on history, civics, and the Constitution. The Board of Education also required that students salute the flag and recite the Pledge of Allegiance. The irony of forcing someone to recite a pledge in praise of "liberty" was not lost on critics. Nevertheless, failure to conform with this requirement constituted insubordination, punishable by expulsion. Readmittance was barred until the child complied with the requirement. Further, the expelled child was treated as legally absent and parents were subject to fines and imprisonment. In the case below, children of Jehovah's Witnesses again refused to comply with the flag-salute requirement on religious grounds and they were penalized in accordance with the statute. They contended that the requirement abridged their religious freedom as applied to the state by way of the Fourteenth Amendment. Writing for a six-to-three majority, Justice Jackson overruled *Gobitis*.

Compulsory flag salutes continue to generate controversy. During the 1988 presidential campaign, the Democratic candidate, Michael Dukakis, was called upon to defend his opposition to a similar proposal in Massachusetts. The conflict arising as it did in the midst of a political campaign probably served to generate more heat than light. More insight into the general issue can be gained from a careful reading of Justice Jackson's opinion.

\* \* \* \* \* \* \* \* \* \* \* \* \* \* \* \* \* \* \* \* \* \* \* \* \* \* \*

Mr. Justice Jackson delivered the opinion of the Court, saying in part:

.... As the present Chief Justice [Stone] said in dissent in the *Gobitis* case, the State may "require teaching by instruction and study of all in our history and in the structure and organization of our government, including the guarantees of civil liberty, which tend to inspire patriotism and love of country." Here, however, we are dealing with a compulsion of students to declare a belief. They are not merely made acquainted with the flag salute so that they may be informed as to what it is or even what it means. The issue here is whether this slow and easily neglected route to aroused loyalties constitutionally may be shortcut by substituting compulsory salute and slogan. . . .

Government of limited power need not be anemic government. . . Without promise of a limiting Bill of Rights it is doubtful if our Constitution could have mustered enough strength to enable its ratification. To enforce those rights today is not to choose weak government over strong government. It is only to adhere as a means of strength to individual freedom of mind in preference to officially disciplined uniformity for which history indicates a disappointing and disastrous end. . . .

The Fourteenth Amendment, as now applied to the States, protects the citizen against the State itself and all of its creatures—Boards of Education not excepted. These have, of course, important, delicate, and highly discretionary functions, but none that they may not perform within the limits of the Bill of Rights. . . .

The very purpose of the Bill of Rights was to withdraw certain subjects from the vicissitudes of political controversy, to place them beyond the reach of majorities and officials and to establish them as legal principles to be applied by the courts. One's right to life, liberty, and property, to free speech, a free press, freedom of worship and assembly, and other fundamental rights may not be submitted to vote; they depend on the outcome of no elections.

. . . . [T]he *Gobitis* opinion . . . reasons that "national unity is the basis of national security," that the authorities have "the right to select appropriate means for its attainment," and hence reaches the conclusion that such compulsory measures toward "national unity" are constitutional. . . .

National unity as an end which officials may foster by persuasion and example is not in question. The problem is whether under our Constitution compulsion as here employed is a permissible means for its achievement.

. . . . Compulsory unification of opinion achieves only the unanimity of the graveyard.

It seems trite but necessary to say that the First Amendment . . . was designed to avoid these ends by avoiding these beginnings. There is no mysticism in the American concept of the State or of the nature or origin of its authority. We set up government by the consent of the governed, and the Bill of Rights denies those in power any legal opportunity to coerce that consent. Authority here is to be controlled by public opinion, not public opinion by authority.

. . . . To believe that patriotism will not flourish if patriotic ceremonies are voluntary and spontaneous instead of a compulsory routine is to make an unflattering estimate of the appeal of our institutions to free minds. . . .

If there is any fixed star in our constitutional constellation, it is that no official, high or petty, can prescribe what shall be orthodox in politics, nationalism, religion, or other matters of opinion or force citizens to confess by word or act their faith therein. If there are any circumstances which permit an exception, they do not now occur to us.

We think the action of the local authorities in compelling the flag salute and pledge transcends constitutional limitations on their power and invades the sphere of intellect and spirit which it is the purpose of the First Amendment to our Constitution to reserve from all official control. . . .

*  *  *  *  *  *  *  *  *  *  *  *  *  *  *  *  *  *  *  *  *  *  *  *  *  *  *  *  *

*Discussion Points:*

1. Compare and contrast the Court's interpretation of the First Amendment in *Schenck*, *Near*, and *Barnette*.
2. Did Jackson think it was ever legitimate for state officials to promote national unity? Explain.
3. In what sense did Jackson maintain that democracy is more than rule by popular majorities? What are the limits of majority rule?

4. How did Jackson apply the concept of "the consent of the governed" to this controversy? How did the compulsory flag salute violate this principle?

# CHAPTER 30

## *KOREMATSU V. UNITED STATES*

### 323 U.S. 2214; 65 S.Ct. 193; 89 L.Ed. 194 (1944)

Following the Japanese attack on Pearl Harbor in December 1941, anti-Japanese sentiment ran high, especially on the West Coast. In February 1942, President Roosevelt's executive order authorized military officials to designate certain military areas and to exclude selected persons from those areas. In March 1942, the entire West Coast was so designated. All persons of Japanese descent were subjected to a curfew. Later, over one-hundred thousand persons of Japanese ancestry were moved to relocation camps. Most were native-born Americans who had not been accused of any specific wrongdoings.

Several cases challenged these regulations on grounds that they deprived American citizens of their civil rights without due process of law. In *Hirabayashi v. United States* (320 U.S. 81, 1943), the Court sustained the curfew as a reasonable military step to combat sabotage. In *Ex Parte Endo* (323 U.S. 283, 1944), the Court ruled that a particular individual, whose loyalty *had* been established, had to be released from a relocation center. In the case below, the Court upheld the evacuation policy itself.

Korematsu, an American of Japanese ancestry, resisted an order to evacuate his home in San Leandro, California. Congress made such resistance a crime. He was convicted for refusing to leave the area. The case was decided by a six-to-three vote. Justice Black's lead opinion deferred to military fears of a Japanese invasion of the West Coast and upheld the conviction. Black accepted the military's contention that there was insufficient time to determine which Japanese Americans were loyal and which ones were disloyal. He saw the relocation policy as within military discretion to take steps needed to conduct a successful war effort. This case, therefore, stands as another example of balancing individual rights against societal interests. The majority position was severely criticized by the three dissenting justices, who assailed the policy as racist and unconstitutional.

On August 10, 1988, President Reagan signed into law a bill offering apologies and reparations to Japanese Americans who were interned. The law authorized payments of $20,000 to every living detainee and acknowledged America's "mistake" and "grave injustice."

* * * * * * * * * * * * * * * * * * * * * * * * * * * * * *

Mr. Justice Black delivered the opinion of the Court, saying in part:
.... It should be noted, to begin with, that all legal restrictions which curtail the civil rights of a single racial group are immediately suspect. That is not to say that all such restrictions are unconstitutional. It is to say that courts must subject them to the most rigid scrutiny. Pressing public necessity may sometimes justify the existence of such restrictions; racial antagonism never can.
.... [E]xclusion from a threatened area ... has a definite and close relationship to the prevention of espionage and sabotage. The military authorities, charged with the primary responsibility of defending our shores, concluded that curfew provided inadequate protection and ordered exclusion. They did so ... in accordance with Congressional authority to the military to say who should, and who should not, remain in the threatened areas.
.... [W]e cannot reject as unfounded the judgment of the military authorities and of Congress that there were disloyal members of that population, whose number and strength could not be precisely and quickly ascertained.
.... That there were members of the group who retained loyalty to Japan has been confirmed by investigations made subsequent to the exclusion. Approximately five thousand American citizens of Japanese ancestry refused to swear unqualified allegiance to the United States and to renounce allegiance to the Japanese Emperor, and several thousand evacuees requested repatriation to Japan.
We uphold the exclusion order as of the time it was made and when the petitioner violated it.... In doing so, we are not unmindful of the hardships imposed by it upon a large group of American citizens.... But hardships are a part of war, and war is an aggregation of hardships. All citizens alike, both in and out of uniform, feel the impact of war in greater or lesser measure. Citizenship has its responsibilities as well as its privileges, and in time of war the burden is always heavier. Compulsory exclusion of large groups of citizens from their homes, except under circumstances of direst emergency and peril, is inconsistent with our basic governmental institution. But when under conditions of

modern warfare our shores are threatened by hostile forces, the power to protect must be commensurate with the threatened danger.

.... To cast this case into outlines of racial prejudice, without reference to the real military dangers which were presented, merely confuses the issue. Korematsu was not excluded from the Military Area because of hostility to him or his race. He was excluded because we are at war with the Japanese Empire, because the properly constituted military authorities feared an invasion of our West Coast and felt constrained to take proper security measures, because they decided that the military urgency of the situation demanded that all citizens of Japanese ancestry be segregated from the West Coast temporarily, and finally, because Congress reposing its confidence in this time of war in our military leaders—as inevitably it must—determined that they should have the power to do just this. There was evidence of disloyalty on the part of some, the military authorities considered that the need for action was great, and time was short. We cannot ... now say that ... these actions were unjustified.

Mr. Justice Roberts, dissenting, stated in part:

I dissent because I think the undisputable facts exhibit a clear violation of Constitutional rights.

.... [I]t is the case of convicting a citizen as a punishment for not submitting to imprisonment in a concentration camp, based on his ancestry, and solely because of his ancestry, without evidence or inquiry concerning his loyalty and good disposition towards the United States....

Mr. Justice Murphy, dissenting, stated in part:

This exclusion of "all persons of Japanese ancestry, both alien and non-alien" ... goes over "the very brink of constitutional power" and falls into the ugly abyss of racism.

In dealing with matters relating to the prosecution and progress of a war, we must accord great respect and consideration to the judgments of the military authorities who are on the scene and who have full knowledge of the military facts....

At the same time, however, it is essential that there be definite limits to military discretion....

Being an obvious racial discrimination, the order deprives all those within its scope of the equal protection of the laws as guaranteed by the Fifth Amendment. It further deprives these individuals of their constitutional rights to live and work where they will, to establish a home where they choose and to move about freely. In excommunicating them without benefit of hearings, this order also deprives them of all their constitutional rights to procedural due process. Yet no reasonable relation to an "immediate, imminent, and impending" public danger is evident to support this racial restriction which is one of the most sweeping and complete deprivations of constitutional rights in the history of this nation in the absence of martial law.

. . . . [T]he exclusion, either temporarily or permanently, of all persons with Japanese blood in their veins has no . . . reasonable relation [to the removal of the dangers of invasion, sabotage, and espionage]. And that relation is lacking because the exclusion order necessarily must rely for its reasonableness upon the assumption that *all* persons of Japanese ancestry may have a dangerous tendency to commit sabotage and espionage and to aid our Japanese enemy in other ways. It is difficult to believe that reason, logic or experience could be marshalled in support of such an assumption.

. . . . No one denies, of course, that there were some disloyal persons of Japanese descent of the Pacific Coast who did all in their power to aid their ancestral land. Similar disloyal activities have been engaged in by many persons of German, Italian and even more pioneer stock in our country. But to infer that examples of individual disloyalty prove group disloyalty and justify discriminatory action against the entire group is to deny that under our system of law individual guilt is the sole basis for the deprivation of rights. . . .

No adequate reason is given for the failure to treat these Japanese Americans on an individual basis by holding investigations and hearings to separate the loyal from the disloyal, as was done in the case of persons of German and Italian ancestry. . . . And the fact that conditions were not such to warrant a declaration of martial law adds strength to the belief that the factors of time and military necessity were not as urgent as they have been presented to be.

Mr. Justice Jackson, dissenting, stated in part:

It would be impracticable and dangerous idealism to expect or insist that each specific military command in an area of probable operations will conform to conventional tests of constitutionality. When an area is so beset that it must be put under military control at all, the paramount consideration is that its measures be successful, rather than legal. The armed services must protect a society, not merely its Constitution. . . .

But if we cannot confine military expedients by the Constitution, neither would I distort the Constitution to approve all the military may deem expedient. That is what the Court appears to be doing. . . . I cannot say from any evidence before me, that the orders of General DeWitt were not reasonably expedient military precautions, nor could

I say that they were. But even if they were permissible military procedures, I deny that it follows that they are constitutional.

. . . . [A] judicial construction of the due process that will sustain this order is a far more subtle blow to liberty than the promulgation of the order itself. A military order, however unconstitutional, is not apt to last longer than the military emergency. . . . But once a judicial opinion rationalizes such an order to show that it conforms to the Constitution, or rather rationalizes the Constitution to show that the Constitution sanctions such an order, the Court for all time has validated the principle of racial discrimination in criminal procedure and of transplanting American citizens. . . .

My duties as a justice as I see them do not require me to make a military judgment as to whether General DeWitt's evacuation and detention program was a reasonable military necessity. I do not suggest that the courts should have attempted to interfere with the Army in carrying out its task. But I do not think they may be asked to execute a military expedient that has no place under the Constitution. . . .

\* \* \* \* \* \* \* \* \* \* \* \* \* \* \* \* \* \* \* \* \* \* \* \* \* \* \* \* \*

*Discussion Points:*

1. Compare and contrast Black's opinion in *Korematsu* with Holmes's opinion in *Schenck.*
2. Why did Black uphold the military exclusion order?
3. Why did Murphy, in dissent, argue that the order was unconstitutional? In what sense was Murphy less deferential to congressional and military judgments than Black?
4. Did Jackson, in dissent, claim that the order was unnecessary? Explain his position fully. He stated that the "armed services must protect a society, not merely its Constitution." How does this remark resemble Lincoln's position in his 1861 Message to the Special Session of Congress?

# PART VII:
# THE WARREN COURT AND
# THE CONSTITUTION

# CHAPTER 31

## *BROWN V. BOARD OF EDUCATION OF TOPEKA*

### 347 U.S. 483; 74 S.Ct. 686; 98 L.Ed. 873 (1954)

In *Plessy v. Ferguson* (1896), the Supreme Court held that state laws requiring "separate but equal" facilities for blacks and whites did not violate the Equal Protection Clause of the Fourteenth Amendment. In fact, separate facilities provided for blacks were often substandard. Considerable attention was directed towards racially-segregated schools.

In *Sweatt v. Painter* (339 U.S. 629, 1950), the Court dealt with the case of a black student who was denied admission to the University of Texas Law School on racial grounds. Instead, he was directed to a separate law school for blacks in Texas. The Court concluded that the black law school was, in fact, not equal to the white law school with respect to library holdings, curriculum, faculty, and alumni attainments. As a result, the Court ordered that the black student be admitted into the University of Texas Law School. The Court did not abandon the separate-but-equal principle in the case; instead, it found that the facilities in question were *not* equal. In *Brown v. Board*, however, the Court did squarely overturn the *Plessy* doctrine.

A series of cases from several states challenged the constitutionality of racially-segregated public schools. The Topeka, Kansas case was taken as the nominal leading case, but all of them were determined by a single decision. Writing for the unanimous Court, Chief Justice Warren did not scrutinize the facilities to evaluate their relative quality. Rather, he concluded that separate educational facilities are "inherently unequal." Subsequently, the Court ordered desegregation to proceed with "all deliberate speed."

Despite this order, many schools remained racially segregated. In *Swann v. Charlotte-Mecklenburg Board of Education* (402 U.S. 1, 1971), the Court confronted a school system in which two-thirds of the district's black students attended schools that were more than 99 percent black. The school district and the local district court failed to agree on a desegregation plan. The district court eventually ordered the school district to implement a massive busing program to effect desegregation. The unanimous Supreme Court upheld the district court's order and supported the use of busing to combat racial segregation. In such cases, the burden would be placed on school authorities to show that their racial composition is not the result of discriminatory actions.

\* \* \* \* \* \* \* \* \* \* \* \* \* \* \* \* \* \* \* \* \* \* \* \* \* \* \* \*

Mr. Chief Justice Warren delivered the opinion of the Court, saying in part:

These cases come to us from the states of Kansas, South Carolina, Virginia, and Delaware. They are premised on different facts and different local conditions, but a common legal question justifies their consideration together in this consolidated opinion.

In each of the cases, minors of the Negro race, through their legal representatives, seek the aid of the courts in obtaining admission to the public schools of their community on a nonsegregated basis. In each instance, they had been denied admission to schools attended by white children under laws requiring or permitting segregation according to race. This segregation was alleged to deprive the plaintiffs of the equal protection of the laws under the Fourteenth Amendment. . . .

The plaintiffs contend that segregated public schools are not "equal" and cannot be made "equal," and that hence they are deprived of equal protection of the laws. . . .

. . . . The doctrine of "separate but equal" did not make its appearance in this Court until 1896 in . . . *Plessy v. Ferguson*, . . . involving not education but transportation. American courts have since labored with the doctrine for over a half century. . . .

In the instant cases, that question is directly presented. Here, unlike *Sweatt v. Painter*, there are findings below that the Negro and white schools involved have been equalized, or are being equalized, with respect to buildings, curricula, qualifications and salaries of teachers, and other "tangible" factors. Our decision, therefore, cannot turn on merely a comparison of these tangible factors in the Negro and white schools involved in each of the cases. We must look instead to the effect of segregation itself on public education.

In approaching this problem, we cannot turn the clock back to 1868 when the Amendment was adopted, or even to 1896 when *Plessy v. Ferguson* was written. We must consider public education in the light of its full development and its present place in American life throughout the Nation. Only in this way can it be determined if segregation in public schools deprives these plaintiffs of the equal protection of the laws.

Today, education is perhaps the most important function of the state and local governments. Compulsory school-attendance laws and the great expenditures for education both demonstrate our recognition of the importance of education to our democratic society. It is required in the performance of our most basic public responsibilities, even service in the armed forces. It is the very foundation of good citizenship. Today it is a principal instrument in awakening the child to cultural values, in preparing him for later professional training, and in helping him to adjust normally to his environment. In these days, it is doubtful any child may reasonably be expected to succeed in life if he is denied the opportunity of an education. Such an opportunity, where the state has undertaken to provide it, is a right which must be made available to all on equal terms.

We come then to the question presented: Does segregation of children in public schools solely on the basis of race, even though the physical facilities and other "tangible" factors may be equal, deprive the children of the minority group of equal educational opportunities? We believe that it does.

. . . . To separate them from others of similar age and qualifications solely because of their race generates a feeling of inferiority as to their status in the community that may effect [sic] their hearts and minds in a way unlikely ever to be undone. The effect of this separation on their educational opportunities was well stated by a finding in the Kansas case by a court which nevertheless felt compelled to rule against the Negro plaintiffs: "Segregation of white and colored children in public schools has a detrimental effect upon the colored children. The impact is greater when it has the sanction of the law; for the policy of separating the races is usually interpreted as denoting the inferiority of the Negro group. A sense of inferiority affects the motivation of a child to learn. Segregation with the sanction of law, therefore, has a tendency to retard the educational and mental development of Negro children and to deprive them of some of the benefits they would receive in a racially integrated school system."

Whatever may have been the extent of psychological knowledge at the time of *Plessy v. Ferguson*, this finding is amply supported by modern authority. Any language in *Plessy v. Ferguson* contrary to this finding is rejected.

We conclude that in the field of public education the doctrine of "separate but equal" has no place. Separate educational facilities are inherently unequal. Therefore, we hold that the plaintiffs and others similarly situated for whom the actions have been brought are, by reason of the segregation complained of, deprived of the equal protection of the laws guaranteed by the Fourteenth Amendment. This disposition makes unnecessary any discussion whether such segregation also violates the Due Process Clause of the Fourteenth Amendment.

Because these are class actions, because of the wide applicability of this decision, and because of the great variety of local conditions, the formulation of decrees in these cases presents problems of considerable complexity. On reargument, the consideration of appropriate relief was necessarily subordinated to the primary questions—the constitutionality of segregation in public education. We have now announced that such segregation is a denial of the equal protection of the laws. In order that we may have the full assistance of the parties in formulating decrees, the cases will be restored to the docket, and the parties are requested to present further argument on Questions 4 and 5 previously propounded by the Court for the reargument this Term. The Attorney General of the United States is again invited to participate. The Attorneys General of the states requiring or permitting segregation in public education will also be permitted to appear as *amici curiae* [friends of the Court who give advice on matters pending before it] upon request to do so by September 15, 1954, and submission of briefs by October 1, 1954.

### Brown v. Board of Education (Second Case; 1955)

These cases were decided on May 17, 1954. The opinions of that date, declaring the fundamental principle that racial discrimination in public education is unconstitutional, are incorporated therein by reference. All provisions of federal, state, or local law requiring or permitting such discrimination must yield to this principle. There remains for consideration the manner in which relief is to be accorded. . . .

Full implementation of these constitutional principles may require solution of varied local school problems. School authorities have the primary responsibility for elucidating, assessing, and solving these problems; courts will have to consider whether the action of school authorities constitutes good faith implementation of the governing constitutional principles. Because of their proximity to local conditions and the possible need for further hearings, the courts which originally heard these cases can best perform this judicial appraisal. Accordingly, we believe it appropriate to remand the cases to those courts.

In fashioning and effectuating the decrees, the courts will be guided by equitable principles. Traditionally, equity has been characterized by a practical flexibility in shaping its remedies and by a facility for adjusting and reconciling public and private needs. These cases call for the exercise of these traditional attributes of equity power. At stake is the personal interest of the plaintiffs in admission to public schools as soon as practicable on a nondiscriminatory basis. To effectuate this interest may call for elimination of a variety of obstacles in making the transition to school systems operated in accordance with the constitutional principles set forth in our May 17, 1954, decision. Courts of equity may properly take into account the public interest in the elimination of such obstacles in a systematic and effective manner. But it should go without saying that the vitality of these constitutional principles cannot be allowed to yield simply because of disagreement with them.

While giving weight to these public and private considerations, the courts will require that the defendants make a prompt and reasonable start toward full compliance with our May 17, 1954 ruling. Once such a start has been made, the courts may find that additional time is necessary to carry out the ruling in an effective manner. The burden rests upon the defendants to establish that such time is necessary in the public interest and is consistent with good faith compliance at the earliest practicable date. . . .

The . . . cases are remanded to the district courts to take such proceedings and enter such orders and decrees consistent with this opinion as are necessary and proper to admit to public schools on a racially nondiscriminatory basis with all deliberate speed the parties to these cases. . . .

\* \* \* \* \* \* \* \* \* \* \* \* \* \* \* \* \* \* \* \* \* \* \* \* \* \* \* \* \* \* \* \*

*Discussion Points:*

1. How did Warren distinguish *Brown* from *Sweatt v. Painter?*
2. How did Warren support the conclusion that there is a *right* to education and it is a right to education "on equal terms"?
3. In *Plessy*, the Court said that segregation did not necessarily stamp blacks with the stigma of inferiority. What did Warren say about the consequences of such racial segregation in *Brown?*
4. Compare and contrast Justice Brown's opinion in *Plessy* with Warren's opinion in *Brown*. Recall Justice Harlan's dissenting opinion in *Plessy*. In what ways did he anticipate the Court's eventual holding in *Brown?*

# CHAPTER 32

## *GIDEON V. WAINWRIGHT*

### 372 U.S. 335; 83 S.Ct. 792;
### 9 L.Ed. 2d 799 (1963)

The Sixth Amendment provides that in "all criminal prosecutions the accused shall . . . have the assistance of counsel for his defense." This Amendment has been interpreted as guaranteeing that if such a defendant cannot afford to hire his own lawyer, one will be appointed to assist him. At the state level, right-to-counsel cases have been considered in light of the Fourteenth Amendment's right to due process. In practice, courts have tried to determine whether or not a defendant was able to receive an essentially fair trial. In some cases, courts have ruled that a defendant received a fair trial without counsel. Some, for example, were deemed capable of conducting their own defense. In *Betts v. Brady* (316 U.S. 455, 1942), the Supreme Court underscored the principle that the state need not necessarily appoint counsel for indigent defendants in all criminal cases. In capital cases, however, courts consistently held that defendants were entitled to the assistance of counsel.

In the case below, Clarence Gideon had been arrested in Florida for breaking and entering. He appeared in court without an attorney. He was indigent and asked the court to appoint an attorney. In light of the fact that Florida law provided for the appointment of counsel for indigents in capital cases only, the court refused Gideon's request. He was convicted and appealed his case, claiming that his constitutionally-guaranteed right to counsel had been violated.

Rejecting the premise of *Betts*, the Supreme Court agreed with Gideon. Writing for the unanimous Court, Justice Black concluded that criminal defendants cannot be assured of receiving fair trials without the aid of counsel. As a result, this right to counsel was applied to both capital and noncapital cases in the state courts.

\* \* \* \* \* \* \* \* \* \* \* \* \* \* \* \* \* \* \* \* \* \* \* \* \* \* \* \* \*

Mr. Justice Black delivered the opinion of the Court, saying in part:

.... Since 1942, when *Betts v. Brady* was decided by a divided Court, the problem of a defendant's federal constitutional right to counsel in a state court has been a continuing source of controversy and litigation.... "Should this Court's holding in *Betts v. Brady* be reconsidered?"...

[in *Betts* [t]he Court said: "Asserted denial [of due process] is to be tested by an appraisal of the totality of facts in a given case..."

... [T]he Court held that refusal to appoint counsel under the particular facts and circumstances in the *Betts* case was not so "offensive to the common and fundamental ideas of fairness" as to amount to a denial of due process.... Upon full reconsideration we conclude that *Betts v. Brady* should be overruled....

We think the Court in *Betts* had ample precedent for acknowledging that those guarantees of the Bill of Rights which are fundamental safeguards of liberty immune from federal abridgment are equally protected against state invasion by the Due Process Clause of the Fourteenth Amendment.... Explicitly recognized to be of this "fundamental nature" and therefore made immune from state invasion by the Fourteenth, or some part of it, are the First Amendment's freedoms of speech, press, religion, association, and petition for redress of grievances. For the same reason ... the Court has made obligatory on the States the Fifth Amendment's command that private property shall not be taken for public use without just compensation, the Fourth Amendment's prohibition of unreasonable searches and seizures, and the Eighth's ban on cruel and unusual punishment....

We accept *Betts v. Brady*'s assumption, based as it was on our prior cases, that a provision of the Bill of Rights which is "fundamental and essential to a fair trial" is made obligatory upon the States by the Fourteenth Amendment. We think the Court in *Betts* was wrong, however, in concluding that the Sixth Amendment's guarantee of counsel is not one of these fundamental rights....

.... Not only ... precedents but also reason and reflection require us to recognize that in our adversary system of criminal justice, any person haled into court, who is too poor to hire a lawyer, cannot be assured of a fair trial unless counsel is provided for him. This seems to us to be an obvious truth.... The right of one charged with crime to counsel may not be deemed fundamental and essential to fair trials in some countries, but it is in ours....

* * * * * * * * * * * * * * * * * * * * * * * * * * * * * * * * *

*Discussion Points:*

1. Review Justice Black's summary of provisions from the Bill of Rights that, to that point, had been absorbed or incorporated into the Fourteenth Amendment and applied at the state level too. Explain how the Court has interpreted the Fourteenth Amendment to accomplish this outcome. In your view, is this a sensible way to interpret the Fourteenth Amendment? Why or why not?
2. Why did Black hold that the absence of counsel denied Gideon a fair trial?
3. Compare and contrast *Betts* with *Gideon*. In both cases, the Court said that "fundamental" and "essential" provisions of the Bill of Rights are protected against state invasion by the Fourteenth Amendment. But the Court reached different conclusions regarding the right to counsel in the respective cases. Why? Discuss the importance of the Court's reliance on the "totality of facts" in *Betts* and the Court's reference to "obvious truth" in *Gideon*.

# CHAPTER 33

## *ABINGTON SCHOOL DISTRICT*
## *V. SCHEMPP*

### 374 US. 203; 83 S.Ct. 1560; 10 L.Ed. 2d 844 (1963)

The First Amendment specifies that "Congress shall make no law respecting an establishment of religion, or prohibiting the free exercise thereof." Jefferson called for a "wall of separation" between church and state. The concept of religious freedom has not always been easy to apply to concrete controversies, however. In *Walz v. Tax Commission* (397 U.S. 664, 1970), a case in which an eight-to-one Supreme Court majority upheld the practice of exempting churches from paying state property and income taxes, Chief Justice Burger explained the situation in this way:

> The course of constitutional neutrality . . . cannot be an absolutely straight line. . . . The general principle deducible from the First Amendment and all that has been said by the Court is this: that we will not tolerate either governmentally established religion or governmental interference with religion. Short of those expressly proscribed governmental acts there is room for . . . a benevolent neutrality which will permit religious exercise to exist without sponsorship and without interference.

In this vein, the Court has allowed the government to "accommodate" a variety of religious activities as long as the government neither sponsors them nor favors one sect over another. These general rules grew out of a series of decisions.

Several cases involved the relationship between church and state in the field of education. The Constitution has been read to require that sectarian religious instruction not be provided in public schools. Further, public funds may not be used to support religious schools. But this latter idea has been applied with flexibility. While public monies cannot be used to aid religion, the Court has sometimes upheld publicly-financed secular programs designed to benefit parochial school *children* (as opposed to parochial *schools*).

In *Everson v. Board of Education* (330 U.S. 1, 1947), for example, the Supreme Court upheld the use of public funds to pay for transporting children to parochial schools as a way of getting children "regardless of their religion, safely and expeditiously to and from accredited schools." But in *McCollum v. Board of Education* (333 U.S. 203, 1948), the Court disallowed a program under which religious instructors provided religious instruction on public school property during school hours for children whose parents signed up for the program. The Court invalidated the program because religious groups were using the public schools to spread their faith. Then, in *Zorach v. Clausen* (343 U.S. 306, 1952), the Court upheld a released-time program in which religious instruction was provided during school hours but away from public-school facilities. The Court found that this program did not aid religion. Here, the public schools did no more "than accommodate their schedules to a program of outside religious instruction." Unlike the establishment of religion, the Court found its accommodation constitutionally acceptable. Additionally, in *Board of Education v. Allen* (392 U.S. 236, 1968), the Court permitted the state to lend textbooks in secular subjects to parochial schools on grounds that such secular books neither inhibited nor advanced religion. Since no funds actually went to the parochial schools, the children were seen as the primary beneficiaries.

In *Lemon v. Kurtzman* (403 U.S. 602, 1971), the Court tried to summarize the judicial criteria employed in evaluating state programs that aided parochial schools. A Pennsylvania program reimbursed parochial schools for the salaries of teachers teaching secular subjects and for secular textbooks and instructional materials. The Court rejected the program—and a similar one in Rhode Island—by unanimous vote. Chief Justice Burger, writing for the Court, said that such aid must have a secular legislative purpose. It must have a primary effect that neither advances nor inhibits religion. And it must not lead to "excessive government entanglement" with religion. In *Lemon*, the Court concluded that the state could not be sure that the parochial-school teachers were teaching in the required neutral manner unless the state continually monitored teacher performance. Such surveillance would constitute excessive entanglement between religious institutions and the state. Burger also held that providing state funds to purchase textbooks was a form of direct aid to the schools.

The Court's "benevolent neutrality" towards state aid for parochial schools, then, means that the aid will be sustained if it is secular in purpose and effect and does not lead to excessive entanglement between church and state. On the other hand, religious instruction, prayer services, and so on in public schools violate the Establishment Clause of the First Amendment (as applied to the states by way of the Fourteenth Amendment).

*Engel v. Vitale* (370 U.S. 421, 1962) stirred a great deal of controversy. The New York State Board of Regents recommended that school districts adopt a denominationally-neutral prayer to be said aloud by students in the presence of a teacher at the start of each school day. The prayer was brief: "Almighty God, we acknowledge our dependence on Thee, and we beg Thy blessings upon us, our parents, our teachers, and our country." The parents of ten students claimed that the program violated their religious beliefs. The Supreme Court, in a six-to-one vote, agreed and found the Regents' Prayer unconstitutional. Writing for the majority, Justice Black said:

> . . . [T]he constitutional prohibition against laws respecting an establishment of religion must at least mean that in this country it is no part of the business of government to compose official prayers for any group of the American people to recite as part of a religious service carried on by the government.

He went on to say that the government "should stay out of the business of writing or sanctioning official prayers and leave that purely religious function to the people themselves and to those the people choose to look to for religious guidance."

But what if the state did not actually compose the prayer? Were other types of religious exercises acceptable in the public schools? The Court addressed such questions in *Abington School District v. Schempp.*

A Pennsylvania law provided for reading from the Bible, without comment, followed by the recitation of the Lord's Prayer and the Pledge of Allegiance at the start of the school day. The Schempps, a Unitarian family, claimed that some of the Bible readings violated their religious beliefs. The Court combined the *Schempp* case with *Murray v. Curlett.* Mrs. Murray and her son, both atheists, thought that a similar Maryland law violated their religious rights on grounds that the daily state-sponsored religious exercises put "a premium on belief as against non-belief." In both cases, therefore, the families claimed that the laws amounted to government endorsement of religious practices. In an eight-to-one decision, the Supreme Court agreed.

\* \* \* \* \* \* \* \* \* \* \* \* \* \* \* \* \* \* \* \* \* \* \* \* \* \* \*

Mr. Justice Clark delivered the opinion of the Court, saying in part:

Applying the Establishment Clause principles to the case at bar we find that the States are requiring the selection and reading at the opening of the school day of verses from the Holy Bible and the recitation of the Lord's Prayer by the students in unison. These exercises are prescribed as part of the curricular activities of students who are required by law to attend school. They are held in school buildings under the supervision and with the participation of teachers employed in those schools. The trial court . . . has found that such an opening exercise is a religious ceremony and was intended by the State to be so. We agree with the trial court's finding as to the religious character of the exercises. Given that finding, the exercises and the law requiring them are in violation of the Establishment Clause.

There is no such specific finding as to the religious character of the exercises . . . and the State contends . . . that the program is an effort to extend its benefits to all public school children without regard to their religious belief. Included within its secular purposes, it says, are the promotion of moral values, the contradiction to the materialistic trends of our times, the perpetuation of our institutions and the teaching of literature. The case came up on demurrer, of course, to a petition which alleged that the uniform practice under the rule had been to read from the King James version of the Bible and that the exercise was sectarian. The short answer, therefore, is that the religious character of the exercise was admitted by the State. But even if its purpose is not strictly religious, it is sought to be accomplished through readings, without comment, from the Bible. Surely the place of the Bible as an instrument of religion cannot be gainsaid, and the State's recognition of the pervading religious character of the ceremony is evident from the rule's specific permission of the alternative use of the Catholic Douay version as well as the recent amendment permitting nonattendance at the exercises. None of these factors is consistent with the contention that the Bible is here used either as an instrument for non-religious moral inspiration or as a reference for the teaching of secular subjects.

The conclusion follows that in both cases the laws require religious exercises and such exercises are being conducted in direct violation of the rights of the appellees and petitioners. Nor are these required exercises mitigated by the fact that individual students may absent themselves upon parental request, for that fact furnishes no defense to a claim of unconstitutionality under the Establishment Clause. Further, it is no defense to urge that the religious practices here may be relatively minor encroachments on the First Amendment. The breach of neutrality that is today a trickling stream may all too soon become a raging torrent and, in the words of Madison, "it is proper to take alarm at the first experiment on our liberties."

It is insisted that unless these religious exercises are permitted a "religion of secularism" is established in the schools. We agree of course that the State may not establish a "religion of secularism" in the sense of affirmatively opposing or showing hostility to religion, thus "preferring those who believe in no religion over those who do believe." We do not agree, however, that this decision in any sense has that effect. In addition, it might well be said that one's education is not complete without a study of comparative religion or the history of religion and its relationship to the advancement of civilization. It certainly may be said that the Bible is worthy of study for its literary and historic qualities. Nothing we have said here indicates that such study of the Bible or of religion, when presented objectively as part of a secular program of education, may not be effected consistently with the First Amendment. But the exercises here do not fall into those categories. They are religious exercises, required by the States in violation of the command of the First Amendment that the Government maintain strict neutrality, neither aiding nor opposing religion.

Finally, we cannot accept that the concept of neutrality, which does not permit a State to require a religious exercise even with the consent of the majority of those affected, collides with the majority's right to free exercise of religion. While the Free Exercise Clause clearly prohibits the use of state action to deny the rights of free exercise to *anyone*, it has never meant that a majority could use the machinery of the State to practice its beliefs....

The place of religion in our society is an exalted one, achieved through a long tradition of reliance on the home, the church and the inviolable citadel of the individual heart and mind. We have come to recognize through bitter experience that it is not within the power of government to invade that citadel, whether its purpose or effect be to aid or oppose, to advance or retard. In the relationship between man and religion, the State is firmly committed to a position of neutrality. Though the application of that rule requires interpretation of a delicate sort, the rule itself is clearly and concisely stated in the words of the First Amendment....

\* \* \* \* \* \* \* \* \* \* \* \* \* \* \* \* \* \* \* \* \* \* \* \* \* \* \* \* \* \*

*Discussion Points:*

1. Explain Clark's reasoning in finding a constitutional violation. Did the fact that parents could ask to have their children excused from the practices make any difference to Clark? What did Clark say to the argument that minor constitutional violations should be tolerated?

2. According to the case facts, was Bible reading conducted as an academic lesson or as a religious exercise? Did Clark rule that the Constitution forbids the objective study of comparative religions or the history of religion in public schools? Explain.

3. In a concurring opinion, Justice Brennan suggested that schools could promote moral values without resorting to religious exercises. Opening exercises could include important documents and writings by prominent Americans about liberty and other fundamental values. A moment of silence might also be utilized. (Note: *Wallace v. Jaffree*, 86 L.Ed. 2d, 1985, raised related issues and the Supreme Court invalidated a moment-of-silence policy after school officials made it clear that the period was intended for prayer.) Discuss some of these alternatives. Can you think of any others?

# CHAPTER 34

## *GRISWOLD V. CONNECTICUT*
### 381 U.S. 479; 85 S.Ct. 1678; 14 L.Ed. 2d 510 (1965)

The Court has sometimes been asked to recognize the fundamental importance of rights that do not appear in the express terms of the Constitution. The right of privacy is an example. In *Griswold v. Connecticut*, the Court acknowledged the existence of such a right and searched for a constitutional basis from which it could be inferred.

The constitutionality of a Connecticut birth-control law was challenged in *Griswold*. It provided that "any person who uses any drug, medicinal article, or instrument for the purpose of preventing conception" would be subject to fine or imprisonment or both. Further, any person who assisted another in preventing conception could be prosecuted as well. In a previous challenge, the Court found no justiciable controversy because the state was not enforcing the law (*Poe v. Ullman*, 367 U.S. 497, 1961). The present case arose after Connecticut began enforcing the law following the opening of birth-control clinics. Estelle Griswold, the Executive Director of the Planned Parenthood League of Connecticut, was convicted of violating the statute.

In a seven-to-two decision, the Supreme Court held that the law violated the right to privacy of husband and wife. Writing for the Court, Justice Douglas suggested that this right is implied by explicit provisions of the Bill of Rights and emanates from the "penumbras" surrounding specific constitutional guarantees. Douglas also referred to the Ninth Amendment, a point stressed by three concurring justices. Justice Black, joined by Justice Stewart, dissented on grounds that there is no explicit right of privacy in the literal text of the Constitution.

\* \* \* \* \* \* \* \* \* \* \* \* \* \* \* \* \* \* \* \* \* \* \* \* \* \* \* \*

Mr. Justice Douglas delivered the opinion of the Court, saying in part:
. . . This law . . . operates directly on an intimate relation of husband and wife and their physician's role in one aspect of that relation.

The association of people is not mentioned in the Constitution nor in the Bill of Rights. The right to educate a child in a school of the parents' choice—whether public or private or parochial—is also not mentioned. Nor is the right to study any particular subject or any foreign language. Yet the First Amendment has been construed to include certain of those rights. . . . In other words, the First Amendment has a penumbra where privacy is protected from governmental intrusion. . . .

The foregoing cases suggest that specific guarantees in the Bill of Rights have penumbras, formed by emanations from those guarantees that help give them life and substance. . . . Various guarantees create zones of privacy. The right of association contained in the penumbra of the First Amendment is one, as we have seen. The Third Amendment in its prohibition against the quartering of soldiers . . . is another facet of that privacy. The Fourth Amendment explicitly affirms the "right of the people to be secure in their persons, houses, papers, and effects, against unreasonable searches and seizures." The Fifth Amendment in its Self-Incrimination Clause enables the citizen to create a zone of privacy which government may not force him to surrender to his detriment. The Ninth Amendment provides: "The enumeration in the Constitution, of certain rights, shall not be construed to deny or disparage others retained by the people."

The present case, then, concerns a relationship lying within the zone of privacy created by several fundamental constitutional guarantees. And it concerns a law which, in forbidding the *use* of contraceptives rather than regulating their manufacture or sale, seeks to achieve its goals by means of having a maximum destructive impact upon that relationship. Such a law cannot stand in light of the familiar principle . . . that a "governmental purpose to control or prevent activities constitutionally subject to state regulation may not be achieved by means which sweep unnecessarily broadly and thereby invade the area of protected freedoms." . . . Would we allow the police to search the sacred precincts of marital bedrooms for telltale signs of the use of contraceptives? The very idea is repulsive to the notions of privacy surrounding the marriage relationship.

We deal with a right of privacy older than the Bill of Rights—older than our political parties, older than our school system. Marriage is a coming together for better or for worse, hopefully enduring, and intimate to the degree of being sacred. . . .

Mr. Justice Goldberg, whom Chief Justice Warren and Mr. Justice Brennan join, concurring, stated in part:

To hold that a right so basic and fundamental and so deep-rooted in our society as the right to privacy in marriage may be infringed because that right is not guaranteed in so many words by the first eight amendments to the Constitution is to ignore the Ninth Amendment and to give it no effect whatsoever. Moreover, a judicial construction that this fundamental right is not protected by the Constitution because it is not mentioned in explicit terms ... would violate the Ninth Amendment, which specifically states that "[t]he enumeration in the Constitution, of certain rights, shall not be *construed* to deny or disparage others retained by the people." (Emphasis added.)

.... [T]he Ninth Amendment shows a belief in the Constitution's authors that fundamental rights exist that are not expressly enumerated in the first eight amendments and an intent that the list of rights included there not be deemed exhaustive....

.... In sum, the Ninth Amendment simply lends strong support to the view that the "liberty" protected by the Fifth and Fourteenth Amendments from infringement by the Federal Government or the States is not restricted to rights specifically mentioned in the first eight amendments....

Mr. Justice Black, whom Mr. Justice Stewart joins, dissented, saying in part:

The Court talks about a constitutional "right of privacy" as though there is some constitutional provision or provisions forbidding any law ever so passed which might abridge the "privacy" of individuals. But there is not....

One of the most effective ways of diluting or expanding a constitutionally guaranteed right is to substitute for the crucial word or words of a constitutional guarantee another word or words more or less flexible and more or less restricted in meaning. This fact is well illustrated by the use of the term "right of privacy" as a comprehensive substitute for the Fourth Amendment's guarantee against "unreasonable searches and seizures." "Privacy" is a broad, abstract and ambiguous concept which can easily be shrunken in meaning but which can also, on the other hand, easily be interpreted as a constitutional ban against many things other than searches and seizures....

I realize that many good and able men have eloquently spoken and written ... about the duty of this Court to keep the Constitution in tune with the times. The idea is that the Constitution must be changed from time to time and that this Court is charged with a duty to make those changes. For myself, I must with all deference reject that philosophy. The Constitution makers knew the need for change and provided for it. Amendments ... can be submitted to the people or their selected agents for ratification. That method of change was good for our Fathers, and being somewhat old-fashioned I must add it is good enough for me. And so, I cannot rely on the Due Process Clause or the Ninth Amendment or any mysterious and uncertain natural law concept as a reason for striking down this state law. . . .

\* \* \* \* \* \* \* \* \* \* \* \* \* \* \* \* \* \* \* \* \* \* \* \* \* \* \* \* \* \*

*Discussion Points:*

1. Explain Justice Douglas's decision to invalidate the challenged law. Where did he find the "right of privacy"? Do you agree that this right is constitutionally protected? Why or why not?
2. Explain Justice Goldberg's decision to invalidate the law.
3. Explain Justice Black's vote to uphold the statute.
4. Recall Brutus and the debate on the question of whether or not a written bill of rights was necessary. In what way was the Ninth Amendment an answer to those who feared that a written bill of rights posed risks and denied widely-held views about the importance of natural law?
5. Compare and contrast the opinions by Douglas, Goldberg, and Black. Which opinion do you find most persuasive? Why?

# CHAPTER 35

## *SOUTH CAROLINA V. KATZENBACK*
### 383 U.S. 301; 86 S.Ct. 803; 15 L.Ed. 769 (1966)

In early years, the right to vote was restricted to white, adult, property-owning males. The Fifteenth Amendment extended the right to vote to black males. Suffrage was extended to women with the ratification of the Nineteenth Amendment in 1920. In 1971, the Twenty-Sixth Amendment lowered the voting age to eighteen. But while the nation has witnessed an expansion of the electorate, this expansion did not proceed at a steady pace.

Congress enacted legislation to enforce the Fifteenth Amendment, but important sections of the Enforcement Act of 1870 were struck down in *United States v. Reese* (92 U.S. 214, 1876). Further, some states employed various measures such as poll taxes, white primaries, and grandfather clauses to defeat the purpose of the Fifteenth Amendment. Citing an interest in ensuring an informed and intelligent electorate, some states also used "literacy tests." Although both blacks and whites were subjected to the tests, they were often administered in ways that kept black voting to a trickle.

Alabama, for example, used a sixty-eight question literacy test composed by the justices of the State Supreme Court. The test was administered by local election officials who could ask as many—or as few—questions as they chose. A single incorrect response could serve as grounds to disqualify the respondent as "illiterate." Some of the test questions follow:

— A United States Senator elected at the general election in November takes office the following year on what date?
— A President elected at the general election in November takes office the following year on what date?
— Does enumeration affect the income tax levied on citizens in various states?
— What words are required by law to be on all coins and paper currency of the United States?

— Appropriation of money for the armed services can be only for a period limited to _____ years.

— Of the original 13 states, the one with the largest representation in the first Congress was _____.

— If a state is a party to a case, the Constitution provides that original jurisdiction shall be in _____.

— The Constitution limits the size of the District of Columbia to _____.

— The only laws which can be passed to apply to an area in a federal arsenal are those passed by _____ provided consent for the purchase of the land is given by the _____.

Clearly, it would be possible for election officials to select such questions to prevent otherwise intelligent and literate citizens from voting. Invalidating a similar test in *Louisiana v. United States* (380 U.S. 145, 1965), Justice Black, writing for the unanimous Supreme Court, said, "This is not a test but a trap, sufficient to stop even the most brilliant man on his way to the voting booth."

Congress again tried to exert federal authority over state officials in the 1950s and early 1960s. Additionally, the Twenty-Fourth Amendment which abolished poll taxes, was ratified in 1964. But some states continued to demonstrate ingenuity in finding ways to minimize black voting. Congress responded in 1965 by passing the Voting Rights Act. The Act abolished literacy tests, erased accumulated poll taxes, and prohibited states from establishing new voting requirements until the Attorney General of the United States certified them as non-discriminatory. It also provided for the appointment of federal examiners and federal poll watchers to guard against voting irregularities. These measures would be used in areas where voting discrimination had been most flagrant. Even in areas not targeted by this triggering formula, the Attorney General was authorized to take steps to protect voting rights.

In this case, South Carolina challenged the constitutionality of the Voting Rights Act. Writing for the Court, Chief Justice Warren saw the Act as an appropriate means for carrying out the Fifteenth Amendment. Several months later, in *Katzenbach v. Morgan* (384 U.S. 641, 1966), the Court upheld sections of the Act which prevented states from disqualifying voters because they could not speak or write English.

By 1980, Southern registration rates for blacks and whites had become roughly equal. As such, some officials in targeted states asserted that the Voting Rights Act should be allowed to expire. In spite of these arguments, Congress approved a twenty-five year extension of the Act in 1982. It remains in place as a mechanism that facilitates the use of federal power to safeguard voting rights in the states.

\* \* \* \* \* \* \* \* \* \* \* \* \* \* \* \* \* \* \* \* \* \* \* \* \* \* \* \*

Mr. Chief Justice Warren delivered the opinion of the Court, saying in part:

. . . . The constitutional propriety of the Voting Rights Act of 1965 must be judged with reference to the historical experience which it reflects. . . .

Two points emerge vividly from the voluminous legislative history of the Act. . . First: Congress felt itself confronted by an insidious and pervasive evil which had been perpetuated in certain parts of our country through unremitting and ingenious defiance of the Constitution. Second: Congress concluded that the unsuccessful remedies which it had prescribed in the past would have to be replaced by sterner and more elaborate measures in order to satisfy the clear commands of the Fifteenth Amendment. . . .

According to the evidence . . . [discriminatory application of voting tests is now the principal] method used to bar Negroes from the polls. . . . Moreover, in almost all of these cases, the courts have held that the discrimination was pursuant to a widespread "pattern or practice." White applicants for registration have often been excused altogether from the literacy and understanding tests or have been given easy versions, have received extensive help from voting officials, and have been registered despite serious errors in their answers. Negroes, on the other hand, have typically been required to pass difficult versions of all the tests, without any outside assistance and without the slightest error. . . .

The previous legislation has proved ineffective for a number of reasons. Voting suits are unusually onerous to prepare. . . Litigation has been exceedingly slow. . . Even when favorable decisions have finally been obtained, some of the States affected have merely switched to discriminatory devices not covered by the federal decrees or have enacted difficult new tests designed to prolong the existing disparity between white and Negro registration. Alternatively, certain local officials have defied and evaded court orders or have simply closed their registration offices to freeze the voting rolls. . . .

During the hearings and debate on the Act, Selma, Alabama, was repeatedly referred to as the pre-eminent example of the ineffectiveness of existing legislation. In Dallas County, of which Selma is the seat, there were four years of litigation by the Justice Department and two findings by the federal courts of widespread voting discrimination. Yet in those four years, Negro registration rose only from 156 to 383, although there are approximately 15,000 Negroes of voting age in the county. Any possibility that these figures were attributable to political apathy was dispelled by the protest demonstrations in Selma in the early months of 1965. . . .

The Voting Rights Act of 1965 reflects Congress's firm intention to rid the country of racial discrimination in voting. The heart of the Act is a complex scheme of stringent remedies aimed at areas where voting discrimination has been most flagrant. . . .

The remedial sections of the Act assailed by South Carolina automatically apply to any State, or to any separate political subdivision such as county or parish, for which two findings have been made: (1) the Attorney General has determined that on November 1, 1964, it maintained a "test or device," and (2) the Director of the Census has determined that less than 50% of its voting-age residents were registered on November 1, 1964, or voted in the presidential election of November 1964. . . .

[The Act provides for the suspension of tests, review of new rules by the Attorney General of the United States, and appointment of federal examiners for such areas.]

These provisions of the Voting Rights Act of 1965 are challenged on the fundamental ground that they exceed the powers of Congress and encroach on an area reserved to the States by the Constitution. . . .

Section 1 of the Fifteenth Amendment declares that "[t]he right of citizens of the United States to vote shall not be denied or abridged by the United States or by any State on account of race, color, or previous condition of servitude." . . . [S]ection 2 . . . expressly declares that "Congress shall have the power to enforce this article by appropriate legislation." By adding this authorization, the Framers indicated that Congress was to be chiefly responsible for implementing the rights created in Section 1. . . .

The basic test to be applied . . . [was laid down by] . . . Chief Justice Marshall, 50 years before the Fifteenth Amendment was ratified:

Let the end be legitimate, let it be within the scope of the Constitution, and all means which are appropriate, which are plainly adapted to that end, which are not prohibited, but consist with the letter and the spirit of the Constitution, are constitutional.

*McCulloch v. Maryland* (1819). . . .

We therefore reject South Carolina's argument that Congress may appropriately do no more than to forbid violations of the Fifteenth Amendment in general terms—that the task of fashioning specific remedies or of applying them to particular localities must necessarily be left entirely to the courts. Congress is not circumscribed by any such artificial rules under Section 2 of the Fifteenth Amendment. . . .

\* \* \* \* \* \* \* \* \* \* \* \* \* \* \* \* \* \* \* \* \* \* \* \* \* \* \* \* \* \* \*

*Discussion Points:*

1. Why did Chief Justice Warren judge the Voting Rights Act with reference to "historical experience?" What did the Act's legislative history demonstrate?
2. Why were literacy tests found to be racially discriminatory?
3. Why had previous legislation been ineffective? How did Warren use Selma, Alabama to illustrate this point? How would the challenged Act's automatic triggering formula help to deal with such difficulties?

# CHAPTER 36

## *MIRANDA V. ARIZONA*
## 348 U.S. 436; 86 S.Ct. 1602; 16 L.Ed. 2d 694 (1966)

The Warren Court made a number of decisions expanding the rights of the accused. For example, in *Mapp v. Ohio* (367 U.S. 643, 1961), the Court held that "all evidence obtained by searches and seizures in violation of the [United States] Constitution is, by that same authority, inadmissible in a state court." In the previously-discussed 1963 *Gideon* decision, the Court ruled that defendants have a right to counsel in state courts. In *Malloy v. Hogan* (378 U.S. 1, 1964), the Court applied the privilege against compulsory self-incrimination at the state, as well as the national, level. In *Escobedo v. Illinois* (378 U.S. 478, 1964), the Court found that once an "investigation is no longer a general inquiry into an unsolved crime but has begun to focus upon a particular suspect," law enforcement officials must honor the suspect's right to remain silent and to consult with an attorney.

These decisions reflect the Court's move to merge the right to counsel and the privilege against self-incrimination. It might be difficult to prove what actually happened during police interrogations of defendants. The presence of counsel at such interrogations is one way to protect against coerced confessions. The *Miranda* decision required the police to inform the accused that he need not assist the police in building a case against him and that he is entitled to legal counsel concerning what he should and should not say.

*Miranda* consolidated four related cases that raised questions about the admissibility of confessions. In the lead case, Ernesto Miranda was suspected of kidnapping and rape. He was arrested at his home and taken to a police station for questioning. He was not advised of his right to remain silent nor of his right to counsel. After two hours of questioning, he provided a written confession. He was subsequently convicted. Writing for a five-to-four majority, Chief Justice Warren ruled that the confession was inadmissible and that such defendants should be informed of their rights.

Miranda was retried and was again convicted, in large part because of testimony from his girlfriend. After spending five years in prison, he was paroled. He went back to prison for parole violations. Following his eventual release, he got into a card game. A fight erupted and Miranda was stabbed to death. On his person were a number of "Miranda Cards." When police arrived on the scene, the arresting officer read one of Miranda's own cards to the suspect arrested for his murder.

\* \* \* \* \* \* \* \* \* \* \* \* \* \* \* \* \* \* \* \* \* \* \* \* \* \*

Mr. Chief Justice Warren delivered the opinion of the Court, saying in part:

The cases before us raise questions which go to the roots of our concepts of American criminal jurisprudence: the restraints society must observe consistent with the Federal Constitution in prosecuting individuals for crime. More specifically, we deal with the admissibility of statements obtained from an individual who is subjected to custodial police interrogation and the necessity for procedures which assure that the individual is accorded his privilege under the Fifth Amendment to the Constitution not to be compelled to incriminate himself.

We start here, as we did in *Escobedo*, with the premise that our holding is not an innovation in our jurisprudence, but is an application of principles long recognized and applied in other settings. We have undertaken a thorough re-examination of the *Escobedo* decision and the principles it announced, and we reaffirm it. That case was but an explication of basic rights that are enshrined in our Constitution—that "No person. . .shall be compelled in any criminal case to be a witness against himself," and that "the accused shall . . . have the Assistance of Counsel"—rights which were put in jeopardy in that case through official overbearing. These precious rights were fixed in our Constitution only after centuries of persecution and struggle. . . .

The constitutional issue we decide in each of these cases is the admissibility of statements obtained from a defendant questioned while in custody or otherwise deprived of his freedom of action in any significant way. In each, the defendant was questioned by police officers, detectives, or a prosecuting attorney in a room in which he was cut off from the outside world. In none of these cases was the defendant given a full and effective warning of his rights at the outset of the interrogation process. In all the cases, the questioning elicited [confessions] which were admitted at their trials. They all thus share salient features—incommunicado interrogation of individuals in a police-dominated atmosphere, resulting in self-incriminating statements without full warnings of Constitutional rights. . . .

In these cases, we might not find the defendants' statements to have been involuntary in traditional terms. Our concern for adequate safeguards to protect precious Fifth Amendment rights is, of course, not lessened in the slightest. In each of the cases, the defendant was thrust into an unfamiliar atmosphere and run through menacing police interrogation procedures. The potentiality for compulsion is forcefully apparent, for example, in *Miranda*, where the indigent Mexican defendant was a serious disturbed individual with pronounced sexual fantasies. . . .

It is obvious that such an interrogation environment is created for no purpose other than to subjugate the individual to the will of his examiner. This atmosphere carries its own badge of intimidation. . . . The current practice of incommunicado interrogation is at odds with one of our Nation's most cherished principles—that the individual may not be compelled to incriminate himself. Unless adequate protective devices are employed to dispel the compulsion inherent in custodial surroundings, no statement obtained from the defendant can truly be the product of his free choice. . . .

Today, then, there can be no doubt that the Fifth Amendment privilege is available outside of criminal court proceedings and serves to protect persons in all settings in which their freedom of action is curtailed in any significant way from being compelled to incriminate themselves. We have concluded that without proper safeguards the process of in-custody interrogation of persons suspected or accused of crime contains inherently compelling pressures which work to undermine the individual's will to resist and to compel him to speak where he would not otherwise do so freely. In order to combat these pressures and to permit a full opportunity to exercise the privilege against self-incrimination, the accused must be adequately and effectively apprised of his rights and the exercise of those rights must be fully honored.

It is impossible for us to foresee the potential alternatives for protecting the privilege which might be devised by Congress or the States in the exercise of their creative rule-making capacities. Therefore we cannot say that the Constitution necessarily requires adherence to any particular solution for the inherent compulsions of the interrogation process as it is presently conducted. Our decision in no way creates a constitutional straitjacket which will handicap sound efforts at reform, nor is it intended to have this effect. We encourage Congress and the States to continue their laudable search for increasingly effective ways of protecting the rights of the individual while promoting efficient enforcement of our criminal laws. However, unless we are shown other procedures which are at least as effective in apprising accused persons of their right of silence and in assuring a continuous opportunity to exercise it, the following safeguards must be observed.

At the outset, if a person in custody is to be subjected to interrogation, he must first be informed in clear and unequivocal terms that he has the right to remain silent. For those unaware of the privilege, the warning is needed simply to make them aware of it—the threshold requirement for an intelligent decision as to its exercise. More important, such a warning is an absolute prerequisite in overcoming the inherent pressures of the interrogation atmosphere. It is not just the subnormal or woefully ignorant who succumb to an interrogator's imprecations, whether implied or expressly stated, that the interrogation will continue until a confession is obtained or that silence in the face of accusation is itself damning and will bode ill when presented to a jury. Further, the warning will show the individual that his interrogators are prepared to recognize his privilege should he choose to exercise it. . . .

. . . More important, whatever the background of the person interrogated, a warning at the time of the interrogation is indispensable to overcome its pressures and to insure that the individual knows he is free to exercise the privilege at that point in time.

The warning of the right to remain silent must be accompanied by the explanation that anything said can and will be used against the individual in court. This warning is needed in order to make him aware not only of the privilege, but also of the consequences of forgoing it. It is only through an awareness of these consequences that there can be any assurance of real understanding and intelligent exercise of the privilege. Moreover, this warning may serve to make the individual more acutely aware that he is faced with a phase of the adversary system—that he is not in the presence of persons acting solely in his interest.

The circumstances surrounding in-custody interrogation can operate very quickly to overbear the will of one merely made aware of his privilege by his interrogators. Therefore, the right to have counsel present at the interrogation is indispensable to the protection of the Fifth Amendment privilege under the system we delineate today. Our aim is to assure that the individual's right to choose between silence and speech remains unfettered throughout the interrogation process. A once-stated warning, delivered by those who will conduct the interrogation, cannot itself suffice to that end among those who most require knowledge of their rights. A mere warning given by the interrogators is not alone sufficient to accomplish that end. Prosecutors themselves claim that the admonishment of the right to remain silent without more "will benefit only the recidivist and the professional . . ."

Accordingly we hold that an individual held for interrogation must be clearly informed that he has the right to consult with a lawyer and to have the lawyer with him during interrogation under the system for protecting the privilege we delineate today. As with the warnings of the right to remain silent and that anything stated can be used in evidence against him, this warning is an absolute prerequisite to interrogation. No amount of circumstantial evidence that the person may have been aware of this right will suffice to stand in its stead. Only through such a warning is there ascertainable assurance that the accused was aware of this right.

If an individual indicates that he wishes the assistance of counsel before any interrogation occurs, the authorities cannot rationally ignore or deny his request on the basis that the individual does not have or cannot afford a retained attorney. The financial ability of the individual has no relationship to the scope of the rights involved here. The privilege against self-incrimination secured by the Constitution applies to all individuals. The need for counsel in order to protect the privilege exists for the indigent as well as the affluent. . . .

In order fully to apprise a person interrogated of the extent of his rights under this system then, it is necessary to warn him not only that he has the right to consult with an attorney, but also that if he is indigent a lawyer will be appointed to represent him. Without this additional warning, the admonition of the right to consult with counsel would often be understood as meaning only that he can consult with a lawyer if he has one or has the funds to obtain one. The warning of a right to counsel would be hollow if not couched in terms that would convey to the indigent—the person most often subjected to interrogation—the knowledge that he too has a right to have counsel present. As with the warnings of the right to remain silent and of the general right to counsel, only by effective and express explanation to the indigent of this right can there be assurance that he was truly in a position to exercise it.

Once warnings have been given, the subsequent procedure is clear. If the individual indicates in any manner, at any time prior to or during questioning, that he wishes to remain silent, the interrogation must cease. . . . If the individual states that he wants an attorney, the interrogations must cease until an attorney is present. At that time, the individual must have an opportunity to confer with the attorney and to have him present during any subsequent questioning. If the individual cannot obtain an attorney and he indicates that he wants one before speaking to the police, they must respect his decision to remain silent. . . . The requirement of warnings and waiver of rights is a fundamental with respect to the Fifth Amendment privilege and not simply a preliminary ritual to existing methods of interrogation. . . .

The principles announced today deal with the protection which must be given to the privilege against self-incrimination when the individual is first subjected to police interrogation while in custody at the station or otherwise deprived of his freedom of action in any significant way. It is at this point that our adversary system of criminal proceedings commences, distinguishing itself at the outset from the inquisitorial system recognized in some countries. Under the system of warnings we delineate today or under any other system which may be devised and found effective, the safeguards to be erected about the privilege must come into play at this point. . . .

\* \* \* \* \* \* \* \* \* \* \* \* \* \* \* \* \* \* \* \* \* \* \* \* \* \* \* \* \* \*

*Reflections and Suggestions:*

1. Do you agree with Warren that custodial police interrogations contain "inherently compelling pressures"? Why or why not?
2. Warren said that "to permit a full opportunity to exercise the privilege against self-incrimination, the accused must be adequately and effectively apprised of his rights." Do you agree that such information should be supplied by the police? If you disagree, what alternatives do you suggest?
3. List the Miranda safeguards. Discuss each in light of the contribution it makes to ensuring fundamentally fair criminal-justice procedures.
4. If the police fail to Mirandize a suspect and he confesses, should the non-Mirandized confession be admissable in court? Before responding, imagine several scenarios in which the police could fail to inform a suspect of his rights. Discuss the implications of your position fully.

# PART VIII:
# THE CONSTITUTION IN
# RECENT TIMES

# CHAPTER 37

## NEW YORK TIMES CO. V. UNITED STATES

### 403 U.S. 713; 91 S.Ct. 2140; 29 L.Ed. 2d 820 (1971)

In the course of the escalation of the American military effort in Vietnam, Secretary of Defense Robert McNamara ordered an internal study of how the United States became involved in the conflict. This top secret study was entitled, "History of the U.S. Decision-Making Process on Viet Nam Policy." Daniel Ellsberg, a Pentagon employee, gave copies of the study to *The New York Times* and the *Washington Post. The New York Times* began to publish excerpts from these so-called "Pentagon Papers." The Justice Department obtained injunctions enjoining *The Times,* the *Washington Post,* and the *Boston Globe* from publishing additional installments on grounds that such publication would harm national security. The Supreme Court lifted the injunctions by a 6-to-3 vote.

The decision was handed down in *Per Curiam* fashion. All nine justices wrote opinions, totaling over eleven-thousand words (the Pentagon Papers themselves ran seven-thousand pages). The justices constructed their arguments carefully for fear that they might otherwise damage the President's authority to safeguard classified information. Ultimately, however, they could not endorse the Justice Department's attempt at prior restraint in light of First-Amendment considerations.

* * * * * * * * * * * * * * * * * * * * * * * * * * * *

*Per Curiam.*

"Any system of prior restraints of expression comes to this Court bearing a heavy presumption against its constitutional validity." *Bantam Books, Inc. v. Sullivan* (1963); see also *Near v. Minnesota* (1931). The Government "thus carries a heavy burden of showing justification for the imposition of such a restraint." *Organization for a Better Austin v. Keefe* (1973). . . .

Mr. Justice Black, whom Mr. Justice Douglas joins, concurring, stated in part:

. . . . [I]t is unfortunate that some of my Bretheren are apparently willing to hold that the publication of news may sometimes be enjoined. Such a holding would make a shambles of the First Amendment. . . .

. . . . Madison and the other Framers of the First Amendment, able men that they were, wrote in language they earnestly believed could never be misunderstood: "Congress shall make no law . . . abridging the freedom of the press. . . ." Both the history and language of the First Amendment support the view that the press must be left free to publish news, whatever the source, without censorship, injunctions, or prior restraints.

In the First Amendment the Founding Fathers gave the free press the protection it must have to fulfill its essential role in our democracy. The press was to serve the governed, not the governors. The Government's power to censor the press was abolished so that the press would remain forever free to censure the Government. . . . In revealing the working of government that led to the Viet Nam war, the newspapers nobly did precisely that which the Founders hoped and trusted they would do.

. . . . To find that the President has "inherent power" to halt the publication of news by resort to the courts would wipe out the First Amendment and destroy the fundamental liberty and security of the very people the Government hopes to make "secure.". . .

The word "security" is a broad, vague generality whose contours should not be invoked to abrogate the fundamental law embodied in the First Amendment . . . .

Mr. Justice Douglas, whom Mr. Justice Black joins, concurring, stated in part:

. . . . [T]he First Amendment provides that "Congress shall make no law . . . abridging the freedom of speech or of the press." That leaves, in my view, no room for governmental restraint on the press.

. . . . The Government says that it has inherent powers to . . . obtain an injunction to protect [the] national interest, which in this case is alleged to be national security.

*Near v. Minnesota* repudiated that expansive doctrine in no uncertain terms.

. . . . Secrecy in government is fundamentally anti-democratic . . . Open debate and discussion of public issues are vital to our national health. . . .

Mr. Justice Brennan, concurring, stated in part:

. . . . [T]he First Amendment tolerates absolutely no prior judicial restraints of the press predicated upon surmise or conjecture that untoward consequence may result. . . . [T]here is a single, extremely narrow class of cases in which the First Amendment's ban on prior judicial restraint may be overridden . . . [S]uch cases may arise only when the Nation "is at war," *Schenck v. United States* (1919), during which times "no one would question but that a government might prevent actual obstruction to its recruiting service or the publication of the sailing dates of transports or the number and location of troops." *Near v. Minnesota* (1931). Even if the present world situation were assumed to be tantamount to a time of war, or if the power of presently available armaments would justify even in peacetime the suppression of information that would set in motion a nuclear holocaust, in neither of these actions has the Government presented or even alleged that publication of . . . the material at issue would cause the happening of an event of that nature. . . . Unless and until the Government has clearly made out its case, the First Amendment commands that no injunction may issue.

Mr. Justice Stewart, whom Mr. Justice White joins, concurring, stated in part:

In the absence of the governmental checks and balances present in other areas of our national life, the only effective restraint upon executive policy and power in the areas of national defense and international affairs may lie in an enlightened citizenry—in an informed and critical public opinion which alone can here protect the values of democratic government. For this reason, it is perhaps here that a press that is alert, aware, and free most vitally serves the basic purpose of the First Amendment. For without an informed and free press there cannot be an enlightened people.

Yet it is elementary that the successful conduct of international diplomacy and the maintenance of an effective national defense require both confidentiality and secrecy. . . .

. . . .We are asked . . . to prevent the publication by two newspapers of material that the Executive Branch insists should not, in the national interest, be published. I am convinced that the Executive is correct with respect to some of the documents involved. But I cannot say that disclosure of any of them will surely result in direct, immediate, and irreparable damage to our Nation or its people. That being so, there can under the First Amendment be but one judicial resolution of the issues before us. I join the judgments of the Court.

Mr. Justice White, whom Mr. Justice Stewart joins, concurring, stated in part:

. . . .I do not say that in no circumstances would the First Amendment permit an injunction against publishing information about government plans or operations. Nor . . . can I deny that revelation of these documents will do substantial damage to public interests. . . . But I nevertheless agree that the United States has not satisfied the very heavy burden which it must meet to warrant an injunction against publication in these cases. . . .

The Government's position is simply stated: The responsibility of the Executive for the conduct of foreign affairs and for the security of the Nation is so basic that the President is entitled to an injunction against publication of a newspaper whenever he can convince a court that the information to be revealed threatens "grave and irreparable" injury to the public interest. . . .

At least in the absence of legislation by Congress, based on its own investigations and findings, I am quite unable to agree that the inherent powers of the Executive and the courts . . . authorize remedies having such sweeping potential for inhibiting publications by the press. . . .

. . . .That the Government mistakenly chose to proceed by injunction does not mean that it could not successfully proceed in another way.

. . . .It is . . . clear that Congress [in considering the Espionage Act in 1917] has addressed itself to the problem of protecting the security of the country and the national defense from unauthorized disclosure of potentially damaging information. . . . It has not, however, authorized the injunctive remedy against threatened publication. It has apparently been satisfied to rely on criminal sanctions and their deterrent effect on the responsible as well as the irresponsible press. . . .

Mr. Justice Marshall, concurring, stated in part:

. . . .[I]t is clear that Congress has specifically rejected passing legislation that would have clearly given the President the power he seeks here and made the current activity of the newspapers unlawful. When Congress specifically declines to make conduct unlawful it is not for this Court to redecide those issues—to overrule Congress.

Mr. Chief Justice Burger, dissenting, stated in part:

....This case is not simple ... We do not know the facts of the case....

I suggest we are in this posture because these cases have been conducted in unseemly haste....

The newspapers make a derivative claim under the First Amendment; they denominate this right as the public right-to-know; by implication, the *Times* asserts a sole trusteeship of that right by virtue of its journalistic "scoop." ... A great issue of this kind should be tried in a judicial atmosphere conducive to thoughtful reflective deliberation, especially when haste ... is unwarranted in light of the long period the *Times*, by its own choice, deferred publication.

It is not disputed that the *Times* has had unauthorized possession of the documents for three to four months, during which it has had its expert analysts studying them, presumably digesting them and preparing the material for publication.... No doubt this was for a good reason; the analysis of 7,000 pages of complex material drawn from a vastly greater volume of material would inevitably take time and the writing of good news stories takes time. But why should ... judges [now] be placed under needless pressure? ...

....[W]e literally do not know what we are acting on. As I see it we have been forced to deal with litigation concerning rights of great magnitude without an adequate record, and surely without time for adequate treatment either in the prior proceedings or in this Court....

....I am in general agreement with much of what Mr. Justice White has expressed with respect to penal sanctions concerning communication or retention of documents or information relating to the national defense.

We all crave speedier judicial processes but when judges are pressured as in these cases the result is a parody of the judicial process.

Mr. Justice Harlan, whom the Chief Justice and Mr. Justice Blackmun join, dissenting, stated in part:

These cases forcefully call to mind the wise admonition of Mr. Justice Holmes, dissenting in *Northern Securities Company v. United States* (1904): "Great cases like hard cases make bad law." ...

With all respect, I consider that the Court has been almost irresponsibly feverish in dealing with these cases....

The power to evaluate the "pernicious influence" of premature disclosure is not ... lodged in the Executive alone. I agree that, in performance of its duty to protect the values of the First Amendment against political pressures, the judiciary must review the initial Executive determination to the point of satisfying itself that the subject matter of the dispute does lie within the proper compass of the President's foreign relations power. . . . Moreover, the judiciary may properly insist that the determination that disclosure of the subject matter would irreparably impair the national security be made by the head of the Executive Department concerned—here the Secretary of State or the Secretary of Defense—after actual personal consideration by that officer. . . . But in my judgment the judiciary may not properly go beyond these two inquiries and redetermine for itself the probable impact of the disclosure on the national security. . . . Pending further hearings . . . I would continue the restraints on publication. I cannot believe that the doctrine prohibiting prior restraints reaches to the point of preventing courts from maintaining the status quo long enough to act responsibly in matters of such national importance as those involved here.

Mr. Justice Blackmun, dissenting, stated in part:
. . . .[The] . . . courts have been pressed into hurried decision of profound constitutional issues on inadequately developed and largely assumed facts without the careful deliberation that, hopefully, should characterize the American judicial process. . . .

* * * * * * * * * * * * * * * * * * * * * * * * * * * * *

*Discussion Points:*

1. Compare and contrast the Court's decisions in *Schenck* and *Near* with its decision in this case.
2. Why did Black oppose restraint of publication of the "Pentagon Papers"? Compare his views on "security" in this case with his views on "privacy" in his dissenting opinion in *Griswold*.
3. Why did Douglas oppose restraint of publication?
4. Why did Brennan oppose restraint of publication? Did he think that the First Amendment would *ever* permit prior restraint? Explain.
5. What position did White and Stewart take? Did they think that injunctions against publication are ever justified? What was the potential relevance of congressional legislation on the matter to these justices? If the government is unable to obtain a restraining order, what other options did White and Stewart see for dealing with the publishers themselves?
6. What was Marshall's position?
7. Why did Burger dissent? Why did Harlan and Blackmun dissent?
8. In the present case, six justices opposed the restraining orders

and three justices dissented. But several members of the majority suggested that they might support restraints on publication under certain conditions. In light of these views, speculate about the kinds of circumstances that could produce a majority in *favor* of restraints on publication.

9. Do you agree with the Court's decision to lift the restraining orders in this case? Why or why not?

# CHAPTER 38

# EQUAL RIGHTS AMENDMENT (1972)

As part of an overall campaign to end discrimination against women, a demand grew to ensure women's equality under the law through an Equal Rights Amendment to the Constitution. After languishing in Congress for 49 years, two-thirds of both houses of Congress approved the Amendment and it was submitted to the states on March 22, 1972. Ratification of constitutional amendments requires the approval of three-fourths of the state legislatures. Thirty-eight states, therefore, were needed to ratify. The first state ratified the Amendment only 32 minutes after it was submitted and a total of thirty states approved it in the first year. But opponents of the Equal Rights Amendment gained momentum and the ratification drive stalled as concerns about the implications of the Amendment mounted. In October 1978, Congress extended the original seven-year deadline for ratification until June 30, 1982. In spite of the extension, the Amendment fell three votes short of passage.

\* \* \* \* \* \* \* \* \* \* \* \* \* \* \* \* \* \* \* \* \* \* \* \* \* \* \*

## AMENDMENT XXVII (Proposed)

SECTION 1: Equality of rights under the law shall not be denied or abridged by the United States or by any State on account of sex.

SECTION 2: The Congress shall have the power to enforce, by appropriate legislation, the provisions of this article.

SECTION 3: This amendment shall take effect two years after the date of ratification.

\* \* \* \* \* \* \* \* \* \* \* \* \* \* \* \* \* \* \* \* \* \* \* \* \* \* \*

*Discussion Points:*

1. What kinds of discrimination have women been subjected to in the United States? Are women discriminated against at present? In what ways and by whom? Some maintain that women do not

receive equal pay for equal work (i.e., that men performing the same or equivalent jobs as women are better paid), that women face special obstacles regarding career choice and advancement, that there are gender-based inequities affecting pensions, social security, and so on. Are these claims accurate? Explain. If you think that such discrimination exists, what steps should be taken to deal with it?

2. Debate over the Equal Rights Amendment has sometimes broadened to include discussion of sexism in more general terms. Consider efforts to change gender-distinctive language (e.g., Ms. instead of Miss or Mrs., chair or chairperson instead of chairman, Hurricane Albert instead of Hurricane Alice, and so on). Consider also efforts to eliminate sexual stereotypes in advertising, entertainment, and popular culture (e.g., office brochures that show all the women sitting at typewriters and all the men in business suits). Think of some additional examples. Are such matters important? Explain. What, if anything, should be done to deal with such issues?

3. Some opponents of the Equal Rights Amendment charged that it would force women to work outside the home to provide half of the family's income, invalidate laws barring homosexual marriage, and eliminate separate prison cells, hospital rooms, locker rooms, and restrooms for men and women. Defenders of the Amendment called these allegations ludicrous and deceptive. What do you think? In light of the language of the proposed Amendment, were these charges reasonable and realistic? Why?

4. Opponents of the Equal Rights Amendment said it would abolish laws that protect women in the labor market. Supporters countered that protective legislation could be enacted to cover men too. Or, they said that the protective laws actually hindered women. When women were "protected" against working long hours or lifting heavy weights, men were protected against job competition from individual women who were strong enough to perform the tasks in question. What do you think? Explain your position.

5. Some opponents of the Equal Rights Amendment said that it would require that men and women be treated the same in all respects. Supporters of the Amendment noted that equality is not necessarily identical to sameness. It is possible to regard citizens as equals before the law while differentiating among them when there is some legitimate reason to do so. We deny the right to vote, drink, retire, and drive to ten-year-old children because it is

reasonable to do so. Likewise, it may prove reasonable to give Widow Jones a special tax break. But this decision should not be based on sexist stereotypes and generalizations. Instead, a careful examination of individual circumstances may reveal that Widower Smith deserves the same kind of tax break. What do you think? Why?

6. The Fourteenth Amendment already says that "No State shall . . . deny to any person in its jurisdiction the equal protection of the laws." Some opponents of the Equal Rights Amendment said that it was unnecessary; an equal rights amendment is already in the Constitution and it can provide the constitutional justification for the kinds of actions that are advocated by the Equal Rights Amendment's proponents. Do you agree that the Equal Rights Amendment is redundant and would add unnecessary clutter to the Constitution? Why or why not?

7. What kinds of laws should be enacted and what other kinds of steps should be taken to combat legal—as opposed to social—forms of sex discrimination? Give some examples.

8. Should the Equal Rights Amendment have been ratified? Why or why not? Should the drive to enact the Amendment continue and should it be ratified in the near future? Why or why not?

# CHAPTER 39

## MILLER V. CALIFORNIA
### 413 U.S. 15; 93 S.Ct. 2067; 37 L.Ed. 419 (1973)

In *Schenck,* Justice Holmes observed that statements that pose a "clear and present danger" that they will produce "substantive evils that Congress has a right to prevent" can be restricted without violating the First Amendment. In later years, the Court was asked to decide if the First Amendment protected obscene materials. Such materials are offensive to many. Certain political statements can be offensive to majority opinion too, but courts usually find that they are protected by the First Amendment because they have social importance and value. Can the same be said of obscene materials?

In *Roth v. United States* (354 U.S. 476, 1957), the Court upheld the conviction of a man charged with violating a federal obscenity law. The Court defined obscene material as that "which deals with sex in a manner appealing to prurient interest." The test of obscenity, the majority agreed, is "whether to the average person, applying contemporary community standards, the dominant theme of the material taken as a whole appeals to prurient interest." Such material, the Court found, is not constitutionally protected as speech or press because it is "utterly without redeeming social importance."

In *Memoirs v. Massachusetts* (383 U.S. 413, 1966), a state court had banned a book as obscene although the court acknowledged that it might have "some minimal literary value." The Supreme Court ruled that a book could be banned only if "(a) the dominant theme of the material taken as a whole appeals to a prurient interest in sex; (b) the material is patently offensive because it affronts contemporary community standards relating to the description or representation of sexual matters; and (c) the material is utterly without redeeming social value." Even though the book was deemed offensive, it was not "utterly without redeeming social value." For this reason, the Supreme Court reversed the state court.

In the case below, the Court relaxed these standards and made it relatively easier for a local community to restrict such materials. In *Miller,* sexually-explicit materials had been mailed to persons who had not requested nor indicated any interest in receiving such mailings. They complained to the police and California applied its criminal obscenity law to the situation. By a five-to-four vote, the Court upheld the conviction.

\* \* \* \* \* \* \* \* \* \* \* \* \* \* \* \* \* \* \* \* \* \* \* \* \* \*

Mr. Chief Justice Burger delivered the opinion of the Court, saying in part:

. . . .In *Roth* . . . the Court sustained a conviction under a federal statute punishing the mailing of "obscene, lewd, lascivious or filthy . . ." materials. The key to that holding was the Court's rejection of the claim that obscene materials were protected by the First Amendment. Five justices joined in the opinion stating: ". . . .[I]mplicit in the history of the First Amendment is the rejection of obscenity as utterly without redeeming social importance." . . .

. . . [I]n *Memoirs* . . . the Court veered sharply away from the *Roth* concept and . . . articulated a new test of obscenity. The plurality held that. . . . "[a] book cannot be proscribed unless it is found to be *utterly* without redeeming social value."

While *Roth* presumed "obscenity" to be "utterly without redeeming social value," *Memoirs* required that to prove obscenity it must be affirmatively established that the material is "*utterly* without redeeming social value." Thus . . . the *Memoirs* plurality produced a drastically altered test that called on the prosecution to prove a negative, i.e., that the material was "*utterly* without redeeming social value"—a burden virtually impossible to discharge under our criminal standards of proof. . . .

. . . .[T]he *Memoirs* test has been abandoned as unworkable . . . and no member of the Court today supports the *Memoirs* foundation.

This much has been categorically settled by the Court, that obscene material is unprotected by the First Amendment. . . . We acknowledge, however, the inherent dangers of undertaking to regulate any form of expression. State statutes designed to regulate obscene materials must be carefully limited. . . .

The basic guidelines for the trier of fact must be: (a) whether "the average person, applying contemporary community standards" would find that the work, taken as a whole, appeals to the prurient interest. . . . (b) whether the work depicts or describes, in a patently offensive way, sexual conduct specifically defined by the applicable state law, and (c) whether the work, taken as a whole, lacks serious literary, artistic, political, or scientific value. We do not adopt as a constitutional standard the *"utterly* without redeeming social value" test of *Memoirs*. . . .

. . . .At a minimum, prurient, patently offensive depiction or description of sexual conduct must have serious literary, artistic, political, or scientific value to merit First Amendment protection. . . . For example, medical books for the education of physicians and related personnel necessarily use graphic illustrations and descriptions of human anatomy. In resolving the inevitably sensitive questions of fact and law, we must continue to rely on the jury system. . . .

Under a national Constitution, fundamental First Amendment limitations on the powers of the States do not vary from community to community, but this does not meant that there are, or should or can be, fixed, uniform, national standards of precisely what appeals to the "prurient interest" or is "patently offensive." . . . [O]ur nation is simply too big and too diverse for this Court to reasonably expect that such standards could be articulated for all 50 states in a single formulation. . . .

It is neither realistic nor constitutionally sound to read the First Amendment as requiring that the people of Maine or Mississippi accept public depiction of conduct found tolerable in Las Vegas or New York City. . . . People in different States vary in their tastes and attitudes and this diversity is not to be strangled by the absolutism or imposed uniformity. . . . We hold that the requirement that the jury evaluate the materials with reference to "contemporary standards of the State of California" serves this protective purpose and is constitutionally adequate. . . .

In sum we (a) reaffirm the *Roth* holding that obscene material is not protected by the First Amendment, (b) hold that such material can be regulated by the States . . . without a showing that the material is *"utterly* without redeeming social value," and (c) hold that obscenity is to be determined by applying "contemporary community standards," . . . not "national standards.". . .

* * * * * * * * * * * * * * * * * * * * * * * * * * * * * * * * *

*Discussion Points:*

1. How did Burger distinguish *Memoirs* from *Roth*? Explain.
2. Obscene material is not protected by the First Amendment. What are the "basic guidelines" for determining if material is "obscene"?

3. Burger believed that it would be unrealistic to insist on a single, uniform, national standard to evaluate offensive material. Instead, he advocated the use of diverse standards developed by the local communities involved. Discuss the implications of this approach. Do you agree with Burger that local communities should be free to develop their own standards? Why or why not?

4. Compare and contrast *Roth, Memoirs,* and *Miller.* Should communities be able to restrict materials only if they are "utterly" without redeeming social value or should they be able to restrict materials that possess some—but not "serious"—social value? Discuss the implications of each approach. Which position do you favor? Why?

# CHAPTER 40

## *ROE V. WADE*

### 410 U.S. 113; 93 S.Ct. 705; 35 L.Ed. 147 (1973)

In *Griswold,* the Court invalidated a state birth control law as infringing upon the "right of privacy." The Court inferred this right from the "penumbras" surrounding specific constitutional guarantees. The Ninth Amendment was also viewed as a source. Eight years later, the Court was asked to decide if this right protected a woman's choice to obtain an abortion.

Texas law prohibited all abortions unless they were needed to preserve the woman's life or health. Jane Roe (the pseudonym used by a Dallas woman) challenged the constitutionality of these anti-abortion statutes. Since her life was not threatened by a continuation of her pregnancy, she was unable to obtain a legal abortion in Texas. By a seven-to-two vote, the Court ruled in her favor, finding that the law violated her privacy right.

Writing for the Court, Justice Blackmun said that the Due Process Clause of the Fourteenth Amendment protects the right of privacy and this right, he added, includes a woman's qualified right to terminate her pregnancy. He observed that the state's interests must be taken into account as well. These interests include protecting the woman's health and protecting potential human life in the form of a viable fetus.

Blackmun reasoned that early-term abortions are relatively safe and the fetus is not yet viable. At this point, the state's interest in the matter is slight. Later-term abortions, however, pose greater risks to the woman's health. Further, the possibility of fetal viability increases at these later stages. For these reasons, the state's interests become weightier during the later stages of pregnancy. In this light, Blackmun concluded that abortion decisions should be left to the woman and her physician during the first three months of pregnancy. During the second three months, the state can adopt reasonable regulations to protect maternal health and fetuses approaching viability. During the last three months, the state can regulate abortions and even prohibit them unless they are necessary to preserve the woman's life or health.

Blackmun's opinion, therefore, permitted regulations that reasonably relate to the "preservation and protection of maternal health" and regulations that protect "fetal life after viability." As such, states could legislate regarding the qualifications of the person performing the abortion, the nature of the facility in which the abortion is performed, and so on. And, in the case of fetal viability, states could prohibit abortions except where necessary to preserve the life or health of the mother. Following *Roe v. Wade*, various regulations were enacted and the Court had several opportunities to review them.

The Court invalidated many state and national regulations. An exception involved the Hyde Amendment that prohibited the use of federal funds for abortions unless they were necessary to save the mother's life. The Court upheld these restrictions in *Maher v. Roe* (432 U.S. 464, 1977) and *Harris v. McRae* (448 U.S. 297, 1980). Justices Stevens, Brennan, and Marshall wrote sharp dissents. In *Harris,* Marshall remarked, for example, that these decisions "deny to the poor the constitutional right recognized in *Roe v. Wade.* . . ."

Then, in *Akron v. Akron Center for Reproductive Health* (462 U.S. 416, 1983), the Court faced abortion regulations that required the following: 1) all abortions performed after the first trimester were to be performed only in hospitals; 2) parents of unmarried minors would be notified before such minors could have abortions; 3) the physician would be required to make certain statements to the patient, including that "the unborn child is a human life from the moment of conception"; and 4) except in an emergency, a twenty-four hour delay would be required between the signing of the consent form and the actual abortion.

Writing for a six-to-three majority, Justice Powell concluded that these regulations failed to advance legitimate state interests. First, a second-trimester abortion "costs more than twice as much in a hospital as in a clinic." Citing statements by the American Public Health Association and the American College of Obstetricians and Gynecologists that such abortions may be performed safely on an outpatient basis in nonhospital facilities, Powell concluded that the regulations unreasonably limited a woman's ability to obtain an abortion. Second, he objected that Akron should not make "a blanket determination that *all* minors under the age of fifteen are too immature to make this decision or that an abortion may never be in the minor's best interests without parental approval." Third, he ruled that the "informed consent" requirement that certain statements be made to the pregnant woman intruded on her physician's discretion. Fourth, he found that Akron failed to show a legitimate interest in its "arbitrary and inflexible" twenty-four hour waiting period. Citing the importance of respect for precedent, Powell reaffirmed *Roe* and invalidated the challenged regulations.

Justice O'Connor, joined by Justices White and Rehnquist, dissented. She assailed the logic of Justice Blackmun's majority opinion in *Roe* in the process, stating that *Akron* "graphically illustrates why the trimester approach is a completely unworkable method." She pointed out that improvements in medical technology "will move *forward* the point at which the state may regulate for reasons of maternal health" and will "move *backward* the point of viability at which the State may proscribe abortions except when necessary to preserve the life and health of the mother." In other words, medical improvements will make later-term abortions safe while simultaneously making fetal viability occur earlier. In this sense, she claimed that "[t]he *Roe* framework . . . is clearly on collision course with itself."

A few years later, the Court again invalidated state restrictions on abortions in *Thornbugh v. American College of Obstetricians and Gynecologists* (90 L.Ed. 2d 779, 1986). This time the vote was five to four. Justice Blackmun was joined by Justices Brennan, Marshall, Powell, and Stevens in finding that the challenged state regulations violated a woman's fundamental right to an abortion. Justices Rehnquist and White, who dissented in *Roe*, again dissented. They were joined by Justice O'Connor and by Chief Justice Burger, a member of the original *Roe* majority.

As the 1980s drew to a close, speculation focused on how the Court would treat the *Roe* precedent. President Reagan, a pro-life advocate, made four Supreme Court appointments—Chief Justice Rehnquist and Justices O'Connor, Scalia, and Kennedy. As such, only three Justices—Blackmun, Brennan, and Marshall—remained from the *Roe* majority.

In *Webster v. Reproductive Health Services* (106 L.Ed. 2d 410, 1989), the Court reviewed a Missouri law that said that human life begins at conception, prohibited the use of public facilities and employees to perform abortions not necessary to save the mother's life, proscribed the use of public funds for "encouraging or counseling" a woman to have an abortion not necessary to save her life, and required the physician to perform tests to determine if the unborn child was viable. Without overruling *Roe,* the Court *upheld* the legislation. Chief Justice Rehnquist was joined by Justices White, O'Connor, Scalia, and Kennedy in sustaining these regulations. The upshot of the case was that it made it relatively easier for states to restrict abortions. Justices Blackmun, Brennan, Marshall, and Stevens were in the minority. Blackmun, the author of the *Roe* opinion, said: "Today, *Roe v. Wade* and the fundamental constitutional right of women to decide whether to terminate a pregnancy, survive but are not secure." He claimed that the Court's decision invited states to enact increasingly restrictive abortion laws "in order to provoke more and more test cases" in the hope of providing the Court with an opportunity to overrule *Roe* squarely and return the matter to the states. He characterized the lead opinion as "deceptive" and accused the Court of "foment[ing] disregard for the law and for our standing decisions."

Clearly, *Roe v. Wade* continues to generate controversy. Regardless of its future fate, the case illustrates the importance of changes in Court personnel.

\* \* \* \* \* \* \* \* \* \* \* \* \* \* \* \* \* \* \* \* \* \* \* \* \* \* \* \*

Mr. Justice Blackmun delivered the opinion of the Court, saying in part:

... We forthwith acknowledge our awareness of the sensitive and emotional nature of the abortion controversy, of the vigorous opposing views, even among physicians, and of the deep and seemingly absolute convictions that the subject inspires. One's philosophy, one's experiences, one's exposure to the raw edges of human existence, one's religious training, one's attitudes toward moral standards ... are all likely to influence and to color one's thinking and conclusions about abortion.

In addition, population growth, pollution, poverty, and racial overtones tend to complicate and not to simplify the problem.

Our task, of course, is to resolve the issue by constitutional measurement free of emotion and of predeliction. We seek earnestly to do this, and because we do, we have inquired into, and in this opinion place more emphasis upon, medical and medical-legal history and what that history reveals about man's attitudes toward the abortive procedure. ...

The Texas statutes that concern us here are Arts. 1191–1194 and 1196 of the State Penal Code. These make it a crime to "procure an abortion," as therein defined, or to attempt one, except with respect to "an abortion procured or attempted by medical advice for the purpose of saving the life of the mother" ....

The principal thrust of appellant's attack on the Texas statutes is that they improperly invade a right, said to be possessed by the pregnant woman, to choose to terminate her pregnancy. Appellant would discover this right in the concept of personal, marital, familial, and sexual privacy said to be protected by the Bill of Right or its penumbras ... or among those rights reserved to the people by the Ninth Amendment... Before addressing this claim, we feel it desirable briefly to survey, in several aspects, the history of abortion, for such insight as that history may afford us, and then to examine the state purposes and interests behind the criminal abortion laws.

It perhaps is not generally appreciated that the respective criminal abortion laws in effect in a majority of States today are of relatively recent vintage... [They] are not of ancient or even common law origin. Instead, they derive from statutory changes effected, for the most part, in the latter half of the nineteenth century....

Three reasons have been advanced to explain historically the enactment of criminal abortion laws in the 19th century and to justify their continued existence.

It has been argued occasionally that these laws were the product of a Victorian social concern to discourage illicit sexual conduct. Texas, however, does not advance this justification in the present case, and it appears that no court or commentator has taken the argument seriously....

A second reason is concerned with abortion as a medical procedure. When most criminal abortion laws were first enacted, the procedure was a hazardous one for the woman.... Abortion mortality was high. Even after 1900, and perhaps until as late as the development of antibiotics in the 1940s, standard modern techniques such as dilation and curettage were not nearly so safe as they are today. Thus it has been argued that a State's real concern ... was to protect the pregnant woman, that is, to restrain her from submitting to a procedure that placed her life in serious jeopardy.

Modern medical techniques have altered this situation. Appellants and various *amici* refer to medical data indicating that abortion in early pregnancy, that is, prior to the end of the first trimester, although not without its risks, is now relatively safe. Mortality rates for women undergoing early abortions, where the procedure is legal, appear to be as low as or lower than the risks for normal childbirth. Consequently, any interest of the State in protecting the woman from an inherently hazardous procedure, except when it would be equally dangerous for her to forego it, has largely disappeared. Of course, important state interests in the area of health and medical standards do remain. The State has a legitimate interest in seeing to it that abortion, like any other medical procedure, is performed under circumstances that insure maximum safety for the patient. This interest obviously extends at least to the performing physician and his staff, to the facilities involved, to the availability of aftercare, and to adequate provision for any complication or emergency that might arise. The prevalence of high mortality rates at illegal "abortion mills" strengthens, rather than weakens, the State's interest in regulating the conditions under which abortions are performed. Moreover, the risk to the woman increases as her pregnancy continues. Thus the State retains a definite interest in protecting the woman's own health and safety when an abortion is proposed at a late stage of pregnancy.

The third reason is the State's interest—some phrase it in terms of duty—in protecting prenatal life. Some of the argument for this justification rests on the theory that a new life is present from the moment of conception. The State's interest and general obligation to protect life then extends, it is argued, to prenatal life. Only when the life of the pregnant mother herself is at stake, balanced against the life she carries within her, should the interest of the embryo or fetus not prevail. Logically, of course, a legitimate State interest in this area need not stand or fall on acceptance of the belief that life begins at conception or at some other point prior to live birth. In assessing the State's interest, recognition may be given to the less rigid claim that as long as at least *potential* life is involved, the State may assert interests beyond the protection of the pregnant woman alone. . . .

The Constitution does not explicitly mention any right of privacy. In a line of decisions, however, . . . the Court has recognized that a right of personal privacy, or a guarantee of certain areas or zones of privacy, does exist under the Constitution. In varying contexts the Court or individual Justices have indeed found at least the roots of that right in the First Amendment; in the Fourth and Fifth Amendments . . .; in the penumbras of the Bill of Rights; in the Ninth Amendment; or in the concept of liberty guaranteed by . . . the Fourteenth Amendment. These decisions make it clear that only personal rights that can be deemed "fundamental" or "implicit in the concept of ordered liberty" are included in this guarantee of personal privacy. They also make it clear that the right has some extension to activities relating to marriage, procreation, [and] contraception. . . . [case citations omitted]

This right of privacy, whether it be founded in the Fourteenth Amendment's concept of personal liberty and restrictions upon state action, as we feel it is, or, as the District Court determined, in the Ninth Amendment's reservation of rights to the people, is broad enough to encompass a woman's decision whether or not to terminate her pregnancy. The detriment that the State would impose upon the pregnant woman by denying this choice altogether is apparent. Specific and direct harm medically diagnosable even in early pregnancy may be involved. Maternity, or additional offspring, may force upon the woman a distressful life and future. Psychological harm may be imminent. Mental and physical health may be taxed by child care. There is also the distress, for all concerned, associated with the unwanted child, and there is the problem of bringing a child into a family already unable, psychologically or otherwise, to care for it. In other cases, as in this one, the additional difficulties and continuing stigma of unwed motherhood may be involved. All these are factors the woman and her responsible physician necessarily will consider in consultation.

On the basis of elements such as these, appellants and some *amici* argue that the woman's right is absolute and that she is entitled to terminate her pregnancy at whatever time, in whatever way, and for whatever reason she alone chooses. With this we do not agree. Appellants' arguments that Texas either has no valid interest at all in regulating the abortion decision, or no interest strong enough to support any limitation upon the woman's sole determination, is unpersuasive. The Court's decisions recognizing a right of privacy also acknowledge that some state regulation in areas protected by that right is appropriate. As noted above, a State may properly assert important interests in safeguarding health, in maintaining medical standards, and in protecting potential life. At some point in pregnancy, these respective interests become sufficiently compelling to sustain regulation of the factors that govern the abortion decision. The privacy right involved, therefore, cannot be said to be absolute. . . .

We therefore conclude that the right of personal privacy includes the abortion decision, but that this right is not unqualified and must be considered against important state interests in regulation. . . .

The appellee and certain *amici* argue that the fetus is a "person" within the language and meaning of the Fourteenth Amendment. In support of this they outline at length and in detail the well-known facts of fetal development. If this suggestion of personhood is established, the appellant's case, of course, collapses, for the fetus' right to life is then guaranteed specifically by the Amendment. The appellant conceded as much on reargument. On the other hand, the appellee conceded on reargument that no case could be cited that holds that a fetus is a person within the meaning of the Fourteenth Amendment.

The Constitution does not define "person" in so many words. Section 1 of the Fourteenth Amendment contains three references to "person." The first, in defining "citizens," speaks of "persons born or naturalized in the United States." The word also appears both in the

Due Process Clause and in the Equal Protection Clause. "Person" is used in other places in the Constitution.... in nearly all these instances, the use of the word is such that it has application only post-natally. None indicates, with any assurance, that it has any possible pre-natal application....

Texas urges that, apart from the Fourteenth Amendment, life begins at conception and is present, throughout pregnancy, and that, therefore, the State has a compelling interest in protecting that life from and after conception. We need not resolve the difficult question of when life begins. When those trained in the respective disciplines of medicine, philosophy, and theology are unable to arrive at any consensus, the judiciary, at this point in the development of man's knowledge, is not in a position to speculate as to the answer....

In areas other than criminal abortion the law has been reluctant to endorse any theory that life, as we recognize it, begins before live birth or to accord legal rights to the unborn except in narrowly defined situations and except when the rights are contingent upon live birth....

In short, the unborn have never been recognized in the law as persons in the whole sense....

In view of all this, we do not agree that, by adopting one theory of life, Texas may override the rights of the pregnant woman that are at stake. We repeat, however, that the State does have an important and legitimate interest in preserving and protecting the health of the pregnant woman, whether she be a resident of the state or a nonresident who seeks medical consultation and treatment there, and that it has still another important and legitimate interest in protecting the potentiality of human life. These interests are separate and distinct. Each grows in substantiality as the woman approaches term and, at a point during pregnancy, each becomes "compelling."

With respect to the State's important and legitimate interest in the health of the mother, the "compelling" point, in the light of present medical knowledge, is at approximately the end of the first trimester. This is so because of the now established medical fact . . . that until the end of the first trimester mortality in abortion is less than mortality in normal childbirth. It follows that, from and after this point, a State may regulate the abortion procedure to the extent that the regulation reasonably relates to the preservation and protection of maternal health. Examples of permissible state regulation in this area are requirements as to the qualifications of the person who is to perform the abortion; as to the licensure of that person; as to the facility in which the procedure is to be performed, that is, whether it must be a hospital or may be a clinic or some other place of less-than-hospital status; as to the licensing of the facility; and the like.

This means, on the other hand, that for the period of pregnancy prior to this "compelling" point, the attending physician, in consultation with his patient, is free to determine without regulation by the State, that in his medical judgment the patient's pregnancy should be terminated. If that decision is reached, the judgment may be effectuated by an abortion free of interference by the State.

With respect to the State's important and legitimate interest in potential life, the "compelling" point is at viability. This is so because the fetus then presumably has the capability of meaningful life outside the mother's womb. State regulation protective of fetal life after viability thus has both logical and biological justifications. If the State is interested in protecting fetal life after viability, it may go so far as to proscribe abortion during that period except when it is necessary to preserve the life or health of the mother.

Measured against these standards, Art. 1196 of the Texas Penal Code, in restricting legal abortions to those "procured or attempted by medical advice for the purpose of saving the life of the mother," sweeps too broadly. The statute makes no distinction between abortions performed early in pregnancy and those performed later, and it limits to a single reason, "saving" the mother' life, the legal justifications for the procedure. The statute, therefore, cannot survive the constitutional attack made upon it here. . . .

To summarize and to repeat:

1. A state criminal abortion statute of the current Texas type, that excepts from criminality only a *life saving* procedure on behalf of the mother, without regard to pregnancy stage and without recognition of the other interests involved, is violative of the Due Process Clause of the Fourteenth Amendment.

(a) For the stage prior to approximately the end of the first trimester, the abortion decision and its effectuation must be left to the medical judgment of the pregnant woman's attending physician.

(b) For the stage subsequent to approximately the end of the first trimester, the State, in promoting its interest in the health of the mother, may, if it chooses, regulate the abortion procedure in ways that are reasonably related to maternal health.

(c) For the stage subsequent to viability the State, in promoting its interest in the potentiality of human life, may, if it chooses, regulate, and even proscribe, abortion except where it is necessary, in appropriate medical judgment, for the preservation of the life or health of the mother. . . .

\* \* \* \* \* \* \* \* \* \* \* \* \* \* \* \* \* \* \* \* \* \* \* \* \* \* \* \* \*

*Discussion Points:*

1. Compare *Roe* with *Griswold.* Where did the Court find the right of privacy in the respective cases? Do you agree that such a right exists? Do you agree with Blackmun that this right "is broad enough to encompass a woman's decision whether or not to terminate her pregnancy"? Why or why not?

2. What legitimate interests does the state have in such cases? Discuss and evaluate Blackmun's trimester approach. Is it sensible? Why or why not?

3. Did *Roe* legalize "abortion on demand," as its critics sometimes maintain? Explain.

4. Consider some of the political, social, and moral dimensions of abortion:

   a) Polls show that most people favor the right to abortion if the pregnancy resulted from rape or incest or when the mother's life is in jeopardy. Poll results are mixed regarding the right to abortion in general. Where do you stand? Why?

   b) Should abortion be legal if the woman is unmarried and marriage to the father is, for some reason, out of the question? Why or why not? Should it be legal if severe economic pressures make childbirth undesirable? Why or why not?

   c) If you think abortion should be illegal, what kinds of penalties should be imposed on women and physicians who violate these laws? Explain.

   d) Courts have upheld the congressional decision to deny federal Medicaid funding for abortions. Critics claim such policies discriminate against the poor because women who can afford to pay for their own abortions can still obtain them. What are your views on this issue?

   e) If *Roe* were overturned, what would happen? If new anti-abortion laws were enacted, would they be obeyed or would women obtain illegal—and perhaps unsafe—abortions? Should such considerations affect the Supreme Court as it reviews attempts by legislators to restrict abortions? Why or why not?

5. In her *Akron* dissent, Justice O'Connor said that "[i]n 1973, viability before 28 weeks was considered unusual." But she predicted that "fetal viability in the first trimester of pregnancy may be possible in the not too distant future." Sixteen years after *Roe,* however, it was still nearly impossible to save infants born before

the twenty-third week. Medical experts explain that fetal lungs are insufficiently developed before that time. In a brief filed in *Webster*, the American Medical Association said that "the earliest point at which an infant can survive has changed little" since *Roe*. Discuss O'Connor's argument. Consider the broader point of the relevance of medical science to judicial decision making in abortion cases.

# CHAPTER 41

## THE WAR POWERS RESOLUTION

### Public Law 93-149, 87 Stat. 555
### (November 7, 1973)

Article Two of the Constitution states that "The President shall be commander in chief of the army and navy of the United States, and of the militia of the several States, when called into the actual service of the United States. . ." The president is also empowered to make treaties and to appoint and receive ambassadors and other public ministers. In light of the need for the Nation to speak with a single and decisive voice when faced with external threats to national security, courts have usually supported presidents in their conduct of international relations. Recall, for example, Justice Sutherland's comment in *Curtiss-Wright* that "the President alone has the power to speak or listen as a representative of the nation." Also recall Sutherland's description of the "plenary and exclusive power of the President as the sole organ of the Federal government in the field of international relations." But such remarks should not lead us to lose sight of the fact that the Framers gave Congress explicit powers over foreign affairs too.

The Constitution requires that treaties be made "by and with the advice and consent of the Senate." Further, while the president is authorized to appoint ambassadors, he is to do so "by and with the consent of the Senate." Furthermore, Congress has the power to "declare war," to "raise and support armies," to "appropriat[e] . . . money" to that end, to "provide and maintain a navy," to "make rules for the government and regulation of the land and naval forces," to "provide for calling forth the militia," and so on. In short, while Article Two identifies the president as commander in chief of the armed forces, Article One (and parts of Article Two) make it clear that Congress has a real and legitimate diplomatic and military role too.

If Congress declares war, the president serves as commander in chief and is entitled to whatever tactical discretion that the position entails. But what if the president wants to deploy troops and Congress has *not* supplied a declaration of war? In today's world of inter-continental ballistic missiles and thermonuclear devices, it might not be possible for Congress to convene and provide the president with a declaration of war in time to meet an enemy attack. Does the Constitution have enough "slack" to cover such contingencies? If one supports the need for presidential command discretion, should that discretion be unbridled? What kinds of limits and congressional involvement would be feasible? Questions concerning the president's powers over the armed forces in the absence of declarations of war have generated much controversy.

In the summer and early fall of 1972, President Nixon expected that his National Security Advisor, Henry Kissinger, would be able to get a peace treaty with North Vietnam before the November elections. When that effort failed and the North Vietnamese proved unreceptive to new efforts in December, Nixon ordered a massive air strike that became known as the "Christmas Bombing." The size of the attack shocked many congressmen and an attempt soon began to limit the president's war powers in the absence of formal declarations of war. When the Watergate story began to unfold in the spring and summer of 1973, the President lost additional political support and sentiment to limit executive authority grew. Against this backdrop, the War Powers Resolution was approved by Congress. Nixon vetoed it on grounds that it unconstitutionally interfered with the President's discretionary powers as commander in chief. Congress overrode his veto on November 7, 1973.

The law attempts to spell out the conditions under which a president can deploy troops and commit them to involvement in "hostilities." The law tries to strike a balance between presidential and congressional war powers. It continues to stimulate lively debate as some urge that it be strengthened, while others urge that it be abolished.

\* \* \* \* \* \* \* \* \* \* \* \* \* \* \* \* \* \* \* \* \* \* \* \* \* \*

## SHORT TITLE

Section 1. This joint resolution may be cited as the "War Powers Resolution."

## PURPOSE AND POLICY

Sec. 2 (a) It is the purpose of this joint resolution to fulfill the interest of the framers of the Constitution ... and insure that the collective judgment of both the Congress and the president will apply to the introduction of United States armed forces into hostilities, or into situations where imminent involvement in hostilities is clearly indicated by the circumstances, and to the continued use of such forces in hostilities or in such situations.

(b) Under article I, section 8, of the Constitution, it is specifically provided that the Congress shall have the power to make all laws necessary and proper for carrying into execution, not only its own powers but also all other powers vested by the Constitution in the government of the United States, or in any department or officer thereof.

(c) The constitutional powers of the president as commander-in-chief to introduce United States armed forces into hostilities, or into situations where imminent involvement in hostilities is clearly indicated by the circumstances, are exercised only pursuant to (1) a declaration of war, (2) specific statutory authorization, or (3) a national emergency created by attack upon the United States, its territories or possessions, or its armed forces.

## CONSULTATION

Sec. 3. The president in every possible instance shall consult with Congress before introducing United States armed forces into hostilities or into situations where imminent involvement in hostilities is clearly indicated by the circumstances, and after every such introduction shall consult regularly with the Congress until United States armed forces are no longer engaged in hostilities or have been removed from such situations.

## REPORTING

Sec. 4. (a) In the absence of a declaration of war, in any case in which United States armed forces are introduced—

(1) into hostilities or into situations where imminent involvement in hostilities is clearly indicated by the circumstances;

(2) into the territory, airspace or waters of a foreign nation, while equipped for combat, except for deployments which relate solely to supply, replacement, repair, or training of such forces; or

(3) In numbers which substantially enlarge United States armed forces equipped for combat already located in a foreign nation; the President shall submit within 48 hours to the Speaker of the House of Representatives and to the President pro tempore of the Senate a report, in writing, setting forth—

(A) the circumstances necessitating the introduction of United States armed forces;

(B) the constitutional and legislative authority under which such introduction took place; and

(C) the estimated scope and duration of the hostilities or involvement.

(b) The president shall provide such other information as the Congress may request in the fulfillment of its constitutional responsibilities with respect to committing the nation to war and to the use of United States armed forces abroad.

(c) Whenever United States armed forces are introduced into hostilities or into any situation described in subsection (a) of this section, the president shall, so long as such armed forces continue to be engaged in such hostilities or situation, report to the Congress periodically on the status of such hostilities or situation as well as on the scope and duration of such hostilities or situation, but in no event shall he report to the Congress less often than once every six months.

## CONGRESSIONAL ACTION

Sec. 5. . . . (b) Within sixty calendar days after a report is submitted or is required to be submitted pursuant to section 4(a) (1), whichever is earlier, the president shall terminate any use of United States armed forces with respect to which such report was submitted (or required to be submitted), unless the Congress (1) has declared war or has enacted a specific authorization for such use of United States armed forces, (2) has extended by law such sixty-day period, or (3) is physically unable to meet as a result of an armed attack upon the United States. Such sixty-day period shall be extended for not more than an additional thirty days if the president determines and certifies to the Congress in writing that unavoidable military necessity respecting the safety of United States armed forces requires the continued use of such armed forces in the course of bringing about a prompt removal of such forces.

(c) Notwithstanding subsection (b), at any time that United States armed forces are engaged in hostilities outside the territory of the United States, its possessions and territories without a declaration of war or specific statutory authorization, such forces shall be removed by the president if the Congress so directs by concurrent resolution. . . .

## INTERPRETATION OF JOINT RESOLUTION

SEC. 8. (a) Authority to introduce United States armed forces into hostilities or into situations wherein involvement in hostilities is clearly indicated by the circumstances shall not be inferred—

(1) from any provision of law (whether or not in effect before the date of the enactment of this joint resolution), including any provision contained in any appropriation Act, unless such provision specifically

authorizes the introduction of United States armed forces into hostilities or into such situations and states that it is intended to constitute specific statutory authorization within meaning of this joint resolution; or

(2) from any treaty heretofore or hereafter ratified unless such treaty is implemented by legislation specifically authorizing the introduction of United States armed forces into hostilities or into such situations and stating that it is intended to constitute specific statutory authorization within the meaning of this joint resolution. . . .

(d) Nothing in this joint resolution—

(1) is intended to alter the constitutional authority of the Congress or of the president, or the provisions of existing treaties; or

(2) shall be construed as granting any authority to the president with respect to the introduction of United States armed forces into hostilities or into situations wherein involvement in hostilities is clearly indicated by the circumstances which authority he would not have had in the absence of this joint resolution.

## SEPARABILITY CLAUSE

Sec. 9. If any provision of this joint resolution or the application thereof to any person or circumstance is held invalid, the remainder of the joint resolution and the application of such provision to any other person or circumstance shall not be affected thereby. . . .

* * * * * * * * * * * * * * * * * * * * * * * * * * * * * * *

*Discussion Points:*

1. Some thought that the War Powers Resolution increased presidential powers by enabling him to conduct a "war" for sixty (or ninety) days. Does Section 8(d) (2) respond adequately to such concerns? Why or why not?
2. It is sometimes said that Congress can declare war but only the president can wage it. Does this distinction make sense? Does it resolve questions concerning the waging of "undeclared wars"?
3. Critics of the War Powers Resolution say that only the president can act with the force and speed necessary to protect national security. The Resolution inhibits his ability to do so. Further, it is unwise to impose a time limit on troop commitments. One should not tell an enemy who is shooting at you that, no matter what happens, your troops will be withdrawn in X days. For these and other reasons, it is argued that the Resolution should be repealed. Do you agree? Explain.

4. Supporters of the Resolution note that it *does* permit the president to respond quickly to crises through its sixty-day provision. It merely specifies that unilateral presidential actions will not be tolerated indefinitely. Congressional involvement is required when the situation permits. What do you think? Explain.
5. Supporters of the Resolution contend that in a checked-and-balanced political system, questions of war and peace cannot be left to a single individual—even the president. The Resolution is a device that permits Congress to play a meaningful role in such matters, while enabling the president to deal with emergencies. What do you think? Explain.
6. In recent years, American troops have been sent to Cambodia to secure the release of the U.S.S. *Mayaguez* and its crew, to Iran in an effort to free American hostages, to Beirut to participate in a multinational peace-keeping force, and to Grenada to quell rebellion and to protect American students. In each instance, congressmen criticized the president for failing to comply with the War Powers Resolution. How can presidents be made to comply? Should they? Do you recommend any statutory changes? Would public opinion and political pressure be more effective? Explain.
7. Should the War Powers Resolution be abolished? Why or why not? Should it be strengthened? Why? How? Should it be modified in some other way? Explain.
8. Congress sometimes grants discretionary powers to the president. To limit such presidential discretion, however, Congress sometimes reserves the right to overrule his decisions. Legislation sometimes provides that one or both houses, or a congressional committee, can "veto" certain executive-branch decisions. In *Immigration and Naturalization Service v. Chadha* (426 U.S. 919, 1983), the Supreme Court invalidated such a legislative veto provision from the 1974 Congressional Budget and Impoundment Control Act. The Court reasoned that Article One requires that legislation be presented to the president for his signature or veto. Since "legislative veto" decisions are themselves legislation and since they are not presented to the president, the Court concluded that they violate the Constitution. Section 5(c) of the War Powers Resolution permits Congress to direct the president to remove American forces from hostilities. Is this provision a legislative veto? If the Supreme Court is presented with a case challenging this provision, should the justices uphold it or should they find it unconstitutional? Why? Consider Section 5(b) of the Resolution. It orders the president to withdraw troops in sixty

(or, perhaps, ninety) days unless he can persuade Congress to *authorize* such continued action. Is this provision different from Section 5(c) in any material way? Does it violate the Constitution? Explain.

# CHAPTER 42

## UNITED STATES V. NIXON

### 418 U.S. 683; 94 S.Ct. 3090; 41 L.Ed. 2d 1039 (1974)

On June 17, 1972, seven men working for the Committee to Reelect the President (CREEP) were caught breaking into Democratic National Party Headquarters at the Watergate apartment and office complex in the nation's capital. They were trying to install electronic listening devices in an apparent effort to gather information about the Democrats' campaign plans. As the investigation proceeded, it seemed that high aides in the White House—and perhaps even President Nixon himself—had been involved and were trying to cover up that involvement. The administration denied such charges, but suspicions grew that some of these officials were obstructing justice.

Congressional investigating committees heard testimony from various White House staffers and former aides. John Dean, former counsel to the President, provided some especially damaging testimony. Dean said that Nixon had congratulated him for limiting the case to the original seven defendants, discussed executive clemency and providing hush money for these defendants, knew about the break-in at an early point, and actively participated in the cover up. Again, the administration denied the charges. Then Alexander Butterfield revealed to Congress that President Nixon tape recorded conversations with his advisors in the Oval Office for the previous two years. Were his conversations with Dean on tape? Such recordings could help establish the truth. The Senate investigating committee and Special Prosecutor Archibald Cox subpoenaed several tapes. Citing separation of powers, Nixon refused to comply. In August 1973, a U.S. District Court ordered Nixon to provide Cox with these tapes. Nixon ordered Cox, who technically worked out of the Justice Department, to drop the matter. When Cox refused, Nixon ordered that he and his staff be fired. Attorney General Elliot Richardson resigned rather than carry out this order. Deputy Attorney General William Ruckelshaus was fired for, likewise, refusing to dismiss Cox. Finally, Solicitor General Robert

Bork carried out the President's order on October 20 in what was dubbed the "Saturday Night Massacre."

Widespread public criticism and the start of formal impeachment proceedings in the House ensued. A new Special Prosecutor, Leon Jaworski, was brought in and Nixon finally agreed to turn over these tapes. The tapes led to additional indictments. Former Attorney General John Mitchell, White House Chief of Staff H. R. Haldeman, and Chief Domestic Advisor John Ehrlichman were among those charged with conspiracy to obstruct justice. Congress then subpoenaed additional tapes, as did Jaworski. Nixon refused to supply them. Instead he carried questions about Jaworski's subpoena to the Supreme Court.

Nixon argued that a president cannot be forced to comply with judicial orders. One branch cannot give orders to a co-equal branch. Further, since the Special Prosecutor operated out of the Justice Department, Nixon categorized the dispute as an entirely intra-Executive Branch matter, as a dispute between the President and one of his own subordinates. He asserted that courts should stay out of such matters. He also argued, on executive-privilege grounds, that a president must be able to protect the confidentiality of his conversations with his aides. Otherwise, his advisors will hesitate to supply him with complete and candid advice and his ability to "faithfully execute the laws" would be impaired. Although the phrase "executive privilege" does not appear in the text of the Constitution, Nixon argued that it is an inherent and constitutionally-based presidential power.

President Nixon indicated that he was hoping for a "definitive" decision from the Supreme Court. Some commentators speculated that he might refuse to comply with a decision that he regarded as "less than definitive." Such speculations were not put to the test as the Court reached a unanimous decision in an opinion issued under the name of Chief Justice Burger.

The Court accepted Nixon's argument that executive privilege is constitutionally based. Further, although the Court was unwilling to say that this privilege is absolute, the justices did agree that the privilege is "presumptive." That is, in such controversies, a court should presume that a president is correct in wanting to protect the confidentiality of his conversations with his advisors and the burden of proof should be placed on the party seeking this information to show a specific and compelling need for it. In the present case, however, the Court concluded that Special Prosecutor Jaworski *had* shown such a need for the tapes and had successfully overcome the presumption that operated in Nixon's favor. Jaworski was able to show that the subpoenaed evidence was necessary to insure that the defendants received their constitutionally-guaranteed right to a fair trial. President Nixon was ordered to furnish the tapes.

A few days after the Court's decision, the House Judiciary Committee approved three articles of impeachment against the President. As Nixon began to comply, it was revealed that he had known about the break-in from the start and that he had misled his political supporters. Impeachment by the full House looked imminent. Before such a vote could be taken, Nixon resigned the presidency. He was subsequently pardoned by his successor, Gerald Ford—the man whom he had appointed to the vice-presidency following Spiro Agnew's earlier resignation.

\* \* \* \* \* \* \* \* \* \* \* \* \* \* \* \* \* \* \* \* \* \* \* \* \* \* \* \* \* \*

Mr. Chief Justice Burger delivered the opinion of the Court, saying in part:

These cases present for review the denial of a motion, filed on behalf of the President of the United States, in the case of *United States v. Mitchell et al.*, to quash a third party subpoena issued by the U.S. District Court for the District of Columbia. . . . The subpoena directed the President to produce certain tape recordings and documents relating to his conversation with aides. . . .

In the District Court, the President's counsel argued that the court lacked jurisdiction to issue the subpoena because the matter was an intrabranch dispute between a subordinate and superior officer of the executive branch and hence not subject to judicial resolution.

That argument has been renewed in this court with emphasis on the contention that the dispute does not present a "case" or "controversy" which can be adjudicated in the federal courts. The President's counsel argues that the federal courts should not intrude into areas committed to the other branches of government.

He views the present dispute as essentially a "jurisdictional" dispute within the executive branch which he analogizes to a dispute between two congressional committees. Since the executive branch has exclusive authority and absolute discretion to decide whether to prosecute a case, . . . it is contended that a President's decision is final in determining what evidence is to be used in a given criminal case.

Our starting point is the nature of the proceeding for which the evidence is sought—here a pending criminal prosecution. It is a judicial proceeding in a federal court alleging violation of federal laws and is brought in the name of the United States as sovereign. Under the authority of Art. II, 2, Congress has vested in the attorney general the power to conduct the criminal litigation of the U.S. Government. . . .

It has also vested in him the power to appoint subordinate officers to assist him in the discharge of his duties. . . . Acting pursuant to those statutes, the attorney general has delegated the authority to represent the United States in these particular matters to a special prosecutor with unique authority and tenure. The regulation gives the special prosecutor explicit power to contest the invocation of executive privilege in the process of seeking evidence deemed relevant to the performance of these specially delegated duties.

So long as this regulation is extant it has the force of law. . . .

Here at issue is the production or non-production of specified evidence deemed by the special prosecutor to be relevant and admissible in a pending criminal case. It is sought by one official of the government within the scope of his express authority; it is resisted by the chief executive on the ground of his duty to preserve the confidentiality of the communications of the President.

In light of the uniqueness of the setting in which the conflict arises, the fact that both parties are officers of the executive branch cannot be viewed as a barrier to justiciability. It would be inconsistent with the applicable law and regulation, and the unique facts of this case to conclude other than that the special prosecutor has standing to bring this action and that a justiciable controversy is presented for decision. . . .

. . .we turn to the claim that the subpoena should be quashed because it demands "confidential conversations between a President and his close advisers that it would be inconsistent with the public interest to produce."

The first contention is a broad claim that the separation of powers doctrine precludes judicial review of a President's claim of privilege. The second contention is that if he does not prevail on the claim of absolute privilege, the court should hold as a matter of constitutional law that the privilege prevails over the subpoena. . . .

In the performance of assigned constitutional duties each branch of the government must initially interpret the Constitution, and the interpretation of its powers by any branch is due great respect from the others. The President's counsel, as we have noted, reads the Constitution as providing an absolute privilege of confidentiality for all presidential communications.

Many decisions of this Court, however, have unequivocally reaffirmed the holding of *Marbury v. Madison* that "it is emphatically the province and duty of the judicial department to say what the law is."

Notwithstanding the deference each branch must accord the others, the "judicial power of the United States" vested in the federal courts by Art. III of the Constitution can no more be shared with the executive branch than the chief executive, for example, can share with the judiciary the veto power, or the Congress share with the judiciary the power to override a presidential veto.

Any other conclusion would be contrary to the basic concept of separation of powers and the checks and balances that flow from the scheme of a tripartite government. . . .

In support of his claim of absolute privilege, the President's counsel urges two grounds one of which is common to all governments and one of which is peculiar to our system of separation of powers. The first ground is the valid need for protection of communications between high government officials and those who advise and assist them in the performance of their manifold duties. . . .

Whatever the nature of the privilege of confidentiality of presidential communications in the exercise of Art. II powers the privilege can be said to derive from the supremacy of each branch within its own assigned area of constitutional duties. Certain powers and privileges flow from the nature of enumerated powers; the protection of the confidentiality of presidential communications has similar constitutional underpinnings.

The second ground asserted by the President's counsel in support of the claim of absolute privilege rests on the doctrine of separation of powers. Here it is argued that the independence of the executive branch within its own sphere . . . insulates a President from a judicial subpoena in an ongoing criminal prosecution, and thereby protects confidential presidential communications.

However, neither the doctrine of separation of powers, nor the need for confidentiality of high level communications, without more, can sustain an absolute, unqualified presidential privilege of immunity from judicial process under all circumstances. The President's need for complete candor and objectivity from advisers call for great deference from the courts.

However, when the privilege depends solely on the broad, undifferentiated claim of public interest in the confidentiality of such conversations, a confrontation with other values arises. Absent a claim of need to protect military, diplomatic or sensitive national security secrets, we find it difficult to accept the argument that even the very important interest in confidentiality of presidential communications is significantly diminished by production of such material for in camera inspection with all the protection that a district court will be obliged to provide.

The impediment that an absolute, unqualified privilege would place in the way of the primary constitutional duty of the judicial branch to do justice in criminal prosecutions would plainly conflict with the function of the courts under Art. III. . . .

To read the Art. II powers of the President as providing an absolute privilege as against a subpoena essential to enforcement of criminal statutes on no more than a generalized claim of the public interest in confidentiality of nonmilitary and non-diplomatic discussions would upset the constitutional balance of "a workable government" and gravely impair the role of the courts under Art. III.

Since we conclude that the legitimate needs of the judicial process may outweigh presidential privilege, it is necessary to resolve those competing interests in a manner that preserves the essential function of each branch. The right and indeed the duty to resolve that question does not free the judiciary from according high respect to the representations made on behalf of the President. . . .

The expectation of a President to the confidentiality of his conversations and correspondence, like the claim of confidentiality of judicial deliberations, for example, has all the values to which we accord deference for the privacy of all citizens and added to those values the necessity for protection of the public interest in candid, objective, and even blunt or harsh opinions in Presidential decision making. A President and those who assist him must be free to explore alternatives in the process of shaping policies and making decisions and to do so in a way many would be unwilling to express except privately. These are the considerations justifying a presumptive privilege for Presidential communications. The privilege is fundamental to the operation of government and inextricably rooted in the separation of powers under the Constitution. In *Nixon v. Sirica,* 487 F. 2d 700 (1973), the Court of Appeals held that such Presidential communications are "presumptively privileged," and this position is accepted by both parties in the present litigation. . . .

But this presumptive privilege must be considered in light of our historic commitment to a rule of law. This is nowhere more profoundly manifest than in our view that "the twofold aim [of criminal justice] is that guilt shall not escape or innocence suffer." *Berger v. United States* (1935). We have elected to employ an adversary system of criminal justice in which the parties contest all issues before a court of law. The need to develop all relevant facts in the adversary system is both fundamental and comprehensive. The ends of criminal justice would be defeated if judgments were to be founded on a partial or speculative representation of the facts. The very integrity of the judicial system and public confidence in the system depend on full disclosure of all the facts, within the framework of the rules of evidence. To ensure that justice is done, it is imperative to the function of courts that compulsory process be available for the production of evidence needed either by the prosecution or by the defense. . . .

The privileges referred to by the court are designed to protect weighty and legitimate competing interests. Thus, the Fifth Amendment to the Constitution provides that no man "shall be compelled in any criminal case to be a witness against himself." And, generally, an attorney or a priest may not be required to disclose what has been revealed in professional confidence.

These and other interests are recognized in law by privileges against forced disclosure, established in the Constitution, by statute, or at common law. Whatever their origins, these exceptions to the demand for every man's evidence are not lightly created nor expansively construed, for they are in derogation of the search for truth.

In this case the President challenges a subpoena served on him as a third party requiring the production of materials for use in a criminal prosecution on the claim that he has a privilege against disclosure of confidential communications. He does not place his claim of privilege on the ground that they are military or diplomatic secrets. As to these areas of Art. II duties the courts have traditionally shown the utmost deference to presidential responsibilities. . . .

No case of the Court, however, has extended this high degree of deference to a President's generalized interest in confidentiality. Nowhere in the Constitution, as we have noted earlier, is there any explicit reference to a privilege of confidentiality, yet to the extent this interest relates to the effective discharge of a President's powers, it is constitutionally based.

The right to the production of all evidence at a criminal trial similarly has constitutional dimensions. The Sixth Amendment explicitly confers upon every defendant in a criminal trial the right "to be confronted with the witness against him" and "to have compulsory process for obtaining witness in his favor.". . .

In this case we must weigh the importance of the general privilege of confidentiality of presidential communications in performance of his responsibilities against the inroads of such a privilege on the fair administration of criminal justice. The interest in preserving confidentiality is weighty indeed and entitled to great respect. However, we cannot conclude that advisers will be moved to temper the candor of their remarks by the infrequent occasions of disclosure because of the possibility that such conversations will be called for in the context of a criminal prosecution.

On the other hand, the allowance of the privilege to withhold evidence that is demonstrably relevant in a criminal trial would cut deeply into the guarantee of due process of law and gravely impair the basic function of the courts. A President's acknowledged need for confidentiality in the communications of his office is general in nature, whereas the constitutional need for production of relevant evidence in a criminal proceeding is specific and central to the fair adjudication of a particular criminal case in the administration of justice.

Without access to specific facts a criminal prosecution may be totally frustrated. The President's broad interest in confidentiality of communications will not be vitiated by disclosure of a limited number of conversations preliminarily shown to have some bearing on the pending criminal cases.

We conclude that when the ground for asserting privilege as to subpoenaed materials sought for use in a criminal trial is based only on the generalized interest in confidentiality, it cannot prevail over the fundamental demands of due process of law in the fair administration of criminal justice. The generalized assertion of privilege must yield to the demonstrated, specific need for evidence in a pending criminal trial.

Accordingly we affirm the order of the District Court that subpoenaed materials be transmitted to that court. . . .

* * * * * * * * * * * * * * * * * * * * * * * * * * * * * * *

*Discussion Points:*

1. Explain President Nixon's separation-of-powers argument. Do you agree with him that courts should not "intrude" into such areas? Why or why not?
2. "Explain the executive-privilege aspect of this case. Where did the Court "find" executive privilege? In what sense is this privilege constitutionally based? What is "presumptive privilege"?
3. If the President had claimed the need to protect "military, diplomatic, or sensitive national security secrets," do you think the case would have been decided differently? Explain.
4. Why did the Court order the President to turn over the tapes? What interests were balanced against his interest in protecting the confidentiality of his conversations with his advisors? Do you agree with the Court's decision in this case? Why or why not?
5. What if the President had refused to comply with the Court's decision in this case? How could he have been forced to comply?

# CHAPTER 43

## *REGENTS OF THE UNIVERSITY OF CALIFORNIA V. BAKKE*

### 438 U.S. 265; 98 S.Ct. 2733; 57 L.Ed. 2d 750 (1978)

The Fourteenth Amendment says that no State shall deny persons "the equal protection of the laws." But virtually any law subjects certain persons to different treatment from that afforded to those who fall outside the statute's coverage. The Equal Protection Clause can be interpreted as requiring that persons be treated in a "fair" or "even-handed" fashion, but such an interpretation places rather ambiguous limits of government actions.

As previously noted, we deny young children the right to drive, vote, and so on. Such "discriminatory" treatment is readily justifiable. But the same could not be said if these rights were denied to blacks or females. The Court has fashioned some standards to employ as it attempts to distinguish permissible legislative classifications from impermissible ones.

For years, the Court deferred to the judgments of legislators about what kinds of economic and social classifications were needed. The Court invalidated laws for compromising equal protection guarantees only if the laws bore no "rational connection" to even some hypothetically "legitimate governmental purpose." The challenging party carried the burden of proving that the law was unreasonable. Most laws could easily survive the minimal levels of judicial scrutiny associated with this old rational-connection test.

During the 1960s, however, the Warren Court used the Equal Protection Clause to protect "fundamental interests" and "suspect classes." If a law affected a suspect class of persons or hampered the exercise of some fundamentally-important right, the Court would subject it to "strict scrutiny." To survive, such laws would have to be drawn narrowly (i.e., they had to be "minimally burdensome") and they had to be "necessary" to "compelling governmental interests." The strict scrutiny associated with this new form of equal protection analysis usually led to the invalidation of the challenged law.

This "two-tier" approach has not been abandoned, but a "newer" approach to equal protection questions has been emerging when a law affects "questionable"—but not suspect—classes or "important"—but not fundamental—interests. Such laws are subjected to an "intermediate" level of scrutiny. To survive, such laws must be "substantially related" to "important" governmental interests. The best example of cases triggering such intermediate review are those involving sex discrimination.

Laws that treat persons differently because of race are generally subjected to strict scrutiny. Hence, most such laws are invalidated. But what about remedial programs? What about laws and voluntary efforts designed to compensate the victims of past racial discrimination for their injuries? Does the Constitution permit such "affirmative action" programs?

Opponents of affirmative action say that these programs are a form of reverse discrimination against white persons. They argue that the Constitution requires that society be "color blind" and that such programs violate this principle. Supporters of affirmative action counter that it is not enough to stop discriminating against minorities. Equal opportunity requires that they be compensated for past injustices. For example, suppose that two men—Mr. W and Mr. B—are preparing for a race. Mr. W, a white man, has been training under the guidance of running and nutrition coaches. Mr. B, a black man, has been chained to a tree and fed a steady diet of bread and water. On the day of the race, B's captors release him, apologize, promise never to do it again, and they lead him to the starting line where he takes his place alongside W. Has B been treated fairly? Does he have an equal opportunity to succeed? Supporters of affirmative action programs think that such victims deserve remedial treatment, at least for a time. One of the Supreme Court's most important decisions in this area emerged from Allan Bakke's application to the medical school of the University of California at Davis.

The Medical School had two admissions programs for its incoming class of 100 students. The special admissions program set aside 16 seats for minority applicants who did not compete with the 84 other applicants. Bakke, a white male, was rejected despite the fact that he had stronger objective scores (grade point average, MCATs, letters of recommendation, and so on) than minority applicants who were accepted. Bakke contended that this special admissions program violated the California Constitution, Title VI of the Civil Rights Act of 1964 (which prohibits racial discrimination in programs that receive federal funding), and the Equal Protection Clause of the Fourteenth Amendment.

Justices Brennan, White, Marshall, and Blackmun found neither constitutional nor Title VI violations and voted to uphold the special admissions program. Justices Stewart, Burger, Rehnquist, and Stevens concluded that the program violated Title VI so they did not address the constitutional questions. Justice Powell's opinion, therefore, proved decisive. He invalidated the Davis program because it operated as a strict racial quota. However, he said that race could be taken into account as one factor when admissions officers screen applicants because racial diversity can enrich an institution. In short, the Court rules that *some* special admissions programs might be acceptable but the Davis one was not.

In a series of subsequent cases, the Court was generally supportive of affirmative action programs. (See, for example, *United Steelworkers of America v. Weber,* 433 U.S. 193, 1979; *Fullilove v. Klutznick,* 448 U.S. 448, 1980; and *Sheetmetal Workers Local 28 v. EEOC,* 92 L.Ed. 2d 344, 1986). But in other cases, the Court was less supportive. For example, in *Memphis Firefighters v. Stotts* (81 L.Ed. 2d 483, 1984) and *Wygant v. Jackson Board of Education* (90 L.Ed. 2d 260, 1986), the Court ruled that white employees with seniority should not be laid off to save jobs for newly-hired minorities. As such, the issue remains somewhat unsettled.

\* \* \* \* \* \* \* \* \* \* \* \* \* \* \* \* \* \* \* \* \* \* \* \* \* \* \*

Mr. Justice Powell stated in part:

... For the reasons stated in the following opinion, I believe that so much of the judgment of the California court as holds petitioner's special admissions program unlawful and directs that respondent be admitted to the Medical School must be affirmed. For the reasons expressed in a separate opinion, my Brothers the Chief Justice, Mr. Justice Stewart, Mr. Justice Rehnquist, and Mr. Justice Stevens concur in this judgment. I also conclude for the reasons stated in the following opinion that the portion of the court's judgment enjoining petitioner from according any consideration to race in its admissions process must be reversed. For reasons expressed in separate opinions, My Brothers Mr. Justice Brennan, Mr. Justice White, Mr. Justice Marshall, and Mr. Justice Blackmun concur in this judgment.

Because the special admissions program involved a racial classification, the Supreme Court held itself bound to apply strict scrutiny. It then turned to the goals the University presented as justifying the special program. Although the court agreed that the goals of integrating the medical profession and increasing the number of physicians willing to serve members of minority groups were compelling state interests, it concluded that the special admissions program was not the least intrusive means of achieving those goals. Without passing on the state constitutional or the federal statutory grounds cited in the trial court,s judgment, the California court held that the Equal Protection Clause required that "no applicant may be rejected because of his race, in favor of another who is less qualified, as measured by standards applied without regard to race". . . .

III . . . Petitioner prefers to view . . . [the special admissions program] as establishing a "goal" of minority representation in the medical school. Respondent, echoing the courts below, labels it a racial quota. This semantic distinction is beside the point: the special admissions program is undeniably a classification based on race and ethnic background. To the extent that there existed a pool of at least minimally qualified minority applicants to fill the 16 special admissions seats, white applicants could compete only for 84 seats in the entering class, rather than the 100 open to minority applicants. Whether this limitation is described as a quota or a goal, it is a line drawn on the basis of race and ethnic status. . . . Racial and ethnic classifications, however, are subject to stringent examination without regard to these additional characteristics. Racial and ethnic distinctions of any sort are inherently suspect and thus call for the most exacting judicial examination. . . .

Petitioner urges us to adopt for the first time a more restrictive view of the Equal Protection Clause and hold that discrimination against members of the white "majority" cannot be suspect if its purpose can be characterized as "benign." The clock of our liberties, however, cannot be turned back to 1868. . . . It is far too late to argue that the guarantee of equal protection to all persons permits the recognition of special wards entitled to a degree of protection greater than that accorded others. . . .

. . . there are serious problems of justice connected with the idea of preference itself. First, it may not always be clear that a so-called preference is in fact benign. Second, preferential programs may only reinforce common stereotypes holding that certain groups are unable to achieve success without special protection based on a factor having no relationship to individual worth. Third, there is a measure of inequity in forcing innocent persons in respondent's position to bear the burdens of redressing grievances not of their making. Also, the mutability of a constitutional principle, based upon shifting political and social judgments, undermines the chances for consistent application of the Constitution from one generation to the next, a critical feature of its coherent interpretation. . . .

C. Petitioner contends that on several occasions this Court has approved preferential classifications without applying the most exacting scrutiny. Most of the cases upon which petitioner relies are drawn from three areas: school desegregation, employment discrimination, and sex discrimination. Each of the cases cited presented a situation materially different from that facts of this case. The school desegregation cases are inapposite. Each involved remedies for clearly determined constitutional violations.

Such preferences also have been upheld where a legislative or administrative body charged with the responsibility made determinations of past discrimination by the industries affected, and fashioned remedies deemed appropriate to rectify the discrimination. But we have never approved preferential classifications in the absence of proven constitutional or statutory violations. . . .

. . . the operation of petitioner's special admissions program is quite different from the remedial measures approved. It prefers the designated minority groups at the expense of other individuals who are totally foreclosed from competition for the 16 special admissions seats in every medical school class. Because of that foreclosure, some individuals are excluded from enjoyment of a state-provided benefit— admission to the medical school—they otherwise would receive. When a classification denies an individual opportunities or benefits enjoyed by others solely because of his race or ethnic background, it must be regarded as suspect.

IV. We have held that in "order to justify the use of a suspect classification, a State must show that its purpose or interest is both constitutionally permissible and substantial, and that its use of the classification is 'necessary [to] the accomplishment' of its purpose or the safeguarding of its interest". . . . The special admissions program purports to serve the purposes of: (i) "reducing the historic deficit of traditionally disfavored minorities in medical schools and the medical profession;" (ii) countering the effects of societal discrimination; (iii) increasing the number of physicians who will practice in communities currently underserved; and (iv) obtaining the educational benefits that flow from an ethnically diverse student body. It is necessary to decide which, if any, of these purposes is substantial enough to support the use of a suspect classification.

A. If petitioner's purpose is to assure within its student body some specified percentage of a particular group merely because of its race or ethnic origin, such a preferential purpose must be rejected not as insubstantial but as facially invalid. Preferring members of any one group for no reason other than race or ethnic origin is discrimination for its own sake. This the Constitution forbids. . . .

B. The State certainly has a legitimate and substantial interest in ameliorating, or eliminating where feasible, the disabling effects of identified discrimination. . . . We have never approved a classification that aids persons perceived as members of relatively victimized groups at the expense of other innocent individuals in the absence of judicial, legislative, or administrative findings of constitutional or statutory violations. . . . Without such findings of constitutional or statutory violations, it cannot be said that the government has any greater interest in helping one individual than in refraining from harming another. Thus, the government has no compelling justification for inflicting such harm.

C. Petitioner does not purport to have made, and is in no position to make, such findings. Its broad mission is education, not the formulation of any legislative policy or the adjudication of particular claims of illegality. For reasons similar to those stated in Part III of this opinion, isolated segments of our vast governmental structures are not competent to make those decisions, at least in the absence of legislative mandates and legislatively determined criteria. Before relying upon these sorts of findings in establishing a racial classification, a governmental body must have the authority and capability to establish, in the record, that the classification is responsive to identified discrimination. Hence, the purpose of helping certain groups whom the faculty of the Davis Medical School perceived as victims of "societal discrimination" does not justify a classification that imposes disadvantages upon persons like respondent, who bear no responsibility for whatever harm the beneficiaries of the special admissions program are thought to have suffered. To hold otherwise would be to convert a remedy heretofore reserved for violations of legal rights into a privilege that all institutions throughout the Nation could grant at their pleasure to whatever groups are perceived as victims of societal discrimination. That is a step we have never approved. . . .

D. The fourth goal asserted by petitioner is the attainment of a diverse student body. This clearly is a constitutionally permissible goal for an institution of higher education. Academic freedom, though not a specifically enumerated constitutional right, long has been viewed as a special concern of the First Amendment. The freedom of a university to make its own judgments as to education includes the selection of its student body. Thus, in arguing that its universities must be accorded the right to select those students who will contribute the most to the "robust exchange of ideas," petitioner invokes a countervailing constitutional interest, that of the First Amendment. In this light, petitioner must be viewed as seeking to achieve a goal that is of paramount importance in the fulfillment of its mission. It may be argued that there is greater force to these views at the undergraduate level than in a medical school where the training is centered primarily on professional competency. But even at the graduate level, our tradition and experience lend support to the view that the contribution of diversity is substantial. . . . An otherwise qualified medical student with a particular background—whether it be ethnic, geographic, culturally advantaged or disadvantaged—may bring to a professional school of medicine experiences, outlooks and ideas that enrich the training of its student body and better equip its graduates to render with understanding their vital service to humanity.

Ethnic diversity, however, is only one element in a range of factors a university properly may consider in attaining the goal of a heterogeneous student body. . . . As the interest of diversity is compelling in the context of a university's admissions program, the question remains whether the program's racial classification is necessary to promote this interest.

V. A. It may be assumed that the reservation of a specified number of seats in each class for individuals from the preferred ethnic groups would contribute to the attainment of considerable ethnic diversity in the student body. But petitioner's argument that this is the only effective means of serving the interest of diversity is seriously flawed. In a most fundamental sense the argument misconceives the nature of the state interest that would justify consideration of race or ethnic background. It is not an interest in simple ethnic diversity, in which a specified percentage of the student body is in effect guaranteed to be members of selected ethnic groups, with the remaining percentage an undifferentiated aggregation of students. The diversity that furthers a compelling state interest encompasses a far broader array of qualifications and characteristics of which racial or ethnic origin is but a single though important element. Petitioner's special admissions program, focused solely on ethnic diversity, would hinder rather than further attainment of genuine diversity. Nor would the state interest in genuine diversity be served by expanding petitioner's two-track system into a multitrack program with a prescribed number of seats set aside for each identifiable category of applicants. Indeed, it is inconceivable that a university would thus pursue the logic of petitioner's two-track program to the illogical end of insulating each category of applicants with certain desired qualifications from competition with all other applicants.

The experience of other university admissions programs, which take race into account in achieving the educational diversity valued by the First Amendment, demonstrates that the assignment of a fixed number of places to a minority group is not a necessary means toward that end. An illuminating example is found in the Harvard College program: "In recent years Harvard College has expanded the concept of diversity to include students from disadvantaged economic, racial and ethnic groups. Harvard College now recruits not only Californians or Louisianans but also blacks and Chicanos and other minority students. In practice, this new definition of diversity has meant that race has been a factor in some admission decisions. When the Committee on Admissions reviews the large middle group of applicants who are 'admissible' and deemed capable of doing good work in their courses, the race of an applicant may tip the balance in his favor just as geographic origin or a life spent on a farm may tip the balance in other candidates' cases. A farm boy from Idaho can bring something to Harvard College that a Bostonian cannot offer. Similarly, a black student can usually bring something that a white person cannot offer.

"In Harvard college admissions the Committee has not set target-quotas for the number of blacks, or of musicians, football players, physicists or Californians to be admitted in a given year. [But in] choosing among thousands of applicants who are not only 'admissible' academically but have other strong qualities, the Committee, with a number of criteria in mind, pays some attention to distribution among many types and categories of students."

In such an admissions program, race or ethnic background may be deemed a "plus" in a particular applicant's file, yet it does not insulate the individual from comparison with all other candidates for the available seats. The file of a particular black applicant may be examined for his potential contribution to diversity without the factor of race being decisive when compared, for example, with that of an applicant identified as an Italian-American if the latter is thought to exhibit qualities more likely to promote beneficial educational pluralism. Such qualities could include exceptional personal talents, unique work or service experience, leadership potential, maturity, demonstrated compassion, a history of overcoming disadvantage, ability to communicate with the poor, or other qualifications deemed important. In short, an admissions program operated in this way is flexible enough to consider all pertinent elements of diversity in light of the particular qualifications of each applicant, and to place them on the same footing for consideration, although not necessarily according them the same weight. Indeed, the weight attributed to a particular quality may vary from year to year depending upon the "mix" both of the student body and the applicants for the incoming class.

This kind of program treats each applicant as an individual in the admissions process. The applicant who loses out on the last available seat to another candidate receiving a "plus" on the basis of ethnic background will not have been foreclosed from all consideration for that seat simply because he was not the right color or had the wrong surname. It would mean only that his combined qualifications, which may have included similar nonobjective factors, did not outweigh those of the other applicant. His qualifications would have been weighed fairly and competitively, and he would have no basis to complain of unequal treatment under the 14th Amendment.

It has been suggested that an admissions program which considers race only as one factor is simply a subtle and more sophisticated—but no less effective—means of according racial preference than the Davis program. A facial intent to discriminate, however, is evident in petitioner's preference program and not denied in this case. No such facial infirmity exists in an admissions program where race or ethnic background is simply one element—to be weighed fairly against other elements—in the selection process. And a Court would not assume that a university, professing to employ a facially nondiscriminatory admissions policy, would operate it as a cover for the functional equivalent of a quota system.

B. In summary, it is evident that the Davis special admissions program involves the use of an explicit racial classification never before countenanced by this Court. It tells applicants who are not Negro, Asian, or "Chicano" that they are totally excluded from a specific percentage of the seats in an entering class. No matter how strong their qualifications, quantitative and extracurricular, including their own potential for contribution to educational diversity, they are never afforded the chance to compete with applicants from the preferred groups for the special admission seats. At the same time, the preferred applicants have the opportunity to compete for every seat in the class. The fatal flaw in petitioner's preferential program is its disregard of individual rights as guaranteed by the 14th Amendment. . . . Such rights are not absolute. But when a State's distribution of benefits or imposition of burdens hinges on the color of a person's skin or ancestry, that individual is entitled to a demonstration that the challenged classification is necessary to promote a substantial state interest. Petitioner has failed to carry this burden. For this reason, that portion of the California court's judgment holding petitioner's special admissions program invalid under the 14th Amendment must be affirmed.

C. In enjoining petitioner from ever considering the race of any applicant, however, the courts below failed to recognize that the State has a substantial interest that legitimately may be served by a properly devised admissions program involving the competitive consideration of race and ethnic origin. For this reason, so much of the California court's judgment as enjoins petitioner from any consideration of the race of any applicant must be reversed.

VI. With respect to respondent's entitlement to an injunction directing his admission to the Medical School, petitioner has conceded that it could not carry its burden of proving that, but for the existence of its unlawful special admissions program, respondent still would not have been admitted. Hence, respondent is entitled to the injunction, and that portion of the judgment must be affirmed.

* * * * * * * * * * * * * * * * * * * * * * * * * * * * * *

*Discussion Points:*

1. What level of scrutiny did Justice Powell employ? Accordingly, what had to be demonstrated before Powell would vote to uphold the challenged program?

2. What goals were advanced in support of the special admissions program? Did the Court find them sufficiently weighty to justify the alleged discrimination? Explain.

3. Discuss some of the "serious problems" associated with preferential treatment cited by Powell.

4. Did Powell regard the attainment of "a diverse student body" as a "constitutionally permissibly goal"? Was the challenged program a legitimate means to this end? If not, why not?

5. Powell cites the following statement: "A farm boy from Idaho can bring something to Harvard College that a Bostonian cannot offer. Similarly, a black student can usually bring something that a white person cannot offer." What is his point? What role can race play in admissions decisions?

6. In his dissenting opinion in *Fullilove*, Justice Stewart objected to an affirmative action program on grounds that the Constitution requires that we be color blind. He said, "I think today's decision is wrong for the same reason that *Plessy v. Ferguson* was wrong." Compare and contrast the *Bakke* decision with *Plessy*. Do you

see Stewart's point? What is your opinion? Is color blindness a realistic standard in the present in light of our past? Explain.

7. Justice Blackmun said that "in order to get beyond racism, we must first take account of race." What was his point? Do you agree or disagree? Why?

8. Critics of affirmative action charge that it is reverse discrimination, it punishes innocent persons just because they are white, it stigmatizes minorities as they pursue professional careers, and it sometimes produces unqualified appointments. What is your opinion of these criticisms? Explain.

9. Supporters of affirmative action say that it is not sufficient for society to stop discriminating; remedial programs are needed to combat the lingering effects of past injustices. They also maintain that these programs help produce needed role models for minority children and they are necessary to help minorities fill positions in proportion to their numbers in the surrounding community. What is your opinion of these arguments? Explain.

# CHAPTER 44

## *BOWERS V. HARDWICK*

### 478 U.S. 186; 106 S.Ct. 2841; 92 L.Ed. 2d 140 (1986)

What are the limits of the constitutionally-protected right of privacy? Can States outlaw homosexual conduct without violating the Constitution or are such laws invalid when they attempt to restrict sexual acts that take place in the privacy of the home? These are some of the questions the Court faced in *Bowers v. Hardwick.*

A Georgia law banned sodomy. The wording of the Act was sufficiently broad to apply to both heterosexual and homosexual conduct, but it was enforced only against homosexuals. In this case, a police officer carrying a warrant for Michael Hardwick's arrest in connection with a public-drinking charge entered Hardwick's house. There he saw Hardwick committing sodomy with another consenting, adult male. Hardwick was arrested under the Georgia statute, but the local district attorney declined to prosecute. Hardwick, attempting to bring a test case, sued in a federal district court seeking an injunction to restrain the state from enforcing this law. He argued that the law deprived him of his rights to privacy and intimate association. The district court dismissed the suit, but a federal appeals court reversed. Georgia then requested review from the Supreme Court.

By a five-to-four vote, the Court upheld the statute. Justice White's lead opinion concluded that the Constitution does not provide "a fundamental right to engage in homosexual sodomy." In his dissenting opinion, Justice Blackmun stressed the importance of the expectation of privacy that a person enjoys in his or her home. He maintained that Justice White understated the nature of the right that was really at issue in this case. Blackmun believed that this case was about "the most comprehensive of rights and the right most valued by civilized men, namely, the right to be let alone."

* * * * * * * * * * * * * * * * * * * * * * * * * * * * * * *

Mr. Justice White delivered the opinion of the Court, saying in part:

. . . .The issue presented is whether the Federal Constitution confers a fundamental right upon homosexuals to engage in sodomy and hence invalidates the laws of the many States that still make such conduct illegal and have done so for a very long time. . . .

We first register our disagreement with the Court of Appeals and with respondent that the Court's prior cases have construed the Constitution to confer a right of privacy that extends to homosexual sodomy . . . [Case citations omitted.] . . . . [These] cases were interpreted as construing the Due Process Clause of the Fourteenth Amendment to confer a fundamental individual right to decide whether or not to beget or bear a child.

Accepting the decisions in these cases . . . we think it evident that none of the rights announced in those cases bears any resemblance to the claimed constitutional right of homosexuals to engage in acts of sodomy that is asserted in this case. No connection between family, marriage, or procreation on the one hand and homosexual activity on the other has been demonstrated. . . .

Precedent aside, however, respondent would have us announce . . . a fundamental right to engage in homosexual sodomy. This we are quite unwilling to do. . . .

. . . [T]he Court has sought to identify the nature of the rights qualifying for heightened judicial protection. In *Palko v. Connecticut* (1937) it was said that this category includes those fundamental liberties that are "implicit in the concept of ordered liberty," such that "neither liberty nor justice would exist if [they] were sacrificed." A different description of fundamental liberties appeared in *Moore v. East Cleveland* (1977) . . . where they are characterized as those liberties that are "deeply rooted in this Nation's history and tradition."

It is obvious to us that neither of these formulations would extend a fundamental right to homosexuals to engage in acts of consensual sodomy. Proscriptions against that conduct have ancient roots. . . . Sodomy was a criminal offense at common law and was forbidden by the laws of the original thirteen States when they ratified the Bill of Rights. . . . In fact, until 1961, all 50 States outlawed sodomy, and today, 24 States and the District of Columbia continue to provide criminal penalties for sodomy performed in private between consenting adults. Against this background, to claim that a right to engage in such conduct is "deeply rooted in this Nation's history and tradition" or "implicit in the concept of ordered liberty" is, at best, facetious.

Nor are we inclined to take a more expansive view of our authority to discover new fundamental rights imbedded in the Due Process Clause. The Court is most vulnerable and comes nearest to illegitimacy when it deals with judge-made constitutional law having little or no cognizable roots in the language or design of the Constitution. . . .

Respondent, however, asserts that the result should be different where the homosexual conduct occurs in the privacy of the home. He relies on *Stanley v. Georgia* (1969), where the Court held that the First Amendment prevents conviction for possessing and reading obscene material in the privacy of his home: "If the First Amendment means anything, it means that a State has no business telling a man, sitting alone in his house, what books he may read or what films he may watch."

*Stanley* did protect conduct that would not have been protected outside the home . . . but the decision was firmly grounded in the First Amendment. The right pressed upon us here has no similar support in the text of the Constitution. . . . Plainly enough, otherwise illegal conduct is not always immunized whenever it occurs in the home. Victimless crime, such as the possession and use of illegal drugs do not escape the law where they are committed at home. *Stanley* itself recognized that its holding offered no protection for the possession in the home of drugs, firearms, or stolen goods. And if respondent's submission is limited to voluntary sexual conduct between consenting adults, it would be difficult, except by fiat, to limit the claimed right to homosexual conduct while leaving exposed to prosecution adultery, incest, and other sexual crimes even though they are committed in the home. We are unwilling to start down that road.

Even if the conduct at issue here is not a fundamental right, respondent . . . insists that majority sentiments about the morality of homosexuality should be declared [an] inadequate [rationale to support the law]. We do not agree and are unpersuaded that the sodomy laws of some 25 States should be invalidated on this basis.

Accordingly, the judgment of the Court of Appeals is reversed.

Mr. Justice Blackmun, with whom Mr. Justice Brennan, Mr. Justice Marshall, and Mr. Justice Stevens join, dissenting, stated in part:

This case is no more about "a fundamental right to engage in homosexual sodomy," as the Court purports to declare, than *Stanley v. Georgia* (1969) was about a fundamental right to watch obscene movies, or *Katz v. United States* (1967) was about a fundamental right to place interstate bets from a telephone booth. Rather, this case is about "the most comprehensive of rights and the right most valued by civilized men," namely, "the right to be let alone." *Olmstead v. United States* (1928) (Brandeis, J., dissenting.)

The statute at issue denies individuals the right to decide for themselves whether to engage in particular forms of private, consensual sexual activity. The Court concludes that [the statute] is valid essentially because "the laws of . . . many States . . . still make such conduct illegal and have done so for a very long time.". . . . Like Justice Holmes, I believe that "[i]t is revolting to have no better reason for a rule of law than that so it was laid down in the time of Henry IV. It is still more revolting if the grounds upon which it was laid down have vanished long since, and the rule simply persists from blind imitation of the past." I believe we must analyze respondent's claim in the light of the values that underlie the constitutional right to privacy. If that right means anything, it means that, before Georgia can prosecute its citizens for making choices about the most intimate aspects of their lives, it must do more than assert that the choice they have made is an "abominable crime not fit to be named among Christians."

. . . . A fair reading of the statute and of the complaint reveals that the majority has distorted the question this case presents.

. . . [T]he Court's almost obsessive focus on homosexual activity is particularly hard to justify in light of the broad language Georgia has used. . . . The sex or status of the persons who engage in [sodomy] is irrelevant as a matter of state law. In fact, to the extent I can discern a legislative purpose . . . that purpose seems to have been to broaden the coverage of the law to reach heterosexual as well as homosexual activity. I therefore see no basis for the Court's decision to treat this case . . . solely on the grounds that it prohibits homosexual activity. . . .

. . . . The Court claims that its decision today merely refuses to recognize a fundamental right to engage in homosexual sodomy; what the Court really has refused to recognize is the fundamental interest all individuals have in controlling the nature of their intimate associations with others.

The behavior for which Hardwick faces prosecution occurred in his own home, a place to which the Fourth Amendment attaches special significance. . . .

. . . . "The right of the people to be secure in their . . . houses," expressly guaranteed by the Fourth Amendment, is perhaps the most "textual" of the various constitutional provisions that inform our understanding of the right to privacy, and thus I cannot agree with the Court's statement that "[t]he right pressed upon us here has no . . . support in the text of the Constitution." Indeed, the right of an individual to conduct intimate relations in the intimacy of his or her own home seems to me to be the heart of the Constitution's protection of privacy. . . .

. . . Essentially, petitioner argues, and the Court agrees, that the fact that the acts described in [the statute] "for hundreds of years, if not thousands, have been uniformly condemned as immoral" is a sufficient reason to permit a State to ban them today.

I cannot agree that either the length of time a majority has held its convictions or the passions with which it defends them can withdraw legislation from this Court's scrutiny. As Justice Jackson wrote so eloquently for the Court in *West Virginia Board of Education v. Barnette* (1943), "we apply the limitations of the Constitution with no fear that freedom to be intellectually and spiritually diverse or even contrary will disintegrate the social organization. . . . [F]reedom to differ is not limited to things that do not matter much. That would be a mere shadow of freedom. The test of its substance is the right to differ as to things that touch the heart of the existing order." It is precisely because the issue raised by this case touches the heart of what makes individuals what they are that we should be especially sensitive to the rights of those whose choices upset the majority.

The assertion that "traditional Judeo-Christian values proscribe" the conduct involved, cannot provide an adequate justification for [the statute]. That certain, but by no means all, religious groups condemn the behavior at issue gives the State no license to impose their judgments on the entire citizenry. The legitimacy of secular legislation depends instead on whether the State can advance some justification for its law beyond its conformity to religious doctrine. . . . No matter how uncomfortable a certain group may make the majority of this Court, we have held that "[m]ere public intolerance or animosity cannot constitutionally justify the deprivation of a person's physical liberty." *O'Connor v. Donaldson* (1975).

. . . . Statutes banning public sexual activity are entirely consistent with protecting the individual's liberty interest in decisions concerning sexual relations: the same recognition that those decisions are intensely private which justifies protecting them from governmental interference can justify protecting individuals from unwilling exposure to the sexual activities of others. But the mere fact that intimate behavior may be punished when it takes place in public cannot dictate how States can regulate intimate behavior that occurs in intimate places. . . .

This case involves no real interference with the rights of others, for the mere knowledge that other individuals do not adhere to one's value system cannot be a legally cognizable interest . . . let alone an interest that can justify invading the houses, hearts, and minds of citizens who choose to live their lives differently. . . .

. . . . I can only hope that . . . the Court soon will reconsider its analysis and conclude that depriving individuals of the right to choose for themselves how to conduct their intimate relationships poses a far greater threat to the values most deeply rooted in our Nation's history than tolerance of nonconformity could ever do. Because I think the Court today betrays those values, I dissent.

* * * * * * * * * * * * * * * * * * * * * * * * * * * * *

*Discussion Points:*

1. Explain Justice White's views about "rights" that have no "cognizable roots in the language" of the Constitutions? What did he say about a "fundamental right" of homosexuals to engage in sodomy? What significance did he place upon majority opinion?

2. Justices White and Blackmun thought that this case was about different things. Blackmun accused White of trivializing the importance of the central issue by the way he chose to frame the question. Explain this point fully. In your opinion, who is more persuasive? What "right" do you think this case is really about?

3. What significance did Blackmun place on historical legislative opposition to homosexual conduct? What did he say about religious opposition to such conduct?

4. Justice Blackmun thought that the language of the Georgia statute was sufficiently broad to apply against heterosexuals and homosexuals alike. However, the law was not being enforced against heterosexuals. In a separate dissenting opinion, Justice Stevens argued that selective application of a law against homosexuals alone must be supported by a legitimate interest more substantial than "a habitual dislike for, or ignorance about, the disfavored group." What do you think of such selective enforcement? Recall that the law that was challenged in *Griswold* had not been enforced for a time either. Discuss the importance of nonenforcement.

5. Why did Blackmun stress the fact that Hardwick's actions occurred in the home? Should other "victimless" crimes (e.g., drug abuse) be tolerated as long as they occur in the home? Why or why not?

6. In a separate concurring opinion, Justice Powell indicated that Hardwick might have been successful had he raised Eighth Amendment claims. The Georgia law authorized a court "to imprison a person for up to 20 years for a single private, consensual act of sodomy." In Powell's view, the possibility of such a long

sentence for this crime raised "serious" Eighth Amendment issues. What do you think?

7. In your opinion, should the constitutional right of privacy have protected Hardwick in this case? Why or why not?

# APPENDIX A:
# THE CONSTITUTION OF THE
# UNITED STATES

# THE CONSTITUTION OF THE
# UNITED STATES

## PREAMBLE

We the People of the United States, in Order to form a more perfect Union, establish Justice, insure domestic Tranquility, provide for the common defence, promote the general Welfare, and secure the Blessings of Liberty to ourselves and our Posterity, do ordain and establish this Constitution for the United States of America.

## ARTICLE I

**Section 1.** All legislative Powers herein granted shall be vested in a Congress of the United States, which shall consist of a Senate and House of Representatives.

**Section 2.** The House of Representatives shall be composed of Members chosen every second Year by the People of the several States, and the Electors in each State shall have the Qualifications requisite for Electors of the most numerous Branch of the State Legislature.

No Person shall be a Representative who shall not have attained to the age of twenty five Years, and been seven Years a Citizen of the United States, and who shall not, when elected, be an Inhabitant of that State in which he shall be chosen.

[Representatives and direct Taxes shall be apportioned among the several States which may be included within this Union, according to their respective Numbers, which shall be determined by adding to the whole Number of free Persons, including those bound to Service for a Term of Years, and excluding Indians not taxed, three fifths of all other Persons.][1] The actual Enumeration shall be made within three Years after the first Meeting of the Congress of the United States, and within every subsequent Term of ten Years, in such Manner as they shall by Law direct. The Number of Representatives shall not exceed one for every thirty Thousand, but each State shall have at Least one Representative; and until such enumeration shall be made, the State of New Hampshire shall be entitled to chuse three, Massachusetts eight,

Rhode-Island and Providence Plantations one, Connecticut five, New-York six, New Jersey four, Pennsylvania eight, Delaware one, Maryland six, Virginia ten, North Carolina five, South Carolina five, and Georgia three.

When vacancies happen in the Representation from any State, the Executive Authority thereof shall issue Writs of Election to fill such Vacancies.

The House of Representatives shall chuse their Speaker and other Officers; and shall have the sole Power of Impeachment.

**Section 3.** The Senate of the United States shall be composed of two Senators from each State, [chosen by the Legislature thereof,]² for six Years; and each Senator shall have one Vote.

Immediately after they shall be assembled in Consequence of the first Election, they shall be divided as equally as may be into three Classes. The Seats of the Senators of the first Class shall be vacated at the Expiration of the second Year, of the second Class at the Expiration of the fourth Year, and of the third Class at the Expiration of the sixth Year, so that one third may be chosen every second Year; [and if Vacancies happen by Resignation, or otherwise, during the Recess of the Legislature of any State, the Executive thereof may make temporary Appointments until the next Meeting of the Legislature, which shall then fill such Vacancies.]³

No Person shall be a Senator who shall not have attained to the Age of thirty Years, and been nine Years a Citizen of the United States, and who shall not, when elected, be an Inhabitant of that State for which he shall be chosen.

The Vice President of the United States shall be President of the Senate, but shall have no Vote, unless they be equally divided.

The Senate shall chuse their other Officers, and also a President pro tempore, in the Absence of the Vice President, or when he shall exercise the Office of President of the United States.

The Senate shall have the sole Power to try all Impeachments. When sitting for that Purpose, they shall be on Oath or Affirmation. When the President of the United States is tried the Chief Justice shall preside: And no Person shall be convicted without the Concurrence of two thirds of the Members present.

Judgment in Cases of Impeachment shall not extend further than to removal from Office, and disqualification to hold and enjoy any Office of honor, Trust or Profit under the United States: but the Party convicted shall nevertheless be liable and subject to Indictment, Trial, Judgment and Punishment, according to Law.

**Section 4.** The Times, Places and Manner of holding Elections for

Senators and Representatives, shall be prescribed in each State by the Legislature thereof; but the Congress may at any time by Law make or alter such Regulations, except as to the Places of chusing Senators.

The Congress shall assemble at least once in every Year, and such Meeting shall [be on the first Monday in December],[4] unless they shall by Law appoint a different Day.

**Section 5.** Each House shall be the Judge of the Elections, Returns and Qualifications of its own Members, and a Majority of each shall constitute a Quorum to do Business; but a smaller Number may adjourn from day to day, and may be authorized to compel the Attendance of absent Members, in such Manner, and under such Penalties as each House may provide.

Each House may determine the Rules of its Proceedings, punish its Members for disorderly Behaviour, and, with the Concurrence of two thirds, expel a Member.

Each House shall keep a Journal of its Proceedings, and from time to time publish the same, excepting such Parts as may in their Judgment require Secrecy; and the Yeas and Nays of the Members of either House on any question shall, at the Desire of one fifth of those Present, be entered on the Journal.

Neither House, during the Session of Congress, shall, without the Consent of the other, adjourn for more than three days, nor to any other Place than that in which the two Houses shall be sitting.

**Section 6.** The Senators and Representatives shall receive a Compensation for their Services, to be ascertained by Law, and paid out of the Treasury of the United States. They shall in all Cases, except Treason, Felony and Breach of the Peace, be privileged from Arrest during their Attendance at the Session of their respective Houses, and in going to and returning from the same; and for any Speech or Debate in either House, they shall not be questioned in any other Place.

No Senator or Representative shall, during the Time for which he was elected, be appointed to any civil Office under the Authority of the United States, which shall have been created, or the Emoluments whereof shall have been encreased during such time; and no Person holding any Office under the United States, shall be a Member of either House during his Continuance in Office.

**Section 7.** All Bills for raising Revenue shall originate in the House of Representatives; but the Senate may propose or concur with amendments as on other Bills.

Every Bill which shall have passed the House of Representatives and the Senate, shall, before it become a Law, be presented to the President of the United States; If he approve he shall sign it, but if not he shall return it, with his Objections to that House in which it shall have originated, who shall enter the Objections at large on their Journal, and proceed to reconsider it. If after such Reconsideration two thirds of that House shall agree to pass the Bill, it shall be sent, together with the Objections, to the other House, by which it shall likewise be reconsidered, and if approved by two thirds of that House, it shall become a Law. But in all such Cases the Votes of both Houses shall be determined by yeas and Nays, and the Names of the Persons voting for and against the Bill shall be entered on the Journal of each House respectively. If any Bill shall not be returned by the President within ten Days (Sunday excepted) after it shall have been presented to him, the Same shall be a Law, in like Manner as if he had signed it, unless the Congress by their Adjournment prevent its Return, in which Case it shall not be a Law.

Every Order, Resolution, or Vote to which the Concurrence of the Senate and House of Representatives may be necessary (except on a question of Adjournment) shall be presented to the President of the United States; and before the Same shall take Effect, shall be approved by him, or being disapproved by him, shall be repassed by two thirds of the Senate and House of Representatives, according to the Rules and Limitations prescribed in the Case of a Bill.

**Section 8.** The Congress shall have Power To lay and collect Taxes, Duties, Imposts and Excises, to pay the Debts and provide for the common Defence and general Welfare of the United States; but all Duties, Imposts and Excises shall be uniform throughout the United States;

To borrow Money on the credit of the United States;

To regulate Commerce with foreign Nations, and among the several States, and with the Indian Tribes;

To establish an uniform Rule of Naturalization, and uniform Laws on the subject of Bankruptcies throughout the United States;

To coin Money, regulate the Value thereof, and of foreign Coin, and fix the Standard of Weights and Measures;

To provide for the Punishment of counterfeiting the Securities and current Coin of the United States;

To establish Post Offices and post Roads;

To promote the Progress of Science and useful Arts, by securing for limited Times to Authors and Inventors the exclusive Right to their respective Writings and Discoveries;

To constitute Tribunals inferior to the supreme Court;

To define and punish Piracies and Felonies commited on the high Seas, and Offences against the Law of Nations;

To declare War, grant Letters of Marque and Reprisal, and make Rules concerning Captures on Land and Water;

To raise and support Armies, but no Appropriation of Money to that Use shall be for a longer Term than two Years;

To provide and maintain a Navy;

To make Rules for the Government and Regulation of the land and naval Forces;

To provide for calling forth the Militia to execute the Laws of the Union, suppress Insurrections and repel Invasions;

To provide for organizing, arming, and disciplining, the Militia, and for governing such Part of them as may be employed in the Service of the United States, reserving to the States respectively, the Appointment of the Officers, and the Authority of training the Militia according to the discipline prescribed by Congress;

To exercise exclusive Legislation in all Cases whatsoever, over such District (not exceeding ten Miles square) as may, by Cession of Particular States, and the Acceptance of Congress, become the Seat of the Government of the United States, and to exercise like Authority over all Places purchased by the Consent of the Legislature of the State in which the Same shall be, for the Erection of Forts, Magazines, Arsenals, dock-Yards, and other needful Buildings;—And

To make all Laws which shall be necessary and proper for carrying into Execution the foregoing Powers, and all other Powers vested by this Constitution in the Government of the United States, or in any Department or Officer thereof.

**Section 9.** The Migration or Importation of such Persons as any of the States now existing shall think proper to admit, shall not be prohibited by the Congress prior to the Year one thousand eight hundred and eight, but a Tax or duty may be imposed on such Importation, not exceeding ten dollars for each Person.

The Privilege of the Writ of Habeas Corpus shall not be suspended, unless when in Cases of Rebellion or Invasion the public Safety may require it.

No Bill of Attainder or ex post facto Law shall be passed.

No capitation, or other direct, Tax shall be laid, unless in Proportion to the Census of Enumeration herein before directed to be taken.[5]

No Tax or Duty shall be laid on Articles exported from any State.

No Preference shall be given by any Regulation of Commerce or Revenue to the Ports of one State over those of another; nor shall Vessels bound to, or from, one State, be obliged to enter, clear or pay Duties in another.

No Money shall be drawn from the Treasury, but in Consequence of Appropriations made by Law; and a regular Statement and Account of the Receipts and Expenditures of all public Money shall be published from time to time.

No Title of Nobility shall be granted by the United States; And no Person holding any Office of Profit or Trust under them, shall, without the Consent of the Congress, accept of any present, Emolument, Office, or Title, of any kind whatever, from any King, Prince or foreign State.

**Section 10.** No State shall enter into any Treaty, Alliance, or Confederation; grant Letters of Marque and Reprisal; coin Money; emit Bills of Credit; make any Thing but gold and silver Coin a Tender in Payment of Debts; pass any Bill of Attainder, ex post facto Law, or Law impairing the Obligation of Contracts or grant any Title of Nobility.

No State shall, without the Consent of the Congress, lay any Imposts or Duties on Imports or Exports, except what may be absolutely necessary for executing it's inspection Laws; and the net Produce of all Duties and Imposts, laid by any State on Imports or Exports, shall be for the Use of the Treasury of the United States; and all such Laws shall be subject to the Revision and Controul of the Congress.

No State shall, without the Consent of Congress, lay any Duty of Tonnage, keep Troops, or Ships of War in time of Peace, enter into any Agreement or Compact with another State, or with a foreign Power, or engage in War, unless actually invaded, or in such imminent Danger as will not admit of delay.

## ARTICLE II

**Section 1.** The executive Power shall be vested in a President of the United States of America. He shall hold his Office during the Term of four Years, and, together with the Vice President, chosen for the same Term, be elected, as follows.

Each State shall appoint, in such Manner as the Legislature thereof may direct, a Number of Electors, equal to the whole Number of Senators and Representatives to which the State may be entitled in the Congress; but no Senator or Representative, or Person holding an Office of Trust or Profit under the United States, shall be appointed an Elector.

[The Electors shall meet in their respective States, and vote by Ballot for two Persons, of whom one at least shall not be an Inhabitant of the same State with themselves. And they shall make a List of all the Persons voted for, and of the Number of Votes for each; which List they shall sign and certify, and transmit sealed to the Seat of the Government of the United States, directed to the President of the Senate. The

President of the Senate shall, in the Presence of the Senate and House of Representatives, open all the Certificates, and the Votes shall then be counted. The Person having the greatest Number of Votes shall be the President, if such Number be a Majority of the whole Number of Electors appointed; and if there be more than one who have such Majority, and have an equal Number of Votes, then the House of Representatives shall immediately chuse by Ballot one of them for President; and if no Person have a Majority, then from the five highest on the list the said House shall in like Manner chuse the President. But in chusing the President, the Votes shall be taken by States, the Representation from each State having one Vote; a quorum for this Purpose shall consist of a Member or Members from two thirds of the States, and a Majority of all the States shall be necessary to a Choice. In every Case, after the Choice of the President, the Person having the greatest Number of Votes of the Electors shall be the Vice President. But if there should remain two or more who have equal Votes, the Senate shall chuse from them by Ballot the Vice President.][6]

The Congress may determine the Time of chusing the Electors, and the Day on which they shall give their Votes; which Day shall be the same throughout the United States.

No Person except a natural born Citizen, or a Citizen of the United States, at the time of the Adoption of this Constitution, shall be eligible to the Office of President; neither shall any Person be eligible to that Office who shall not have attained to the Age of thirty five Years, and been fourteen Years a Resident within the United States.

In Case of the Removal of the President from Office, or of his Death, Resignation, or Inability to discharge the Powers and Duties of the said Office,[7] the Same shall devolve on the Vice President, and the Congress may by Law provide for the Case of Removal, Death, Resignation or Inability, both of the President and Vice President, declaring what Officer shall then act as President, and such Officer shall act accordingly, until the Disability be removed, or a President shall be elected.

The President shall, at stated Times, receive for his Services, a Compensation, which shall neither be encreased nor diminished during the Period for which he shall have been elected, and he shall not receive within that Period any other Emolument from the United States, or any of them.

Before he enter on the Execution of his Office, he shall take the following Oath or Affirmation:—"I do solemnly swear (or affirm) that I will faithfully execute the Office of President of the United States, and will to the best of my Ability, preserve, protect and defend the Constitution of the United States."

**Section 2.** The President shall be Commander in Chief of the Army and Navy of the United States, and of the Militia of the several States, when called into the actual Service of the United States; he may require the Opinion, in writing, of the principal Officer in each of the executive Departments, upon any Subject relating to the Duties of their respective Offices, and he shall have Power to grant Reprieves and Pardons for Offenses against the United States, except in Cases of Impeachment.

He shall have Power, by and with the Advice and Consent of the Senate, to make Treaties, provided two thirds of the Senators present concur; and he shall nominate, and by and with the Advice and Consent of the Senate, shall appoint Ambassadors, other public Ministers and Consuls, Judges of the supreme Court, and all other Officers of the United States, whose Appointments are not herein otherwise provided for, and which shall be established by Law: but the Congress may by Law vest the Appointment of such inferior Officers, as they think proper, in the President alone, in the Courts of Law, or in the Heads of Departments.

The President shall have Power to fill up all Vacancies that may happen during the Recess of the Senate, by granting Commissions which shall expire at the End of their next Session.

**Section 3.** He shall from time to time give to the Congress Information of the State of the Union, and recommend to their Consideration such Measures as he shall judge necessary and expedient; he may, on extraordinary Occasions, convene both Houses, or either of them, and in Case of Disagreement between them, with Respect to the Time of Adjournment, he may adjourn them to such Time as he shall think proper; he shall receive Ambassadors and other public Ministers; he shall take Care that the Laws be faithfully executed, and shall Commission all the Officers of the United States.

**Section 4.** The President, Vice President and all Civil Officers of the United States, shall be removed from office on Impeachment for, and Conviction of, Treason, Bribery, or other high Crimes and Misdemeanors.


## ARTICLE III

**Section 1.** The judicial Power of the United States, shall be vested in one supreme Court, and in such inferior Courts as the Congress may from time to time ordain and establish. The Judges, both of the supreme and inferior Courts, shall hold their Offices during good Behaviour, and shall, at stated Times, receive for their Services, a Compensation, which shall not be diminished during their Continuance in Office.

**Section 2.** The judicial Power shall extend to all Cases, in Law and Equity, arising under this Constitution, the Laws of the United States, and Treaties made, or which shall be made, under their Authority;—to all Cases affecting Ambassadors, other public Ministers and Consuls;—to all Cases of admiralty and maritime Jurisdiction;—to Controversies to which the United States shall be a Party;—to Controversies between two or more States;—between a State and Citizens of another State;[8]—between Citizens of different States;—between Citizens of the same State claiming Lands under Grants of different States, and between a State, or the Citizens thereof, and foreign States, Citizens or Subjects.[8]

In all Cases affecting Ambassadors, other public Ministers and Consuls, and those in which a State shall be Party, the supreme Court shall have original Jurisdiction. In all the other Cases before mentioned, the supreme Court shall have appellate Jurisdiction, both as to Law and Fact, with such Exceptions, and under such Regulations as the Congress shall make.

The Trial of all Crimes, except in cases of Impeachment, shall be by Jury; and such Trial shall be held in the State where the said Crimes shall have been committed; but when not committed within any State, the Trial shall be at such Place or Places as the Congress may by Law have directed.

**Section 3.** Treason against the United States, shall consist only in levying War against them, or in adhering to their Enemies, giving them Aid and Comfort. No Person shall be convicted of Treason unless on the Testimony of two Witnesses to the same overt Act, or on Confession in open Court.

The Congress shall have Power to declare the Punishment of Treason, but no Attainder of Treason shall work Corruption of Blood, or Forfeiture except during the Life of the Person attainted.

## ARTICLE IV

**Section 1.** Full Faith and Credit shall be given in each State to the public Acts, Records, and judicial Proceedings of every other State. And the Congress may by general Laws prescribe the Manner in which such Acts, Records and Proceedings shall be proved, and the Effect thereof.

**Section 2.** The Citizens of each State shall be entitled to all Privileges and Immunities of Citizens in the several States.

A Person charged in any State with Treason, Felony, or other Crime, who shall flee from Justice, and be found in another State, shall on Demand of the executive Authority of the State from which he fled, be delivered up, to be removed to the State having Jurisdiction of the Crime.

[No Person held to Service or Labour in one State, under the Laws thereof, escaping into another, shall, in Consequence of any Law or Regulation therein, be discharged from such Service or Labour, but shall be delivered up on Claim of the Party to whom such Service or Labour may be due.]⁹

**Section 3.** New States may be admitted by the Congress into this Union; but no new State shall be formed or erected within the Jurisdiction of any other State; nor any State be formed by the Junction of two or more States, or Parts of States, without the Consent of the Legislatures of the States concerned as well as of the Congress.

The Congress shall have Power to dispose of and make all needful Rules and Regulations respecting the Territory or other Property belonging to the United States; and nothing in this Constitution shall be so construed as to Prejudice any Claims of the United States, or of any particular State.

**Section 4.** The United States shall guarantee to every State in this Union a Republican Form of Government, and shall protect each of them against Invasion; and on Application of the Legislature, or of the Executive (when the Legislature cannot be convened) against domestic Violence.

## ARTICLE V

The Congress, whenever two thirds of both Houses shall deem it necessary, shall propose Amendments to this Constitution, or, on the Application of the Legislatures of two thirds of the several States, shall call a Convention for proposing Amendments, which, in either Case, shall be valid to all Intents and Purposes, as Part of this Constitution, when ratified by the Legislatures of three fourths of the several States, or by Conventions in three fourths thereof, as the one or the other Mode of Ratification may be proposed by the Congress; Provided [that no Amendment which may be made prior to the Year One thousand eight hundred and eight shall in any Manner affect the first and fourth

Clauses in the Ninth Section of the first Article; and][10] that no State, without its Consent, shall be deprived of its equal Suffrage in the Senate.

## ARTICLE VI

All Debts contracted and Engagements entered into, before the Adoption of this Constitution, shall be as valid against the United States under this Constitution, as under the Confederation.

This Constitution, and the Laws of the United States which shall be made in Pursuance thereof; and all Treaties made, or which shall be made, under the Authority of the United States, shall be the supreme Law of the Land; and the Judges in every State shall be bound thereby, any Thing in the Constitution or Laws of any State to the Contrary notwithstanding.

The Senators and Representatives before mentioned, and the Members of the several State Legislatures, and all executive and judicial Officers, both of the United States and of the several States, shall be bound by Oath or Affirmation, to support this Constitution; but no religious Test shall ever be required as a Qualification to any Office or public Trust under the United States.

## ARTICLE VII

The Ratification of the Conventions of nine States, shall be sufficient for the Establishment of this Constitution between the States so ratifying the Same. Done in Convention by the Unanimous Consent of the States present the Seventeenth Day of September in the Year of our Lord one thousand seven hundred and Eighty seven and of the Independence of the United States of America the Twelfth In witness whereof We have hereunto subscribed our Names, George Washington, President and deputy from Virginia.

| | |
|---|---|
| New Hampshire: | John Langdon, |
| | Nicholas Gilman. |
| Massachusetts: | Nathaniel Gorham, |
| | Rufus King. |
| Connecticut: | William Samuel Johnson, |
| | Roger Sherman. |
| New York: | Alexander Hamilton. |

| | |
|---|---|
| New Jersey: | William Livingston, |
| | David Brearley, |
| | William Paterson, |
| | Jonathan Dayton. |
| Pennsylvania: | Benjamin Franklin, |
| | Thomas Mifflin, |
| | Robert Morris, |
| | George Clymer, |
| | Thomas FitzSimons, |
| | Jared Ingersoll, |
| | James Wilson, |
| | Gouverneur Morris. |
| Delaware: | George Read, |
| | Gunning Bedford Jr., |
| | John Dickinson, |
| | Richard Bassett, |
| | Jacob Broom. |
| Maryland: | James McHenry, |
| | Daniel of St. Thomas Jenifer, |
| | Daniel Carroll. |
| Virginia: | John Blair, |
| | James Madison Jr. |
| North Carolina: | William Blount, |
| | Richard Dobbs Spaight, |
| | Hugh Williamson. |
| South Carolina: | John Rutledge, |
| | Charles Cotesworth Pinckney, |
| | Charles Pinckney, |
| | Pierce Butler. |
| Georgia: | William Few, |
| | Abraham Baldwin. |

[The language of the original Constitution, not including the Amendments, was adopted by a convention of the states on Sept. 17, 1787, and was subsequently ratified by the states on the following dates: Delaware, Dec. 7, 1787; Pennsylvania, Dec. 12, 1787; New Jersey, Dec. 18, 1787; Georgia, Jan. 2, 1788; Connecticut, Jan. 9, 1788; Massachusetts, Feb. 6, 1788; Maryland, April 28, 1788; South Carolina, May 23, 1788; New Hampshire, June 21, 1788.

Ratification was completed on June 21, 1788.

The Constitution subsequently was ratified by Virginia, June 25,

1788; New York, July 26, 1788; North Carolina, Nov. 21, 1789; Rhode Island, May 29, 1790; and Vermont, Jan. 10, 1791.]

# AMENDMENTS

## Amendment I
*(First ten amendments ratified Dec. 15, 1791.)*

Congress shall make no law respecting an establishment of religion, or prohibiting the free exercise thereof; or abridging the freedom of speech, or of the press; or the right of the people peaceably to assemble, and to petition the Government for a redress of grievances.

## Amendment II

A well regulated Militia, being necessary to the security of a free State, the right of the people to keep and bear Arms, shall not be infringed.

## Amendment III

No Soldier shall, in time of peace be quartered in any house, without the consent of the Owner, nor in time of war, but in a manner to be prescribed by law.

## Amendment IV

The right of the people to be secure in their persons, houses, papers, and effects, against unreasonable searches and seizures, shall not be violated, and no Warrants shall issue, but upon probable cause, supported by Oath or affirmation, and particularly describing the place to be searched, and the persons or things to be seized.

## Amendment V

No person shall be held to answer for a capital, or otherwise infamous crime, unless on a presentment or indictment of a Grand Jury, except in cases arising in the land or naval forces, or in the Militia, when in actual service in time of War or public danger; nor shall any person be subject for the same offence to be twice put in jeopardy of life or limb; nor shall be compelled in any criminal case to be a witness against himself, nor be deprived of life, liberty, or property, without due process of law; nor shall private property be taken for public use, without just compensation.

## Amendment VI

In all criminal prosecutions, the accused shall enjoy the right to a speedy and public trial, by an impartial jury of the State and district wherein the crime shall have been committed, which district shall have been previously ascertained by law, and to be informed of the nature and cause of the accusation; to be confronted with the witnesses against him; to have compulsory process for obtaining witnesses in his favor, and to have the Assistance of Counsel for his defence.

## Amendment VII

In Suits at common law, where the value in controversy shall exceed twenty dollars, the right of trial by jury shall be preserved, and no fact tried by a jury, shall be otherwise re-examined in any Court of the United States, than according to the rules of the common law.

## Amendment VIII

Excessive bail shall not be required, nor excessive fines imposed, nor cruel and unusual punishments inflicted.

## Amendment IX

The enumeration in the Constitution, of certain rights, shall not be construed to deny or disparage others retained by the people.

## Amendment X

The powers not delegated to the United States by the Constitution, nor prohibited by it to the States, are reserved to the States respectively, or to the people.

## Amendment XI *(Ratified Feb. 7, 1795)*

The Judicial power of the United States shall not be construed to extend to any suit in law or equity, commenced or prosecuted against one of the United States by Citizens of another State, or by Citizens or Subjects of any Foreign State.

## Amendment XII *(Ratified June 15, 1804)*

The Electors shall meet in their respective states and vote by ballot for President and Vice-President, one of whom, at least, shall not be an inhabitant of the same state with themselves; they shall name in their ballots the person voted for as President, and in distinct ballots the person voted for as Vice-President, and they shall make distinct lists of all persons voted for as President, and of all persons voted for as Vice-President, and of the number of votes for each, which lists they shall sign and certify, and transmit sealed to the seat of the government of the United States, directed to the President of the Senate;—The President of the Senate shall, in the presence of the Senate and House of Representatives, open all the certificates and the votes shall then be counted;—The person having the greatest number of votes for President, shall be the President, if such number be a majority of the whole number of Electors appointed; and if no person have such majority, then from the persons having the highest numbers not exceeding three on the list of those voted for as President, the House of Representatives shall choose immediately, by ballot, the President. But in choosing the President, the votes shall be taken by states, the representation from each state having one vote; a quorum for this purpose shall consist of a member or members from two-thirds of the states, and a majority of all the states shall be necessary to a choice. [And if the House of Representatives shall not choose a President whenever the right of choice shall devolve upon them, before the fourth day of March next following, then the Vice-President shall act as President, as in the case of the death or other constitutional disability of the President—][11] The person having the greatest number of votes as Vice-President, shall be the Vice-President, if such number be a majority of the whole number of Electors appointed, and if no person have a majority, then from the two highest numbers on the list, the Senate shall choose the Vice-President; a quorum for the purpose shall consist of two-thirds of the whole number of Senators, and a majority of the whole number shall be necessary to a choice. But no person constitutionally ineligible to the office of President shall be eligible to that of Vice-President of the United States.

## Amendment XIII *(Ratified Dec. 6, 1865)*

**Section 1.** Neither slavery nor involuntary servitude, except as a punishment for crime whereof the party shall have been duly convicted, shall exist within the United States, or any place subject to their jurisdiction.

**Section 2.** Congress shall have power to enforce this article by appropriate legislation.

## Amendment XIV *(Ratified July 9, 1868)*

**Section 1.** All persons born or naturalized in the United States and subject to the jurisdiction thereof, are citizens of the United States and of the State wherein they reside. No State shall make or enforce any law which shall abridge the privileges or immunities of citizens of the United States; nor shall any State deprive any person of life, liberty, or property, without due process of law; nor deny to any person within its jurisdiction the equal protection of the laws.

**Section 2.** Representatives shall be apportioned among the several States according to their respective numbers, counting the whole number of persons in each State, excluding Indians not taxed. But when the right to vote at any election for the choice of electors for President and Vice President of the United States, Representatives in Congress, the Executive and Judicial officers of a State, or the members of the Legislature thereof, is denied to any of the male inhabitants of such State, being twenty-one years of age,[12] and citizens of the United States, or in any way abridged, except for participation in rebellion, or other crime, the basis of representation therein shall be reduced in the proportion which the number of such male citizens shall bear to the whole number of male citizens twenty-one years of age in such State.

**Section 3.** No person shall be a Senator or Representative in Congress, or elector of President and Vice President, or hold any office, civil or military, under the United States, or under any State, who, having previously taken an oath, as a member of Congress, or as an officer of the United States, or as a member of any State legislature, or as an executive or judicial officer of any State, to support the Constitution of the United States, shall have engaged in insurrection or rebellion against the same, or given aid or comfort to the enemies thereof. But Congress may by a vote of two-thirds of each House, remove such disability.

**Section 4.** The validity of the public debt of the United States, authorized by law, including debts incurred for payment of pensions and bounties for services in suppressing insurrection or rebellion, shall not be questioned. But neither the United States nor any State shall assume or pay any debt or obligation incurred in aid of insurrection or rebellion against the United States, or any claim for the loss or emancipation of any slave; but all such debts, obligations and claims shall be held illegal and void.

**Section 5.** The Congress shall have power to enforce, by appropriate legislation, the provisions of this article.

**Amendment XV** *(Ratified Feb. 3, 1870)*

**Section 1.** The right of citizens of the United States to vote shall not be denied or abridged by the United States or by any State on account of race, color, or previous condition of servitude.

**Section 2.** The Congress shall have power to enforce this article by appropriate legislation.

## Amendment XVI *(Ratified Feb. 3, 1913)*

The Congress shall have power to lay and collect taxes on incomes, from whatever source derived, without apportionment among the several States, and without regard to any census or enumeration.

## Amendment XVII *(Ratified April 8, 1913)*

The Senate of the United States shall be composed of two Senators from each State, elected by the people thereof, for six years; and each Senator shall have one vote. The electors in each State shall have the qualifications requisite for electors of the most numerous branch of the State legislatures.

When vacancies happen in the representation of any State in the Senate, the executive authority of such State shall issue writs of election to fill such vacancies: *Provided,* That the legislature of any State may empower the executive thereof to make temporary appointments until the people fill the vacancies by election as the legislature may direct.

This amendment shall not be so construed as to affect the election or term of any Senator chosen before it becomes valid as part of the Constitution.

## Amendment XVIII *(Ratified Jan. 16, 1919)*

**Section 1.** After one year from the ratification of this article the manufacture, sale, or transportation of intoxicating liquors within, the importation thereof into, or the exportation thereof from the United States and all territory subject to the jurisdiction thereof for beverage purposes is hereby prohibited.

**Section 2.** The Congress and the several States shall have concurrent power to enforce this article by appropriate legislation.

**Section 3.** This article shall be inoperative unless it shall have been ratified as an amendment to the Constitution by the legislatures of the several States, as provided in the Constitution, within seven years from the date of the submission hereof to the States by the Congress.][13]

## Amendment XIX *(Ratified Aug. 18, 1920)*

The right of citizens of the United States to vote shall not be denied or abridged by the United States or by any State on account of sex.

Congress shall have power to enforce this article by appropriate legislation.

## Amendment XX *(Ratified Jan. 23, 1933)*

**Section 1.** The terms of the President and Vice President shall end at noon on the 20th day of January, and the terms of Senators and Representatives at noon on the 3d day of January, of the years in which such terms would have ended if this article had not been ratified; and the terms of their successors shall then begin.

**Section 2.** The Congress shall assemble at least once in every year, and such meeting shall begin at noon on the 3d day of January, unless they shall by law appoint a different day.

**Section 3.**[14] If, at the time fixed for the beginning of the term of the President, the President elect shall have died, the Vice President elect shall become President. If a President shall not have been chosen before the time fixed for the beginning of his term, or if the President elect shall have failed to qualify, then the Vice President elect shall act as President until a President shall have qualified; and the Congress may by law provide for the case wherein neither a President elect nor a Vice President elect shall have qualified, declaring who shall then act as President, or the manner in which one who is to act shall be selected, and such person shall act accordingly until a President or Vice President shall have qualified.

**Section 4.** The Congress may by law provide for the case of the death of any of the persons from whom the House of Representatives may choose a President whenever the right of choice shall have devolved upon them, and for the case of the death of any of the persons from whom the Senate may choose a Vice President whenever the right of choice shall have devolved upon them.

**Section 5.** Sections 1 and 2 shall take effect on the 15th day of October following the ratification of this article.

**Section 6.** This article shall be inoperative unless it shall have been ratified as an amendment to the Constitution by the legislatures of three-fourths of the several States within seven years from the date of its submission.

## Amendment XXI *(Ratified Dec. 5, 1933)*

**Section 1.** The eighteenth article of amendment to the Constitution of the United States is hereby repealed.

**Section 2.** The transportation or importation into any State, Territory or possession of the United States for delivery or use therein of intoxicating liquors, in violation of the laws thereof, is hereby prohibited.

**Section 3.** This article shall be inoperative unless it shall have been ratified as an amendment to the Constitution by conventions in the several States, as provided in the Constitution, within seven years from the date of the submission hereof to the States by the Congress.

### Amendment XXII *(Ratified Feb. 27, 1951)*

**Section 1.** No person shall be elected to the office of the President more than twice, and no person who has held the office of President, or acted as President, for more than two years of a term to which some other person was elected President shall be elected to the office of the President more than once. But this Article shall not apply to any person holding the office of President when this Article was proposed by the Congress, and shall not prevent any person who may be holding the office of President, or acting as President, during the term within which this Article become operative from holding the office of President or acting as President during the remainder of such term.

**Section 2.** This Article shall be inoperative unless it shall have been ratified as an amendment to the Constitution by the legislatures of three-fourths of the several States within seven years from the date of its submission to the States by the Congress.

### Amendment XXIII *(Ratified March 29, 1961)*

**Section 1.** The District constituting the seat of Government of the United States shall appoint in such manner as the Congress may direct:

A number of electors of President and Vice President equal to the whole number of Senators and Representatives in Congress to which the District would be entitled if it were a State, but in no event more than the least populous State; they shall be in addition to those appointed by the States, but they shall be considered, for the purposes of the election of President and Vice President, to be electors appointed by a State; and they shall meet in the District and perform such duties as provided by the twelfth article of amendment.

**Section 2.** The Congress shall have power to enforce this article by appropriate legislation.

### Amendment XXIV *(Ratified Jan. 23, 1964)*

**Section 1.** The right of citizens of the United States to vote in any primary or other election for President or Vice President, for electors for President or Vice President, or for Senator or Representative in Congress, shall not be denied or abridged by the United States or any State by reason of failure to pay any poll tax or other tax.

**Section 2.** The Congress shall have power to enforce this article by appropriate legislation.

### Amendment XXV *(Ratified Feb. 10, 1967)*

**Section 1.** In case of the removal of the President from office or of his death or resignation, the Vice President shall become President.

**Section 2.** Whenever there is a vacancy in the office of the Vice President, the President shall nominate a Vice President who shall take office upon confirmation by a majority vote of both Houses of Congress.

**Section 3.** Whenever the President transmits to the President pro tempore of the Senate and the Speaker of the House of Representatives his written declaration that he is unable to discharge the powers and duties of his office, and until he transmits to them a written declaration to the contrary, such powers and duties shall be discharged by the Vice President as Acting President.

**Section 4.** Whenever the Vice President and a majority of either the principal officers of the executive departments or of such other body as Congress may by law provide, transmit to the President pro tempore of the Senate and the Speaker of the House of Representatives their written declaration that the President is unable to discharge the powers and duties of his office, the Vice President shall immediately assume the powers and duties of the office as Acting President.

Thereafter, when the President transmits to the President pro tempore of the Senate and the Speaker of the House of Representatives his written declaration that no inability exists, he shall resume the powers and duties of his office unless the Vice President and a majority of either the principal officers of the executive department or of such other body as Congress may by law provide, transmit within four days to the President pro tempore of the Senate and the Speaker of the House of Representatives their written declaration that the President is unable to discharge the powers and duties of his office. Thereupon Congress shall decide the issue, assembling within forty-eight hours for that purpose if not in session. If the Congress, within twenty-one days after receipt of the latter written declaration, or, if Congress is not in session, within twenty-one days after Congress is required to assemble, determines by two-thirds vote of both houses that the President is unable to discharge the powers and duties of his office, the Vice President shall continue to discharge the same as Acting President; otherwise, the President shall resume the powers and duties of his office.

## Amendment XXVI *(Ratified July 1, 1971)*

**Section 1.** The right of citizens of the United States, who are eighteen years of age or older, to vote shall not be denied or abridged by the United States or by any State on account of age.

**Section 2.** The Congress shall have power to enforce this article by appropriate legislation.

---

**Footnotes**

1. The part in brackets was changed by section 2 of the Fourteenth Amendment.
2. The part in brackets was changed by section 1 of the Seventeenth Amendment.
3. The part in brackets was changed by the second paragraph of the Seventeenth Amendment.
4. The part in brackets was changed by section 2 of the Twentieth Amendment.
5. The Sixteenth Amendment gave Congress the power to tax incomes.
6. The material in brackets has been superseded by the Twelfth Amendment.
7. This provision has been affected by the Twenty-fifth Amendment.
8. These clauses were affected by the Eleventh Amendment.
9. This paragraph has been superseded by the Thirteenth Amendment.
10. Obsolete.
11. The part in brackets has been superseded by section 3 of the Twentieth Amendment.
12. See the Twenty-sixth Amendment.
13. This Amendment was repealed by section 1 of the Twenty-first Amendment.
14. See the Twenty-fifth Amendment.

Source: U.S. Congress, House, Committee on the Judiciary, *The Constitution of the United States of America, As Amended Through July 1971*, H. Doc. 93-215, 93rd Cong., 2nd sess., 1974.

# APPENDIX B:
# SELECTED BIBLIOGRAPHY

# SELECTED BIBLIOGRAPHY

## I. GENERAL WORKS

Bowen, Catherine Drinker. *Miracle in Philadelphia: The Story of the Constitutional Convention, May to September 1787.* Boston: Atlantic Monthly Press, 1986 [1st ed., 1966].
A very readable narrative of the events of the Philadelphia Convention.

Collier, Christopher and James Lincoln Collier. *Decision in Philadelphia: The Constitutional Convention of 1787.* New York: Random House/Reader's Digest Press, 1986.
A lively contemporary account of the actions and personalities in the Constitutional Convention.

Rodell, Fred. *55 Men: The Story of the Constitution,* with an introduction by Charles Alan Wright. Harrisburg, PA: Stackpole Books, 1986 [1st ed., 1937].
A day-by-day chronicle of the Constitutional Convention, which gives a dramatic rendering of the dynamics of the Convention's business.

Rossiter, Clinton. *1787: The Grand Convention.* New York: Macmillan, 1966.
An account of the Constitutional Convention against the larger background of the conditions and events of the year 1787.

Rutland, Robert. *The Ordeal of the Constitution: The Antifederalists and the Ratification Struggle of 1787-88.* Boston: Northeastern University Press, 1983.
Details the political strategies, compromises, and disappointments of the Constitution's opponents, and presents some materials on the broader political philosophy of the Antifederalists.

Van Doren, Carl. *The Great Rehearsal.* Westport, CT: Greenwood Press, 1982 (reprint of 1948 edition).
A readable popular history of the Philadelphia Convention and the delegates who framed the Constitution.

Wood, Gordon S. *The Creation of the American Republic, 1776–1787.* New York: W. W. Norton, 1972 [1st ed., 1969].

Important contemporary account of the influence of republican ideas in America in the decade preceding the writing of the Constitution.


## II. NEW RELEASES (RECENT AND FORTHCOMING TITLES)

Adler, Mortimer. *We Hold These Truths.* New York: Macmillan, 1987.

Barbash, Fred. *The Founding: A Dramatic Account of the Writing of the Constitution.* New York: The Linden Press/Simon & Schuster, 1987.

Kammen, Michael. *A Machine That Would Go of Itself: The Constitution in American Culture.* New York: Alfred A. Knopf, 1986.

McDonald, Forrest. *Novus Ordo Seclorum: The Intellectual Origins of the Constitution.* Lawrence, KS: University of Kansas Press, 1985.

Mee, Charles L., Jr. *The Genius of the People.* New York: Harper & Row, 1987.

Peters, William. *A More Perfect Union: The Men and Events That Made the Constitution.* New York: Crown Publishers, 1987.

Preiss, Byron and David Osterlund, eds. *The Constitution of the United States of America.* New York: Bantam Books, 1987.

Project '87. *This Constitution: Our Enduring Legacy.* Washington, DC: CQ Press/Project '87, 1986.

Vetterli, Richard and Gary Bryner. *In Search of the Republic.* Totowa, NJ: Roman and Littlefield, 1987.


## III. BIOGRAPHIES

For brief biographies of each of the members of the Convention, see:

Ferris, Robert G., and James H. Charleton. *The Signers of the Constitution.* With a foreword by Warren E. Burger. Arlington, VA: Interpretive Publications, Inc., 1986 [1st ed., 1976]. (Distributed by the National Park Service.)

McGee, Dorothy Horton. *Framers of the Constitution.* New York: Dodd, Mead, 1987 [1st ed., 1968].

Cooke, Jacob E. *Alexander Hamilton: A Biography.* New York: Scribners, 1982.

Flexner, James T. *Washington: The Indispensable Man.* Boston: Little, Brown, & Co., 1974.

Ketcham, Ralph. *James Madison: A Biography*. New York: Macmillan, 1971.

Morris, Richard B. *Witnesses at the Creation: Hamilton, Madison, Jay and the Constitution*. New York: Holt, Rinehart, and Winston, 1985.

Peterson, Merrill D. *Thomas Jefferson and the New Nation: A Biography*. New York: Oxford University Press, 1970.

Wright, Esmond. *Franklin of Philadelphia*. Cambridge: Harvard University Press, 1986.

## IV. CONSTITUTIONAL LAW

The basic source for Supreme Court interpretations of the Constitution is the *U.S. Reports* (over 400 volumes to date), available at many college and law libraries. There are also many casebooks which give selections from leading cases. A convenient reference is Paul C. Bartholomew and Joseph F. Menez, *Summaries of Leading Cases on the Constitution*, 12th ed. Totowa, NJ: Rowman and Allanheld, 1983.

## V. PRIMARY SOURCES AND REFERENCE BOOKS

Farrand, Max, ed. *The Records of the Federal Convention of 1787*. 4 vols. New Haven: Yale University Press, 1987.
    The complete record of the debates in the Philadelphia Convention, compiled from James Madison's notes and other sources.

Hamilton, Alexander, James Madison, and John Jay. *The Federalist Papers*, ed. with an introduction by Clinton Rossiter. New York: New American Library, 1961. (Many other editions are also in print.)
    The most famous defense of the Constitution, written in 1787-88 to secure ratification in New York and still among the best guides to interpreting the document.

Ketcham, Ralph, ed. *The Anti-Federalist Papers and the Constitutional Convention Debates*. New York: New American Library, 1986.
    Designed as a companion volume to the Rossiter edition of *The Federalist Papers*, this book presents key Anti-Federalist writings together with selections from the debates in the Federal Convention. It also contains a useful bibliography and index.

Kurland, Philip B., and Ralph Lerner, eds. *The Founders' Constitution*. 5 vols. Chicago: University of Chicago Press, 1987.
> The editors have brought together a large collection of documents to illustrate how the Constitution was conceived, ratified, and interpreted by those responsible for founding the nation.

Levy, Leonard W., ed. *The Encyclopedia of the American Constitution*. 4 vols. New York: Macmillan, 1986.
> 2,200 signed, original articles by 262 leading constitutional scholars, on every constitutional topic from "*Abington Township School District v. Schempp*" to "*Zurcher v. Stanford Daily*" with a complete index and suggestions for further reading.

Madison, James. *Notes of Debates in the Federal Convention of 1787*. Edited, with an introduction by Adrienne Koch. Athens, OH: Ohio University Press, 1985.
> The most complete single record of the events in the Philadelphia Convention.

Padover, Saul K., and Jacob W. Landynski. *The Living U.S. Constitution*. New York: New American Library, second revised edition, 1983.
> This book presents basic information about the Constitution. It contains a brief section on the Convention, together with the text of the Constitution and amendments, excerpts from major Supreme Court decisions, and an indexed guide to the Constitution.

Storing, Herbert J., ed. *The Anti-Federalist: Writings by the Opponents of the Constitution*. Selected by Murray Dry from *The Complete Anti-Federalist*. Chicago: University of Chicago Press, 1985.
> A one-volume selection from Storing's seven-volume edition of the writings of the Anti-Federalists.


## VI. BOOKS FOR YOUNG READERS

Commager, Henry Steele. *The Great Constitution: A Book for Young Americans*. Indianapolis: Bobbs-Merrill, 1961.
> Relying on original sources, the author describes the purposes of the Constitutional Convention and the drafting of the Constitution.

Cooke, Donald E. *America's Great Document: The Constitution*. Edmond, Inc., 1973.
> A narrative account of the Constitutional Convention interspersed with brief biographies of the delegates. Includes sections on the ratification debates, amendments, and the text of the Constitution.

Cullop, Floyd G. *The Constitution of the United States: An Introduction.* New York: New American Library, 1984.
   A clause-by-clause examination of the U.S. Constitution specifically designed for high school students.

Findlay, Bruce and Esther. *Your Rugged Constitution.* Stanford: Stanford University Press, 1969.
   Contains a clause-by-clause explanation of the Constitution with illustrations from American history.

Morris, Richard B. *The Constitution.* Minneapolis: Lerner Publications Co.; revised edition, 1985.
   Beginning with the difficulties of the new American nation under the Articles of Confederation, this book discusses the steps leading to the Constitutional Convention, the Convention itself, and the ratification debates. It also discusses the Bill of Rights, the establishment of the Cabinet, and the concept of judicial review. The last part of the book contains a simplified outline of the Constitution.

Prolman, Marilyn. *The Story of the Constitution.* Chicago: Children's Press, 1969.
   The book begins in 1776, covers the war, the Confederation period, and the Constitutional Convention. The book concludes with a discussion of the amendments (through Amendment 25).

Williams, Selma R. *Fifty-Five Fathers.* New York: Dodd, Mead & Co., 1987.
   A readable, dramatic account of the Philadelphia Convention based on Madison's notes.

## VII. BIBLIOGRAPHIES

Kermit L. Hall, comp., *A Comprehensive Bibliography of American Constitutional and Legal History*, 5 vols. Millwood, NY: Kraus Thomson International, 1984.

McCarrick, Earlean M., ed. *U.S. Constitution: A Guide to Information Sources.* Gale Research Company, 1980.

Stephen M. Millett, ed. *A Selected Bibliography of American Constitutional History.* ABC/Clio Press, 1975.

This list of books is drawn largely from a bibliography of the National Endowment for the Humanities. It was selected by a committee of scholars. It is illustrative of books on the constitutional period and is not necessarily endorsed by the Commission on the Bicentennial of the United States Constitution.

---

NOTE: This bibliography was compiled by The Commission on the Bicentennial of the United States Constitution and it is reprinted here by permission. For additional information, write the Commission at 808 Seventeenth Street, NW, Washington, D.C. 20006.